Alan A. Lew, PhD
Lawrence Yu, PhD
John Ap, PhD
Zhang Guangrui
Editors

Tourism in China

Pre-publication
REVIEWS,
COMMENTARIES,
EVALUATIONS . . .

"The People's Republic of China is emerging as the most exciting tourist destination and tourist source market of the twenty-first century. In this context, *Tourism in China* is essential reading for all people interested in what is happening in this previously little-known destination.

The editors and contributors are to be congratulated for providing a timely and comprehensive insight into the historical development of tourism and it's infrastructure in the world's most populous country. The carefully selected contributions cover a wide spectrum of tourism issues in China, including: transport, hotels, theme parks, travel agencies, ecotourism, marketing, leisure, economic impact, the historical development of tourism, and an analysis of in- and outbound visitor flow.

This book will appeal to tourism academics and students as well as to tourism professionals in organizations that seek to enter the Chinese tourism market to capitalize on the tourism opportunities that have been created by China's entry into the WTO. Managers of NTOs of countries that have been approved as destinations for travelers from China will also greatly benefit from this excellent publication."

Thomas Bauer, PhD
Assistant Professor,
School of Hotel and Tourism
Management, The Hong Kong
Polytechnic University;
Author, *Tourism in the Antarctic*

More pre-publication
REVIEWS, COMMENTARIES, EVALUATIONS . . .

"**B**y the title, *Tourism in China* is a book on China's tourism. However, its contents, rich and comprehensive, are not limited to tourism in China. In fact, it provides a wide window through which readers may not only learn about China's tourism in the past, present, and future, but also know more about China itself.

Among the contributors, there are noted scholars who are active in China, Chinese scholars who have lived overseas for a long while, and foreign scholars who have profound interests in China studies. Their academic fields are extensive, from economics, management, and geography, to planning, sociology, environment, and other sciences. As a result, this book may not only help readers study China's tourism from various angles, but also understand China in various aspects such as that of economy, society, culture, and environment. Foreign readers will find it useful in better understanding China, while Chinese readers will learn more about how the outside world observes China's tourism and the country as a whole."

Professor Liu Rongcang
Director, Institute of Finance
and Trade Economics,
Chinese Academy of Social Sciences

"**A**ny book that attempts to cover China holistically faces an ambitious task, and few rise to the challenge successfully. This book is an exception. The editors have compiled a comprehensive and wide-ranging series of chapters, logically ordered and presented, which together provide an excellent understanding of tourism and its development in China, the world's largest nation. While the focus of this volume is on tourism development, in fact it should be read by all those interested in the tensions and processes of modernization and national identity as China forges head."

Trevor H. B. Sofield, PhD
Professor and Chair,
Department of Tourism,
University of Tasmania

"**S**ince becoming open to international visitors, albeit initially with a variety of constraints, China has become an increasingly important player in world tourism, both as a destination for and origin of international tourists. This work addresses a country and a topic that is of substantial and growing international significance.

Through discussion of national trends and specific chapters on such topics as amusement parks and nature preserves, this work provides an up-to-date introduction to the status of tourism in China. The contributors attempt to provide a balanced perspective through discussion of the challenges that must be overcome if the potential of tourism in China is to be fully realized. This work constitutes an extremely useful point of departure for those interested in gaining a current and critical understanding of tourism in this important, but poorly understood, part of the world."

Geoffrey Wall, PhD
Associate Dean,
Graduate Studies and Research,
Faculty of Environmental Studies,
University of Waterloo

More pre-publication
REVIEWS, COMMENTARIES, EVALUATIONS . . .

"To date, the rich and diverse history and character of tourism in China has scarcely touched the English language discourse of tourism. The potential contribution of an understanding of tourism to, from, and within mainland China to established theory and practice is enormous. In bringing together leading Chinese and Western scholars to review the current state of tourism, *Tourism in China* is a historic publication. It is the first significant text in English on tourism in China, which is expected to be the world's largest tourism-receiving country by 2020.

The editors have assembled an impressive and comprehensive range of contributing chapters, covering fields as diverse as ecotourism, literature, education and research, industry, structure, and China's entry into the World Trade Organization. The chapters are of exceptionally high caliber, and are well referenced and accessible. The structure of the book is a key strength and the comprehensive coverage will ensure that the work retains its currency well into the future. This impressive book is essential reading for anyone with a serious interest in the future of tourism in China, in the Asia Pacific region, and globally."

Brian King, PhD
Professor and Head,
School of Hospitality,
Tourism, and Marketing,
Victoria University, Australia

The Haworth Hospitality Press®
An Imprint of The Haworth Press, Inc.
New York • London • Oxford

Tourism in China

Tourism in China

Alan A. Lew, PhD
Northern Arizona University

Lawrence Yu, PhD
The George Washington University

John Ap, PhD
The Hong Kong Polytechnic University

Zhang Guangrui
The Chinese Academy of Social Sciences

Editors

The Haworth Hospitality Press®
An Imprint of The Haworth Press, Inc.
New York • London • Oxford

Published by

The Haworth Hospitality Press®, an imprint of The Haworth Press, Inc., 10 Alice Street, Binghamton, NY 13904-1580.

Cover design by Lora Wiggins.

Library of Congress Cataloging-in-Publication Data

Tourism in China / Alan A. Lew ... [et al.].
    p. cm.
Includes bibliographical references (p.) and index.
ISBN 0-7890-1281-2 (hard : alk. paper) — ISBN 0-7890-1282-0 (soft)
1. Tourism—China. I. Lew, Alan A.

G155.C55 T68 2002
338.4'79151046—dc21

2002068768

CONTENTS

SECTION III: INDUSTRY AND DEVELOPMENT

SECTION V: CONCLUSION

      Lawrence Yu
      John Ap
      Zhang Guangrui
      Alan A. Lew

ABOUT THE EDITORS

Alan A. Lew is Professor of Geography and Public Planning at Northern Arizona University in Flagstaff and has been a visiting scholar at the National University of Singapore, the Hong Kong Polytechnic University, and Tübingen University in Germany. He is the author of *Tourism in China, Sustainable Tourism: A Geographical Perspective, Tourism and Gaming on American Indian Lands,* and *Seductions of Place.* Professor Lew is editor-in-chief of *Tourism Geographies* and serves as Web master for the tourism groups of the International Geographical Union and the Association of American Geographers.

Larry Yu, PhD, is Associate Professor at the Department of Tourism and Hospitality Management, School of Business and Public Management, George Washington University in Washington, DC. Dr. Yu is the author of *The International Hospitality Business: Management and Operations* and co-editor of *A Host of Opportunities: Introduction to Hospitality Management and Tourism in China: Geographic, Political and Economic Perspectives.* He also serves on the editorial boards of *Journal of Vacation Marketing* and *Journal of Hospitality and Tourism Education.* Dr. Yu was lead researcher for the White House Conference on Travel and Tourism in 1995 and serves as a consultant to international hotel firms, such as Choice Hotels International and United States government agencies.

John Ap, PhD, is Associate Professor in Tourism Management at the Hong Kong Polytechnic University. Prior to joining the academic world, Dr. Ap spent eleven years as a certified town planner in Australia and was Project Manager with the Tourism Commission of New South Wales. He has produced more than 60 scholarly publications and received the 1998 Journal of Travel Research Best Article Award for "Developing and Testing a Tourism Impact." As a consultant, Dr. Ap's clients have included the International Association of Amusement Parks and Attractions, Ocean Park, the Hong Kong Tourist Association, the Business and Professionals Federation of Hong Kong, the Hong Kong Association of Registered Tour Coordinators, and UNESCO.

Zhang Guangrui is Director of the Tourism Research Centre, Chinese Academy of Social Sciences in Beijing, China. He is a widely published author and is a member of the international editorial board of Tourism Management and Tourism Recreation Research, and is a member of the editorial board of Finance & Trade Economics. Professor Zhang has worked as a consultant for the China National Tourism Administration as well as local governments and industries in China and developed a master plan in 1998 for tourism in the Shanxi Province. He is a member of the China National Tourism Standardization Technological Committee and is Senior Advisor for the Travel Development Centre of Finland.

CONTRIBUTORS

Carson L. "Kit" Jenkins is Professor of International Tourism at the University of Strathclyde. His teaching, research, and consultancy interests focus on tourism policy, planning, and development in the developing countries.

Claudia Kruse holds an MA in Chinese and Business Studies and an MSc in Tourism, Environment, and Development (SOAS, University of London). Currently, she researches tourism and globalization for an ethical investment research company and also works as a tutor at SOAS.

Kreg Lindberg is a Senior Research Fellow with the Cooperative Research Centre (CRC) for Sustainable Tourism and the School of Tourism and Hotel Management at Griffith University, Australia. His research interests include the economic and other aspects of ecotourism, as well as the economic and social impacts of tourism in general. He was lead editor for both volumes of the book *Ecotourism: A Guide for Planners and Managers.*

Dr. Barry Mak is currently Assistant Professor of the School of Hotel and Tourism Management, The Hong Kong Polytechnic University. Dr. Mak earned his MS and PhD degrees in tourism at the Scottish Hotel School of Strathclyde University, U.K. Prior to his academic career, Dr. Mak worked for the biggest travel agency in Hong Kong for three years. Dr. Mak is an independent director of the Travel Industry of Hong Kong and the Chief Examiner of Travel and Tourism of Examinations and Assessment Authority of Hong Kong.

Qian Wei majored in English at Hangzhou University from 1956 to 1960 and subsequently taught English at the same school until 1971. He then became involved in travel and tourism as well as foreign affairs in Hangzhou until 1991, when he joined the China Tourism Institute in Beijing. There he served as the Vice President in charge of academic affairs and taught courses in hotel marketing, tourism management, tour guiding as an art, creativity, and translation until his retirement in 1999.

Hailin Qu is a native-born Chinese. He is currently a Professor and the William E. Davis Distinguished Chair in the School of Hotel and Restaurant Administration at Oklahoma State University. He is also a Visiting Chair Professor in the Department of Hotel and Tourism Management of The Hong Kong Polytechnic University and a Senior International Academic Advisor in the Tourism Research Center of the Chinese Academy of Social Sciences. He has also been awarded an Honorary Professor title by several universities in China. His research interests are travel and tourism marketing, consumer behavior, hotel and tourism service quality, and tourism economic impact and forecasting.

Xiaoping Shen is an Associate Professor at Central Connecticut State University. She received her PhD degree in geography at the University of Ottawa in Canada. Her research interests are economic and tourism geography and regional development of China, as well as GIS applications and spatial analysis.

Clem Tisdell is Professor of Economics at The University of Queensland. His research interests include tourism economics, the development of China, and environmental economics. He recently co-authored the book *Tourism and China's Development*.

Ning Wang is Associate Professor in the Department of Sociology, Zhongshan University, Guangzhou, People's Republic of China. He earned his PhD from the University of Sheffield, UK. His research interests include the sociology of tourism and consumer culture. He is the author of the book *Tourism and Modernity: A Sociological Analysis* (Pergamon, 2000).

Suosheng Wang is a PhD student specializing in tourism marketing research at Oklahoma State University. He previously worked for ten years at the China National Tourism Administration. He received his MPhil from the Hong Kong Polytechnic University.

Xiaolun Wang received his PhD in geography from Arizona State University. He was a Visiting Assistant Professor at Arizona State University from 1994 to 1997 and a postdoctoral fellow in the Department of History at Fudan University from 1997 to 1999.

Honggen Xiao is a graduate student in the Department of Recreation and Leisure Studies at the University of Waterloo in Canada. He was formerly with the Tourism Department at Huaqiao University in Fujian Province, China. His research interests are leisure and tourism, tourism in China, perception and impact studies of tourism, and tourism anthropology.

Xu Gang is Assistant Professor in the Nanyang Business School at the Nanyang Technological University, Singapore. His research interests include tourism management, international trade and investment, and economic integration in East Asia.

Dayuan Xue is Professor at the Nanjing Institute of Environmental Science, China State Environmental Protection Administration. His work has focused on biodiversity conservation and protected area management in China. He recently completed a two-year postdoctoral research fellowship in the Department of Economics at The University of Queensland.

Hanqin Qiu Zhang is Assistant Professor of International Tourism at the Hong Kong Polytechnic University. She received her BA (Hons) from Nankai University in mainland China, her MA degree from the University of Waterloo in Canada, and her PhD from the University of Strathclyde in the UK. Her research interests are in consumer behavior and China's hotel and tourism development and policy issues.

Foreword

Being asked to write the foreword for a publication such as *Tourism in China* is naturally a great honor for me. However, upon further reflection, I realized what a privilege I had been given. This publication has been prepared by four renowned professors in the international tourism community—professors whose works I have read and studied and whom I respect and admire greatly. Furthermore, this publication, probably the most in-depth analysis of China's tourism industry, will, I am sure, serve as a significant reference for Chinese tourism.

Having worked in the tourism sector for over twenty-five years, I have been a witness to not only the accelerated growth of the tourism industry worldwide but also to the spectacular development of China's tourism industry. Let us look at some bare facts: In 2000, 698 million international tourists worldwide generated US$476 billion in receipts. This has made tourism, at the turn of the millennium, one of the most dynamic industries of the world. No wonder that a number of Asia Pacific countries have identified tourism as a vehicle for socioeconomic growth and poverty alleviation.

During the past decade, China surpassed all possible forecasts with its high and constant growth in international and domestic tourism activity. By 2000, China became the leader in Asian tourism, surpassing its neighbors in the region in both international tourist arrivals and receipts. Furthermore, World Tourism Organization (WTO) forecasts indicate that by 2020, China will become the world's leading tourism destination, overtaking traditional destinations such as France, Spain, and the United States. The country's invaluable cultural and natural heritage, pristine mountains, extensive river valleys, lakes, beaches, rich cuisine, arts and crafts, and, above all, very warm and hospitable people, form a mighty attractive tourism product—a product that can appeal to a wide cross section of tourist markets and segments within these markets. The country has everything that a tourist destination can aspire to have.

China is making concerted efforts to develop its tourism industry to match the projected tourist arrivals. According to the China National Tourism Administration, the country aims to receive 145 million visitors by 2020, of which foreign tourists would comprise 33.5 million with receipts of US$75 billion. On the other hand, domestic tourism is expected to generate Renminbi (RMB) 2,700 billion. Thus, tourism revenues would represent 8 percent of the country's GDP. China's main development strategies focus on increasing inbound tourism, fostering more domestic tourism, improving tourist facilities and services, diversifying and broadening its tourism product base, and undertaking intensive development of the western region.

Another feature of Chinese tourism that will have great implications for global tourism affairs is the growth of Chinese outbound tourism. The Chinese market is being increasingly targeted all over the world, and the Chinese government is encouraging and facilitating overseas travel of Chinese people, thereby making a significant contribution to the international tourism industry. I am sure that the day is not very far when China will become a reference point in the tourism markets for both inbound and outbound tourism.

With these excellent forecasts in mind, I would like to take a moment to discuss the benefits that a strong tourism industry can provide to a country of the size and diversity of China. Tourism is a "people's industry" in which people are the essence of tourism activity. People constitute the market, require services from other people, and generate the social, cultural, and economic interactions that have made tourism such an important activity. One of the most immediate benefits of the tourism industry is its ability to create employment and, as an added benefit, it requires both skilled and unskilled employment. China is the most populous destination in the world. As a labor-intensive industry, tourism has the potential to create more jobs per unit of investment than most other industries, and tourism can be a useful source of employment for women and ethnic minority groups.

Other related benefits of the tourism industry include foreign revenue receipts and attraction of national and international investment in the development of tourism infrastructure, which can also be exploited for local use. It is therefore no surprise to me that the Chinese government identified tourism as a major engine for the development of its western provinces. In this manner, it is not only diversifying its tourism product beyond its traditional destinations, but is also ensuring that these provinces develop an industry that can provide immediate benefits with relatively little investment and using existing resources. Furthermore, tourism, when properly developed and managed, can serve as a mechanism for protecting natural environments; preserving historical, archaeological, and religious monuments; and stimulating the practice of local cultures, folklore, traditions, arts and crafts, and cuisine.

I firmly believe that this publication could not have been produced at a better time or by more qualified professionals. I commend Dr. Alan Lew, Dr. Lawrence Yu, Dr. Zhang Guangrui, and Dr. John Ap for having the foresight to prepare an in-depth analysis of China's tourism industry, including the successful policies and practices that have shaped it, as well as identifying the path the industry will take over the next few years. The combined expertise in China's tourism affairs of the four editors is probably unmatched. I have had the personal pleasure of meeting and working with two of them and can attest to their wealth of experience and capacity to objectively analyze tourism trends in China.

Tourism in China paints a clear picture of the key elements behind China's success story in tourism and identifies the main challenges faced by the country in its efforts in becoming the leading tourism destination of the world, as well as in maintaining this position for many years to come.

I recommend this book to academics and practitioners alike.

Dr. Harsh Varma
Regional Representative
for Asia and the Pacific
World Tourism Organization
Madrid, Spain

SECTION I: INTRODUCTION AND HISTORICAL DEVELOPMENT

Chapter 1

Introduction:
China's Tourism Boom

Zhang Guangrui
Alan A. Lew

Travel and tourism has become a strategic industry in China's development toward a socialist market economy. Two decades of development have yielded both positive experiences and hard lessons. The country is still probing better ways of developing a strong travel and tourism industry that can compete successfully in regional and global markets. China faces many opportunities and challenges in developing its tourism in this new century, although they may be quite different from those in the decade before. China's tourism has a bright future, although arduous efforts will be required to develop it effectively. The compilation of chapters in this book presents the diverse opportunities and challenges that China faces, as well as some of the strategies that help to bring about more successful future development.

CHINA'S TOURISM ENVIRONMENT

China is rich in tourism resources. An incredible diversity of landscapes and cultures stretches across the vastness of the country. Every type of tourist will find something: densely crowded cities with modern skylines and old traditional structures, UNESCO-recognized natural and cultural heritage sites, agricultural villages nestled in lush tropical vegetation, nomadic horse riders galloping across open grasslands and deserts, snow- and ice-covered mountains offering challenging adventures for "new tourists," and quality resorts with world-class golf and other entertainment activities. Most of the many cultures are old and very traditional. There is great potential in China for specialized tourism, focusing on ethnic groups and colorful cultures, as well as environmental adventure. The growing market in *ecotourism* in the developed world will find considerable opportunities in China, as well.

Sound economic growth supports the tourism industry. Further deepening of the recent economic reforms and increasing openness to the outside world have helped China's economy grow quickly. The country's gross domestic product (GDP) was RMB 8940.4 billion (bn) yuan in 2000 (US$1.00 = RMB 8.30 yuan), and China experienced an annual growth of 8.3 percent in the latter half of the 1990s (Zhu 2001). It is expected to grow at 7 percent per year in the first five years of the new century. The stronger economy will afford further improvement in infrastructure for tourism development and, at the same time, will foster more Chinese tourists, both domestic and outbound.

Positive government policies advance tourism. The Chinese government first made clear that tourism was an important part of the tertiary (service) industry in the 1980s. Tourism was further designated as a growth point of the national economy in the late 1990s. So far, over two-thirds of the provincial governments have committed to making tourism one of their pillar industries. In the national campaign for the development of western China, tourism has also been made a priority among industrial sectors. In his report on the "10th Five-Year Plan for the National Economy and Social Development," Premier Zhu Rongji stressed that the development of the service sector should be sped up, and more efforts should be given to the service industries directly related to resident consumption such as real estate, community service, travel and tourism, catering, entertainment and recreation, and health (Zhu 2001). Therefore, more preferential government policies have been, or will be, worked out to support tourism development at both central and local levels. For example, the central government has increased public holidays, and purposely made three weeklong holidays per year (one each during the Spring Festival, May Day Festival, and the National Day holiday, which starts October 1) to give residents more leisure time. Indeed, this practice has proved that domestic tourism can be a driving force for increasing domestic consumption, and further stimulating production.

INTERNATIONAL TOURISM ENVIRONMENT

China's entry into the World Trade Organization will expand tourism. China joined the World Trade Organization in November 2001. This may provide other opportunities for its tourism development, including:

- fewer formalities and barriers for cross-border travelers,
- reductions in traveling costs as a result of global competition,
- removal of some protectionist policies, and
- upgrade of communication, financial, and information facilities.

China will remain more open to the outside world, and more international management practices will be introduced. The removal of barriers to trade and travel will enhance China's position as a country for financial investment, international business, and business and leisure travel.

The international climate is improving for China's tourism development. China is located in the rapidly growing Asia Pacific realm. Both economies and tourist travel are expected to grow faster in this region than in the rest of the world, although the unexpected financial crisis cast some shadows on the region's economy in the late 1990s. According to the WTO, the worldwide average growth of international tourism during the 1990s was less than 5 percent, while growth in the Asia Pacific region was over 8.3 percent in the first half of the decade, and 2.7 percent in the latter half due to the financial crisis (WTO 2000).

China is the largest country in the Asia Pacific region and an active member of the Pacific Asia Travel Association (PATA). In terms of international tourism, China enjoyed the fastest growth in arrivals in the region in the last decade, and such trends will develop in the years to come. In addition to Japan, which is expected to continue to be a major tourist market for China, other countries in the region, and the close neighboring countries in particular, are expected to bring even more leisure tourists and business travelers to China. According to the WTO, China's top ten markets will include Japan, the Republic of Korea, United States, the Russian Federation, Mongolia, Singapore, Malaysia, the Philippines, the United Kingdom, and Germany by 2020, and China's annual growth rate from 2000 to 2010 will be 9.5 percent (WTO 2000). The return of Hong Kong and Macao to their motherland has been a success, making movements of people easier and more frequent. As a unique and interesting destination, China will be a major factor in the future development of regional tourism throughout Asia, as well as throughout the world. According to the forecast by WTO, China will be the top international destination country in the world with about 137 million international arrivals by the year 2020, and with over 1 million outbound visitors a year, China will rank fourth on the list of countries generating tourism (Tables 1.1 to 1.4).

The success of China's market-oriented reforms has drawn attention worldwide, from politicians to business circles and the general public. China's rapidly developing business environment is already responsible for a major part of the growth in tourism in recent years. Not only are foreign investments flowing into the country, but they also are increasing the numbers of entrepreneurs, who typically combine pleasure with their business trips. This component of the visitor market will likely increase in the coming years. There is little doubt that, barring any unpredictable upheavals, China will soon be as successful in the tourism business as any competitor in the international marketplace. Based on the WTO's bright forecasts, and adjusted for the specific goals and conditions, the China National Tourism Ad-

TABLE 1.1. World's Top Ten International Tourism Destinations (2000)

Rank	Country	Int'l Tourist Arrivals (millions)	Growth (%)
1	France	74.5	2.0
2	United States	52.7	8.7
3	Spain	48.5	3.7
4	Italy	41.2	12.8
5	**China**	**31.2**	**15.5**
6	United Kingdom	24.9	−15.5
7	Russian Fed.	22.8	23.2
8	Canada	20.4	4.9
9	Mexico	20.0	5.0
10	Germany	18.9	10.5

Source: World Tourism Organization (WTO) (2001). *Tourism Highlights 2001.* Madrid: WTO.

TABLE 1.2. World's Top Ten International Tourism Earners (1999)

Rank	Country	Int'l Tourism Receipt (US$ million)	Annual Growth (%)
1	United States	74, 881	5.0
2	Spain	32, 497	8.9
3	France	31, 507	5.3
4	Italy	28, 359	−5.0
5	United Kingdom	20, 223	−3. 6
6	Germany	16, 730	−0.2
7	**China**	**14, 098**	**11.9**
8	Austria	12, 533	−0.8
9	Canada	10, 171	8.2
10	Mexico	7, 223	−3.6

Source: World Tourism Organization (WTO) (2001). *Tourism Highlights 2001.* Madrid: WTO.

TABLE 1.3. Top Ten World Tourism Destinations in 2020

Rank	Country/Region	Int'l Tourist Arrivals (thousands)	Market Share (%)	1995-2020 Growth (%)
1	**China**	**137,100**	**8.6**	**8.0**
2	United States	102,400	6.4	3.5
3	France	93,300	5.8	1.8
4	Spain	71,000	4.4	2.4
5	Hong Kong, SAR, China	59,300	3.7	7.3
6	Italy	52,900	3.3	2.2
7	United Kingdom	52,800	3.3	3.0
8	Mexico	48,900	3.1	3.6
9	Commonwealth of Independent States	47,100	2.9	6.7
10	Czech Republic	44,000	2.7	4.0
TOTAL		**708,800**	**44.2**	

Source: World Tourism Organization (WTO) (1997). *Tourism: 2020 Vision.* Madrid: WTO.

TABLE 1.4. Top Ten World Tourist-Generating Countries in 2020

Rank	Country/Region	Outbound Tourist Departures (thousands)	Market Share (%)
1	Germany	163,500	10.2
2	Japan	141,500	8.8
3	United States	123,300	7.7
4	**China**	**100,000**	**6.2**
5	United Kingdom	96,100	6.0
6	France	37,600	2.3
7	Holland	35,400	2.2
8	Canada	31,300	2.0
9	Commonwealth of Independent States	30,500	1.9
10	Italy	29,700	1.9
TOTAL		**788,900**	**49.2**

Source: World Tourism Organization (WTO) (1997). *Tourism: 2020 Vision.* Madrid: WTO.

ministration (CNTA) developed the "10th Five-Year Plan and Long-Term Goal Outlines up to 2015 and 2020 for Tourism Development in China" (CNTA 2001). Over the next twenty years, according to this ambitious plan, China will move from being a *big tourism country* to becoming a *powerful tourism country.* Specific quantitative goals set in the plan include the following:

- By 2020, China will have 210 to 300 million inbound tourist arrivals, 2.5 to 3.6 times greater than the figure of 2000. Among them, "foreign" tourist arrivals will reach 31 to 45 million, 3 to 4.4 times greater than that of 2000.
- International tourism earnings will be US$58 to 82 billion, 3.6 to 5 times above the figure of 2000.
- During the same period, domestic tourism revenue will reach RMB 2100 billion yuan, 6.6 to 9.4 times that in 2000.
- Therefore, the total output of both inbound and domestic tourism will be RMB 3600 billion yuan, 8 times of that of 2000, equivalent to 11 percent of China's GDP by 2020. Indeed, the tourism industry will become the pillar of the country's economy.

For the first five years in the new century, the foundation stage, international tourism revenue will grow by 8 to 10 percent annually, while domestic tourism revenue will grow by 8 to 9 percent. The second five years will be an upgrading stage, with international tourism revenue growing by 6 to 8 percent, and domestic tourism revenue growing by 10 to 12 percent. The third five years, from 2011 to 2015, will be a stage of consolidation. International tourism revenue will reach US$43 to 56 bn with an annual growth of 6 to 8 percent, while domestic tourism revenue will grow by 10 to 12 percent. The last five years of the plan, from 2016 to 2020, will be the stage of perfection. By 2020, the total tourism output will be RMB 2500 to 3600 bn yuan, accounting for 7.9 to 11.4 percent of China's GDP. The plan has been approved, and detailed implementation measures have been developed by the CNTA.

THE CHAPTERS

The contributions in this book describe many of the forms and challenges of tourism throughout the modern history of China. In Chapter 2, Zhang Guangrui provides an overview of the key period of modern tourism development in China, which essentially began in 1978. Comparisons to the earlier Maoist Communist period show the remarkable changes that were unleashed in that year. In Chapter 3 Xiaolun Wang then takes us back in time more than a century to examine how international tourists from the West viewed China at that time. Interesting corollaries with modern tourists show how some aspects of the human travel experience transcend time and space. The introductory section of this book concludes with Ning Wang's (Chapter 4) look at the modern vernacular landscape in China—a landscape that seems to be rapidly disappearing in the modernizing city of Beijing while it also becomes a tourist attraction. The tension between modernization and traditional values and places are evident throughout this introductory section.

Section II addresses some of the more empirical impacts of tourism in China. In Chapter 5, Zhang Guangrui provides another insightful overview with a look at the state of tourism research in China and the variety of agencies and levels at which this takes place. Xu Gang and Claudia Kruse focus in Chapter 6 on the economics of tourism that have been so important in driving this growing sector in China. In Chapter 7, Kreg Lindberg, Clem Tisdell, and Dayuan Xue provide insight into ecotourism in China and its sometimes problematic role in the management of China's nature reserves.

The chapters in the third section of the book assess major segments of China's tourism industry. Lawrence Yu (Chapter 8) describes the development and challenges of China's accommodations industry, which has struggled over the years to meet the needs of growing tourist demand. Even more of a challenge has been the complex development of travel agencies in China, which Qian Wei so well describes in Chaper 9. In Chapter 10, Barry Mak gives a comprehensive overview and analysis of the development of the varied forms of transportation that tourists and other long-distance travelers use in China. Each form has had its own distinct development history through China's transition from communist to market orientations. John Ap (Chapter 11) provides several case studies in his description of the occasional successes, but more common failures, in rapid growth of theme and amusement park development in China. He provides a detailed and useful description of how China, and its investors, might improve the success of future man-made attractions.

The chapters in Section IV explore the tourists themselves, both international and domestic. The tremendous growth in China's tourism has actually occurred with limited organized marketing on the part of the Chinese, as Suosheng Wang and John Ap describe in Chapter 12. They explain how China has tried to manipulate the tourism market, in a rather basic manner so far. In Chapter 13, Xiaoping Shen describes the number and characteristics of international tourists to China. She notes the distinct market segments that exist, especially the difference between short-haul (mostly from Asian countries) and long-haul visitors. In Chapter 14, Honggen Xiao looks at leisure in China, providing insight into the lifestyle of contemporary Chinese, for whom domestic and outbound travel have now become major life goals. Outbound travel is described in Zhang Qiu Hanqin, Carson L. Jenkins, and Hailin Qu's contribution (Chapter 15), with a focus on Hong Kong's role in the development of this potentially huge market for Asia and the world.

The editors of this book combine their collective expertise with the insights that the contributing authors provided to lay out the challenges that China's tourism faces and the future development strategies that could enhance its success in Chapter 16. No one can predict the future, but much can be learned from the past. That being said, tourism is a huge phenomenon in China, and not all of its facets are covered in this book. This book was intended to be a second edition to *Tourism in China* (Lew and Yu 1995.) However, reflecting the many changes that China's tourism has undergone since the earlier book was published, this volume contains mostly new chapters and has a distinctly different focus. One major difference is that this new effort focuses primarily on the core region of China's tourism development, which is situated in the Han Chinese area of eastern China. Due to space limitations, the non-Han Chinese regions of China's southwest, north, and west were intentionally omitted, even though they have very important roles to play in China's overall tourism economy. With the exception of Chinese outbound travelers to Hong Kong, the "compatriot Chinese" regions of Hong Kong, Macao, and Taiwan were also intentionally omitted, as was border tourism along China's enormous international land boundary. These are all key areas in the future development of tourism in China and Asia, but their inclusion would have easily doubled the length of the current book—although it may justify a future sister volume. Despite these limitations, we hope you find the book useful in your efforts to understand China's tourism.

REFERENCES

CNTA (2001). *zhongguo lvyouye fazhan shiwu jihua he 2015/2020 nian yuan-jing mubiao gangyao* (The 10th five-year plan and the long-term goal outlines up to 2015 and 2020 for tourism development in China). Beijing: China Tourism Publishing House.

Lew, Alan A. and Yu, Lawrence, eds. (1995). *Tourism in China: Geographical, Political, and Economic Perspectives.* Boulder, CO: Westview Press.

World Tourism Organization (WTO) (1997). *Tourism: 2020 Vision.* Madrid: WTO.

World Tourism Organization (WTO) (2000). *Tourism 2020 Vision East Asia and Pacific.* Madrid, Spain.

World Tourism Organization (WTO) (2001). *Tourism Highlights 2001.* Madrid: WTO.

Zhu Rongji (2001). Report on the 10th five-year plan for the national economy and social development on March 5, 2001. *People's Daily* (Beijing), March 17.

Chapter 2

China's Tourism Since 1978: Policies, Experiences, and Lessons Learned

Zhang Guangrui

Leisure travel in China dates back thousands of years. Emperors, scholars, monks, and other religious people were frequent travelers in ancient times, since they had positions of power, intellectual interests, or free time. In modern times, international travel to China was once controlled by wealthy or adventurous foreigners. They dominated the leisure travel industry, both as participants and as business operators. Thomas Cook and Sons, among other early international travel companies, opened an office in China during the 1920s (Hibbort 1990). Initially located in Shanghai, the company moved later to the old Hotel de Pekin in the country's capital. These offices handled ground services for international and domestic tours in China. The earliest Chinese travel agency was initially set up as a travel division in the Shanghai Commercial and Savings Bank in 1923 by Chen Guangpu, a banker who advocated the services after being poorly served by Thomas Cook and Sons. That division was later separated from the bank and renamed the China Travel Service, becoming the first-ever travel agency owned and run by the Chinese in China (Zhang 1995). However, the seemingly endless and ruthless wars of the late 1930s and 1940s essentially put an end to all pleasure travel in the country.

The People's Republic of China was established in 1949, bringing an end to the civil and international wars that had so disrupted the country. For the first three decades, up to 1978, the travel and tourism industry was for all intents and purposes considered a form of politi-

cal activity. Travel services (including both agents and tour operators) were set up immediately after the new Communist government
was formed, but only provided services for visiting overseas Chinese
residents and for foreigners with special permission to visit the country. Hence, for a long time, tourism in China was a "diplomatic activity," serving political rather than economic goals. Domestic tourism
hardly existed, and outbound travel was limited almost exclusively to
diplomats and government officials. The Great Cultural Revolution
(1966-1976) forced this nascent travel industry to be almost entirely
suspended. In the early 1970s, however, Mao Zedong, the founder of
the People's Republic and Chairman of the Communist Party of
China (CPC), did begin to permit a few "rightists" to visit China. The
term "rightists" referred to people who opposed the Chinese political
system, especially from countries such as the United States of America.

The year 1978 had great significance for China. In that year, the
CPC held the Third Plenary Session of its eleventh Congress, at which
an epoch-making decision was made to shift emphasis from political
struggle to economic reconstruction. This was based on the concept of
"Four Modernizations" of industry, agriculture, science and technology, and national defense. In addition, China declared that it would
"open its door" to the outside world. These decisions are often referred
to as China's "second revolution" (the first being the Communist vic-
tory in 1949). Tourism in China would never have become what it is today without these historical policy changes. The following discussion
outlines the context of China's tourism development and the evolution
of related tourism policies, including analysis of experiences gained,
lessons learned, and future prospects of the tourist industry in China.

TOURIST MOVEMENT

Despite many global problems, including economic recessions,
conflicts and wars in the Persian Gulf and among former Yugoslavian
states, political crises in the former Soviet Union, financial crises in
Asia, and various environmental catastrophes, worldwide tourism experienced a respectable growth throughout the 1980s and 1990s. The
average annual growth of international visitor arrivals has been approximately 4 percent through these decades, while international
tourism receipts from 1980 to 2000 increased by a total of only 10 per-

cent (WTO 2000). In sharp contrast to the world situation at large, China's tourism over the past two decades has grown rapidly in arrivals and expenditures.

From 1978 to 2000, both China's inbound visitor arrivals and its foreign exchange earnings from international visitors averaged an annual growth of 20 percent (Tables 2.1 and 2.2) (CNTA 2000). In 1999, China received some 72.8 million international visitor arrivals, among which some 8.4 million were foreigners (the remainder were "compatriots" from Hong Kong, Macao, and Taiwan). Total foreign exchange earnings from these visitors were close to US$14 billion. (Note that China's official numbers include day excursionists and, therefore, are not comparable to World Tourism Organization figures.) From an almost insignificant beginning only some twenty years ago, China now ranks among the top ten world international tourism destinations, and, of course, is number one among Asian and Pacific countries (Tables 2.3 and 2.4).

Domestic and Outbound Tourism

For most of the period since 1949, leisure travel had been considered representative of a bourgeois capitalist lifestyle and, therefore, contrary to communist ethics. Being considered socially and politically taboo for the Chinese people before 1978, domestic tourism hardly existed before the mid-1980s. Since that time, and especially in the 1990s, the central government has issued several policies to encourage the Chinese to travel domestically, as a means of stimulating consumption and growing the country's economy. In 1999, over 700 million trips were made by domestic tourists with a spending over RMB 283 billion (CNTA 2000). Domestic tourism today is clearly contributing to the economic development of many Chinese cities and regions (Table 2.5).

Outbound tourism by Chinese citizens is a more recent phenomenon. Successful economic reforms, especially in urban areas, more openness to the outside world, and increasing disposable money and time have all contributed to rising demand by Chinese to see the world. This trend started with tours to visit friends and relatives (VFR) in Hong Kong and Macao in the early 1980s. This was followed by an increase in cross-border day trips in the late 1980s to the frontier areas of Russia, Korea, and Mongolia in the north, and to

TABLE 2.1. Overseas Visitor Arrivals in China (1978-2000)*

Year	Total	Foreigners	Overseas Chinese	Compatriots** Total	Taiwanese
1978	1,809,200	229,600	18,100	1,561,500	
1979	4,203,901	362,389	20,910	3,820,602	
1980	5,702,536	529,124	34,413	5,138,999	
1981	7,767,096	675,153	38,856	7,053,087	
1982	7,924,261	764,497	42,745	7,117,019	
1983	9,477,005	872,511	40,352	8,564,142	
1984	12,852,185	1,134,267	47,498	11,670,420	
1985	17,833,097	1,370,462	84,827	16,377,808	
1986	22,819,450	1,482,276	68,133	21,269,041	
1987	26,902,267	1,727,821	87,031	25,087,415	
1988	31,694,804	1,842,206	79,348	29,773,250	437,700
1989	24,501,394	1,460,970	68,556	22,971,868	541,000
1990	27,461,821	1,747,315	91,090	25,623,416	948,000
1991	33,349,757	2,710,103	133,427	30,506,227	946,632
1992	38,114,945	4,006,427	165,007	33,943,441	1,317,770
1993	41,526,945	4,655,857	166,182	36,704,906	1,526,969
1994	43,684,456	5,182,060	115,245	36,996,690	1,390,215
1995	46,386,511	5,886,716	115,818	40,383,977	1,532,309
1996	51,127,516	6,744,334	154,601	44,228,581	1,733,897
1997	57,587,923	7,428,006	99,004	50,060,913	2,117,576
1998	63,478,401	7,107,747	120,704	56,249,950	2,174,602
1999	72,795,594	8,432,296	108,141	64,255,157	2,584,648
2000	83,443,881	10,160,432	75,487	73,207,962	3,108,643

Source: China Ministry of Public Security, published in China National Tourism Administration (CNTA) (2000). *Yearbook of China Tourism Statistics (2000-2001).* Beijing: China's Tourism Press.

*These figures are international border frontier records including both overnight visitors and day-trippers.

**Compatriots include residents from Hong Kong, Macao, and Taiwan.

TABLE 2.2. International Tourism Receipts in China (1978-1999)

Year	Receipts (US$ mn)	Indices (1978 = 100)	Annual Growth (%)
1978	262.9	100.00	–
1979	449.3	170.90	70.90
1980	616.7	234.60	37.30
1981	784.9	298.60	27.30
1982	843.2	320.70	7.40
1983	941.2	358.00	11.60
1984	1,131.3	430.30	20.20
1985	1,250.0	475.50	10.50
1986	1,530.9	582.30	22.50
1987	1,861.5	708.10	21.60
1988	2,217.6	854.60	20.70
1989	1,860.5	707.70	−17.20
1990	2,217.6	843.50	19.20
1991	2,844.9	1,082.10	28.30
1992	3,946.9	1,501.30	38.70
1993	4,683.2	1,781.40	18.70
1994	7,323.0	2,786.10	*
1995	8,733.0	3,321.70	19.25
1996	10,200.0	3,879.98	16.81
1997	12,074.0	4,592.67	18.37
1998	12,602.0	4,793.36	4.37
1999	14,099.0	5,362.70	11.88
2000	16,224.0	6,171.17	15.08

Source: China National Tourism Administration (CNTA) (2000). *Yearbook of China Tourism Statistics (2000-2001).* Beijing: China's Tourism Press.
*Owing to the change of statistical methodology of foreign exchange receipts, the data for this year are incomparable with those of previous years.

TABLE 2.3. World's Ten Top International Tourism Destinations (1999)

Rank	Country	Int'l Tourist Arrivals (thousands)	Growth (%)
1	France	71, 400	2.0
2	Spain	51, 958	8.8
3	United States	46, 983	1.3
4	Italy	35, 839	2.9
5	China	27, 047	7.9
6	United Kingdom	25, 740	0.0
7	Mexico	20, 216	2 0
8	Canada	19, 556	3.8
9	Poland	17, 940	− 4.5
10	Austria	17, 630	1.6

Source: WTO (2000).

TABLE 2.4. World's Ten Top International Tourism Earners (1999)

Rank	Country	Int'l Tourism Receipt (US$ mn)	Annual Growth (%)
1	United States	74, 881	5.0
2	Spain	32, 497	8.9
3	France	31, 507	5.3
4	Italy	28, 359	− 5.0
5	United Kingdom	20, 223	− 3.6
6	Germany	16, 730	− 0.2
7	China	14, 098	11. 9
8	Austria	12, 533	− 0.8
9	Canada	10, 171	− 8.2
10	Mexico	7,223	− 3.6

Source: WTO (2001).

TABLE 2.5. Domestic Tourism (1978-1999)

Year	Domestic Tourists (mn)	Annual Growth (%)	Domestic Revenue (RMB mn)	Annual Growth (%)
1978	–	–	1,840	–
1984	200	–	–	–
1985	240	20.0	8,000	–
1986	270	12.5	10,600	32.5
1987	290	7.4	14,000	32.1
1988	300	3.4	18,700	33.5
1989	240	−20.0	15,000	−19.7
1990	280	16.7	17,000	13.3
1991	300	7.1	20,000	17.6
1992	330	10.0	25,000	25.0
1993	410	24.2	86,400	–*
1994	524	27.8	102,350	18.5
1995	629	20.0	137,570	34.4
1996	639	1.6	163,840	19.1
1997	644	0.8	211,270	29.0
1998	694	7.8	239,100	13.2
1999	719	3.6	283,192	18.4

Source: China National Tourism Administration (CNTA) (2000). *Yearbook of China Tourism Statistics (2000-2001).* Beijing: China's Tourism Press.
*Because the sample survey replaced the previous statistical method in collecting data of domestic revenue, the data are incomparable with the previous years'.

Vietnam, Laos, and Myanmar in the south. In the 1990s, control over Chinese outbound tourism gradually and cautiously relaxed. By the end of 1999, fourteen countries and regions had been recognized as designated overseas tourist destinations for Chinese residents, namely South Korea, Singapore, Thailand, Malaysia, the Philippines, Japan, Australia, New Zealand, Vietnam, Laos, Myanmar, and Brunei, in addition to the special administrative regions of Hong Kong and Macao. Because of the potential of China as the last and largest unopened tourist market, many other countries are now negotiating with the Chinese authorities, including some European countries. Outbound package tours during the holidays have become family favorites for many. For various reasons, such as size and quality control, only some sixty-five travel agencies have been authorized to organize outbound tours to officially designated destination countries and regions, with a fixed quota each year. Compared with inbound and domestic tourism, much less information on outbound travel is available in terms of length of stay and spending (Table 2.6).

TOURISM INFRASTRUCTURE

China boasts a long history and rich culture, and there is no lack of tourist attractions of all descriptions. However, tourism infrastructure and service facilities were not adequate when the country decided to promote tourism in the late 1970s. Both quantity and quality were lacking. Arduous nationwide efforts over the past two decades have resulted in great improvements to China's tourism infrastructure.

Accommodations

In 1978 there were only 76,192 bedspaces in 203 hotels throughout the entire country, of which only about 60 percent were suitable to accommodate overseas visitors (Sun 1992). Most of these hotels were built in the early postliberation days only for foreign experts working in China and for state leaders. In fact, they did not really fit the needs of modern tourists. The nightmare of extremely short supply of hotel rooms in the early years of 1980s is still fresh in the minds of some veteran hotel managers. Due to the special attention of both the central and local governments, and efforts from both the public and private sectors, the problem of China's hotel supply has fundamentally changed. The introduction of foreign capital and management in this sector has provided a good example for other sectors of China's economy in terms of opening to the outside world. By the end of 1999, there were 7,035 hotels with 889,430 rooms in China. Among all these hotels, 3,856 were higher quality "starred" hotels with 524,894 rooms. The number of hotel rooms has increased by over fifty-seven times in the period from 1978 to 1999, not including

TABLE 2.6. Outbound Travel by Chinese Residents

Year	Departures (thousands)	Annual Growth (%)	Departures for Business (thousands)	Annual Growth (%)	Departures for Private Affairs (thousands)	Annual Growth (%)
1993	3,740.0	27.7	2,273.8	–	1,466.2	–
1994	3,733.6	– 0.2	2,091.1	– 0.8	1,642.3	12.0
1995	4,520.5	21.1	2,466.6	17.9	2,053.9	25.1
1996	5,060.7	12.0	2,646.8	7.3	2,413.9	17.5
1997	5,323.9	5.2	2,884.3	9.0	2,439.6	1.1
1998	8,425.6	58.3	5,235.3	81.5	3,190.2	30.8
1999	9,232.4	9.6	4,966.3	– 5.1	4,266.1	33.7

Source: China Ministry of Public Security, published in China National Tourism Administration (CNTA) (2000). *Yearbook of China Tourism Statistics (2000-2001).* Beijing: China's Tourism Press.

a great many hotels and other forms of accommodations that are not registered with the China National Tourism Administration (CNTA).

Transportation

China has the largest population of any country in the world and is one of the largest in terms of land area. Transportation has been a long-standing problem in the country, and at the beginning of China's tourism development this proved to be an acute headache for the tourism industry. International airline capacity was inadequate and domestic air transport was even worse. Problems included poor connections and a shortage of planes and airports, to say nothing about the quality of service. Railways were the principal means of passenger transport for long-distance travel by domestic travelers, although most of the trains were slow and crowded.

Because of the importance of transportation to all forms of economic development, this situation has been greatly improved over the past two decades. In addition to Air China, which is the national carrier and is controlled by the central government, there are over a dozen large regional airlines serving both domestic and international routes. Most of China's provinces and regions have set up their own local airline. By 1999, China had a fleet of over 510 aircraft, which made 1,115 regularly scheduled flights, of which 150 were international. Foreign carriers offered additional routes to and from China.

Meanwhile, railway authorities have been working hard to meet the increasing demands of domestic tourism by enhancing the speed of trains and adjusting their timetables. As a result, most large cities are now connected by direct express trains, many departing in the evening and arriving at their destinations the next morning. Special tourist or chartered trains to some famous destinations have become very popular, especially during the recent expansion of weeklong holidays. At the same time, more expressways have been constructed, and a nation-wide expressway network is taking shape, allowing coach service to play an important role in domestic transportation. For most of the country, transport is no longer a bottleneck for tourism development. In fact, owing to an oversupply on some air routes, discount airfares are now commonplace.

Tourist Attractions

In the early days of opening to the outside world, only a selected number of Chinese cities were accessible to foreign tourists and special permits were needed to travel to some areas in China. By the end of 1978, only 107 cities or regions were open to foreign visitors, and the major attractions being offered were model factories, schools, neighborhoods, and communes. These made up the majority of a tour group's visit, regardless of the visitors' interests. Although some historical and cultural sites were opened to early foreign visitors, most were largely imitations of one another, such as the many history museums found in Beijing as well as in every provincial capital. By the mid-1980s, visits to factories, schools, communes, and other working units became increasingly rare, yet the similarity of sights everywhere still made for a rather dull itinerary. A saying among international visitors was that in China they "see nothing but temples in the daytime, and do nothing but sleep at night."

That situation changed considerably in the 1990s. Almost all cities in China are now open to foreign visitors and no additional permission is needed to travel within most of the country. For incoming visitors, numerous special interest tours nationwide meet every requirement, and travel companies now vie with one another in offering more innovative tours to attract incoming tourists. Among many others, favorite tours include the Silk Road Tour in the northwest, Tibet's Root of the World Tour, the Three Gorges cruise along the Yangtze River, the Tour of Ancient Capitals, the Southwest Minorities Folklore Tour, Ice and Snow Tours in the northeast, and newly emerging ecotours. In the last fifteen years, some twenty-seven sites in China have been listed as World Natural and Cultural Heritage Sites. Added to these attractions are interesting festivals and shopping, live entertainment, and other amusements and activities that sometimes prove to be too much for tired tourists to pack into their limited time of stay in China.

THE CONTEXT OF CHINA'S TOURISM POLICIES

In the course of political reform and greater openness, great changes have taken place in China's economic policies. The government discarded its long-standing closed-door policy and became more open to the outside world. The highly centralized and planned economy has gradually given way to the "invisible hand" of market forces. Under the leadership of the CPC, the government of China has shifted its emphasis from endless ideological campaigns to concrete economic construction as a way to make the country more successful, prosperous, and powerful. As a component of the country's social and economic development, tourism policies have been adopted in line with the general orientation of the entire nation. These policies have transformed tourism in China in the following ways.

Recognition—From a Diplomatic Activity to an Industry of Importance

Over the past two decades or so, the official purpose of tourism development in China has undergone three major changes:

- *Politics only.* From the early establishment of travel services shortly after 1949, until the eve of present reform in 1978, tourist activities, in fact, only overseas tourist activities in China, were nothing more than an activity serving the foreign affairs of China. They typically centered on "people-to-people diplomacy," seeking no economic returns for the country in any way. Tourists then were either overseas Chinese or "foreign friends and guests." Tourism was a useful means for the young People's Republic to cultivate friendship, understanding, and sympathy from the international community. Overseas tourists, although small in number, were treated as VIPs, with endless banquets, meetings with leaders, courtesy calls, and visits to the working units that presented the achievements and ethics of the government. These were all arranged by the host, regardless of the real interests of the visitors. In China the destination selected the tourists rather than the other way around.
- *Politics plus economics.* During the early stages of reform (from 1978 to 1985), tourism was considered both a part of foreign affairs and an economic activity. However, tourism policies and practices still put politics before economic gains. One example of this was the application of discriminatory pricing policies. Overseas Chinese and compatriots from Hong Kong, Macao, and Taiwan paid much less than non-Chinese-origin foreign

tourists, even if they received the same services. Consequently, prices and services varied according to the race of the person rather than the willingness to pay. Very often, overseas Chinese or compatriots were refused by hotels or transport ticket offices, or given less than proper services, because they paid less than foreign visitors. Foreign visitors, on the other hand, complained of being embarrassed and annoyed by their preferential treatment.

- *Economics over politics.* In 1986, the national government declared tourism to be a comprehensive economic activity with the direct purpose of earning foreign exchange for China's modernization. For the first time ever, tourism was included in China's national plan for social and economic development. In the early 1980s, the national government stressed the importance of tourism as an important service industry that was seen to require less investment, yet have quicker results, better efficiency, larger employment potential, and a greater potential to improve people's livelihood than many other tertiary service sectors (CPC 1993). The development of tourism has been made a key industrial policy since then, which placed its economic impact foremost, as opposed to the political emphasis of the past. At a national economy conference called by the Central Committee of CPC in December of 1998, it was clearly stated that tourism should be considered as a new growth point of the national economy. Since then, most provinces and regions in the country have made tourism one of the pillar industries in their local economic development planning.

Administration—From Micromanagement and Control to Macromanagement and Service

From 1949 to the mid-1960s, there was no single state organ responsible for tourism due to its small scale. The Bureau for Travel and Tourism (BTT) was set up in the mid-1970s under the jurisdiction of the Foreign Ministry. Travel to China by overseas Chinese was treated as a foreign affairs activity and was controlled by the office of Overseas Chinese Affairs under the State Council. Therefore, all aspects of tourism were tightly controlled by the national government, including visas, travel permits, tour pricing, places to visit, and tour guides. Local foreign affairs offices or overseas Chinese affairs offices were responsible for the local arrangements of incoming tours, based upon instructions given by their superior administrations.

With the rapid growth of tourism in the late 1970s, and a deeper understanding of its significance in the course of reform, the National Tourism Administration of the People's Republic of China (CNTA) was set up in 1981 to replace the BTT. CNTA became China's principal national tourism organization (NTO) under the direct jurisdiction of the country's State Council. As such, it became entirely independent from the foreign ministry. The function of the CNTA was different from that of its predecessor. It concentrated on the macro-management of the tourism industry through the development of long-term, medium-term, and yearly tourism plans for the whole nation. CNTA was also involved in the formulation of rules and regulations governing tourism, conducting major overseas travel promotions, education, and training services. Like all other government departments in China, CNTA has gradually cast off its older, monolithic ways of administration. As a new state organ born in the course of reform, it has paid much more attention to the economic and legal aspects of business management. Since the mid-1980s, the business operations of the CNTA have been separated from its governmental functions. It no longer directly owns any companies and its former enterprises have been turned into independent corporate entities with their own decision-making power.

Priority—From Inbound Only to Both International and Domestic Travel

The mode of China's tourism development is quite different from that in most of the developed countries in the world. For political and economic purposes, China started its tourism activities based on inbound travel only. Until the mid-1980s, domestic tourism hardly existed, and pleasure travel was considered a taboo among the Chinese people. As a developing country, China still gives priority to inbound tourism for its foreign exchange earnings.

To meet the growing demand for leisure travel among China's own citizens and to encourage personal consumption for economic growth, the central government has issued a number of policies to promote domestic tourism. Weeklong holidays were first introduced in 1992 and a five-day work week was introduced in 1995. Starting in 1999, three weeklong holidays were established around May 1 (May Day/ Labor Day), October 1 (National Day), and the lunar Spring Festival of Chinese New Year. The stated purpose of these weeks was to encourage people to travel and vacation. According to Lin (2000), during the first seven-day holiday (October 1-7, 1999), over 40 million trips were made with a spending of RMB 14.1 billion yuan (US$1.7 billion); during the second seven-day holiday (May 1-7, 2000), 46 million trips were made with a spending of RMB 18.1 billion yuan; and during the National Day holiday of 2000, domestic trips increased to 59.8 million, and spending was up to over RMB 23 billion yuan (US$1.8 billion).

Parallel with the development of both incoming and domestic tourism, control of outbound travel has been relaxed, and some Southeast and East Asian countries have become popular destinations for Chinese visitors. Although the overseas destinations are limited and the size and mode of outbound travel has been tightly controlled, the number of outbound visitors has been increasing with each year and the number of open destinations will certainly grow. As a result, China's tourism accounts will increasingly be more balanced, with tourist flows in both directions. Nowadays, equal attention is paid to both international and domestic tourism in terms of their contribution to local and regional social and economic development within China.

Business—From Monopoly to Standardization in Tourism Business Operations

When China was still under a strong, centrally planned economic system, with tourism being treated as a political activity, tourism business operations were tightly held in the hands of state organizations. All travel business was monopolized by a handful of centrally controlled travel services. The earliest were the China International Travel Service (CITS) and China Travel Service (CTS). These were later joined by the China Youth Travel Service (CYTS). These were known as the "three magnates" of travel services in China. In fact, they were not independent business operators as such, but part of the government bureaucracy. Most hotels and transport operators were also state enterprises. With the deepening reform and booming tourism of the 1980s, government control has been gradually relaxed.

The days when the "three magnates" dominated travel business are now gone, and there were over 7,000 travel services in operation scattered all over the country in 1999.

Generally speaking, travel services in China are businesses that are operated independently from any direct government organizations, even though many are still state owned. There are some travel service groups with branches in different locations, of which a few have been listed on the stock market. Some are privately owned or are joint ventures with overseas partners. In 1997, the State Council issued the *Regulations of Travel Service Management,* which has served as a milestone for standardization of the business management. Since then, China's travel services have been classified into two categories (international and domestic) instead of the more complicated three (Classes A, B, C, which had two different types of agencies that dealt with overseas travel), indicating that more legalistic mechanisms have replaced the older administrative structure of the travel industry.

Similar changes have taken place also in other tourism-related sectors such as hotel and transport industries. Among all of China's registered hotels in 1999, 61 percent of the rooms were state owned while those that were owned, partly and wholly, by overseas investors accounted for 15.8 percent (CNTA 2000). China's airline industry has undergone a similar decentralized restructuring, as discussed previously.

Actions—From a Product-Oriented to a Market-Oriented Mode

Due to nearly three decades of being closed to the outside world, combined with a limited receiving capacity, China's tourism in the late 1970s and early 1980s was a seller's market. When China first opened its doors to the Western world, tourists, particularly from the United States and Japan, flooded in regardless of facilities, programs, or prices offered. Taking advantage of this demand, China exercised a product-oriented management policy. The practice of rationing and quotas, which served as the traditional means of market control in the planned economy, was also implemented in the international tourism business. This both vexed and puzzled overseas tour operators. Intoxicated with the temporary and abnormal situation of excessive demand, China showed little interest in marketing or market research, and was hardly troubled with the problem of who its tourists were, except that there were more than the infrastructure could handle.

However, with the increase in China's receiving capacity and the easing of the rush to visit China (especially after the Tiananmen Square incident in 1989), the seller's market was replaced by a buyer's market. China realized the importance of the tourism market, which could be influenced or guided but not controlled at will. Only in the late 1980s did China begin to take the international tourist market seriously, and later the widespread financial crisis in Southeast and East Asia forced China to pay much more attention to tourism promotion and marketing. Three year-long national tourism promotion campaigns were launched in 1992, 1997, and 1999, and China is increasingly vying with its neighboring countries for visitors.

EXPERIENCES AND LESSONS

China is a latecomer on the stage of world tourism, and, in reality, it has only been an active player in world tourism since the early 1980s. In the past twenty years or so, China has become one of the world's top international tourism destinations, and the tourism industry has played an important role in the country's economy. During this period, tourism has experienced the embarrassment of an unprepared takeoff, the joy of a surprising boom, the panic of an unexpected slide, then an all-around development. Nevertheless, through practice and experience, China has taken important steps in its tourism development. Outstanding progress has been made in understanding tourism and in seeking a way of developing tourism that is in accordance with the socialist politics and economics of China. The Chinese have gained experience in their successes and have learned many lessons from their failures. Some of these lessons may offer insight and guidance for tourism development in other developing countries. Some of the basic principles that guide tourism development in China today are as follows.

Capitalize on the Country's Comparative Advantages

As a developing country, China is still backward economically and technologically when compared to most industrialized economies.

Yet its vast area, diverse landscapes, ancient history, rich culture, and distinctive political and economic systems constitute China's tourism resources. These abundant resources, many of which are unique, serve the country well in developing tourism. As a matter of fact, China missed several opportunities for tourism development before the reform of 1978, when the country favored heavy industries over the service sector, and preferred international trading in goods rather than services. Although China may not build its economy entirely on tourism, a much more important role for the tourism industry has now been recognized by the central and local governments. China can best compete with other destinations in international tourism by giving full play to its comparative advantages in cultural and historical resources, instead of beach resorts, amusement parks, or other costly projects, at least in the near term.

Develop Tourism in Line with National Economic Development Policies

China's tourism development followed the Chinese principles of "being active, acting according to one's abilities, and maintaining a steady advance" for some years before it was considered a major growth point of the national economy. Tourism is a highly diverse industry, and only policies that encourage the development of all of its related components will result in success. Tourism development may stimulate and promote other industries, yet it is also heavily dependent on the concurrent growth of other sectors. In fact, the tourism industry in China has long been ignored, and it is actually smaller than most other major economic sectors. Therefore, a strategy of "appropriately faster growth" for tourism than other industries in the national economy should be adopted for a certain number of years to come (Sun 1992). Specific policies favorable to the tourism industries would be required to realize this goal. At the same time, it will do no good to develop tourism without regard to the ability of related economic sectors to support it. China's experience has shown that the large-scale construction of tourist attractions, accommodations, and recreational facilities, before the necessary infrastructure (e.g., transportation and education/training) is available, will not achieve a sound development of tourism, but will probably waste resources and damage the destination's image.

Boldly Introduce Outside Capital and Modern Management

Access to overseas capital and the use of management techniques and technologies from abroad can provide a shortcut to increasing tourism in underdeveloped countries. Due to political unrest and past government policies, China has lagged behind the world's advanced countries in many ways. It is not easy for China to catch up in the short term. Tourism, especially international tourism, is a business full of intense competition. Facilities and services for more seasoned and sophisticated tourists must be attractive and distinctive. Above all, they must be up to world standards. Since 1978, China has gradually introduced policies to encourage overseas capital investment and the adoption of modern technology and management techniques to build its hotel industry. The practice of overseas involvement in China has helped to greatly speed up hotel construction, improve the image of China's tourism industry, strengthen links with the rest of the world, and enhance the world's awareness of China. More important, joint ventures with international hotel developers have widened the horizons of the Chinese hoteliers and other businessmen in the country. In fact, the first joint venture hotels served as models for the country's hotel industry. An example of this is the Jianguo Hotel, which was the first Sino-United States joint venture hotel in Beijing, and was originally managed by Peninsular Hotel Corporation of Hong Kong.

Without the introduction of modern overseas management and technology, China's hotel business could not be what it is today. To some extent, the hotel industry in China serves as a pioneer and vanguard in carrying out the policies of reform and openness to the outside world. The success in this field has become an outstanding example of China's current socialist market-oriented economic reforms. So far, outside capital and management has been introduced in almost all sectors of tourism industry, including catering, transport, shopping, travel services, and entertainment, in addition to accommodations. It is believed that more overseas investment and management will flow in now that China has obtained membership in the World Trade Organization.

Beware of the Negative Impacts of Tourism

Tourism has brought foreign exchange and other economic benefits to many destinations in China. Many historical sites and natural features, which had long been left idle, have become surprising moneymakers. However, this is not the whole story. With increasing tourist arrivals and business growth, some negative impacts have become visible and have drawn popular attention. Experience has shown that in terms of the economy, tourism is not always an industry that will generate quick economic results from limited investment, as described by some early writers. With rather poor infrastructure in some Chinese cities and regions, considerable capital must be invested to build the necessary facilities and services before profits from the industry can be realized. Adequate facilities for tourism development, including airplanes, airports, roads, deluxe coaches, cruise ships, and accommodations, are rather costly, and the capital returns of some of them are very marginal, requiring a long development period. In addition, the tourist industry is subject to negative influences from a variety of factors, including natural disasters, economic fluctuations, and political unrest, most of which are beyond the control of tourist destinations and business operators. Tourism, therefore, can be a risky business.

The social and environmental impacts of tourism, which often may be insignificant when the business is very small, cannot be ignored with the expansion of the industry. To describe tourism as a "smokeless" industry in terms of pollution is not an accurate picture. In a developing country such as China, which lacks both experience and funds, pollution as a result of rapid tourism growth would be hard to avoid without careful planning. Major environmental impacts of tourism in China result from too many people producing excessive wear on facilities and causing considerable waste problems. Poorly located and built hotels and other structures can also be a problem. Some tour operators promote so-called "mass" ecotourism, bringing large numbers of people into fragile ecological systems in (so-called) protected areas. Because of its potential negative impacts, the tourist industry is often used as a scapegoat in China for larger social problems. Prostitution, drug trafficking, airport con artists, and even the commodification of traditional folkways would probably be less of a problem in China without the flood of overseas tourists. It is true, as stated in the Manila Declaration on World Tourism in 1980, that "the economic returns of tourism, however real and significant they may be, do not and cannot constitute the only criterion for the decision by States to encourage this activity" (Zhang 1990: 533). It is, therefore, necessary to keep an eye on the negative impacts of tourism.

CONCLUSION

The consistent growth in world tourism serves as an indication of the state of world peace and economic development in general. China's political stability and the sustained growth of its economy will continue to boost the country's tourist industry. Thanks to an abundance of unique and valuable resources, and favorable government development policies, China's tourism (both foreign and domestic) has a promising future. However, arduous efforts must still be made to meet the serious challenge of competition from other major tourist destinations and to guard against the negative impacts that tourism can bring to the country and people. Assuming that the current favorable situation will continue, China will continue to strive to be the top tourist destination in Asia and the world in the coming twenty-first century—as has been forecasted and expected.

REFERENCES

China National Tourism Administration (CNTA). *Yearbook of China Tourism Statistics* (2000-2001). Beijing: China's Tourism Press.

Communist Party of China (CPC) (1993). "Decision of the Central Committee of the CPC and the State Council on Speeding Up the Development of Tertiary Industries," June 16 (in Chinese).

Hibbort, Peter (1990). Cook's Peking home. *Time Traveller* (15):8-9 (Thomas Cook Travel Archive and Library, United Kingdom).

Lin Changrong (2000). Holiday tourism. *China Tourism News* (December 22) (original in Chinese).

Sun, Shangqing, ed. (1992). *Choices in the 21st Century: China's Tourism Development Strategies*. Beijing: People's Publishing House (original in Chinese).

World Tourism Organization (WTO) (2000). *Tourism Highlights*. Madrid: WTO.

World Tourism Organization (WTO) (2001). *Tourism Highlights 2001*. Madrid: WTO.

Zhang, Lili (1998). *Jindai Zhongguo Luyoufazhande Jingi toushi* (Analysis of China's Tourism Development in Modern History). Tianjin: Tianjin University Publishing House.

Zhang, Yuji (1990). *Luyou Jingji Gongzuo Shouce* (Handbook for Tourism Economy). Beijing: China Cyclopedia Publishing House.

Chapter 3

China in the Eyes of Western Travelers, 1860-1900

Xiaolun Wang

Western understanding of China dates from ancient times, and foreign travelers have played a central role in shaping Western perceptions of China. Many early travelers, mostly missionaries and some merchants from Italy, came to China through central Asia between the thirteenth and fifteenth centuries. More missionaries came from Italy and other Western countries after the sixteenth century via ocean travel, and they wrote books and letters about their experiences in China. It was not until the late 1700s, however, that western Europeans came to China for predominantly secular reasons. Led by the British, the last quarter of the nineteenth century was the beginning of modern travel in China; the next half century was also the heyday of Western travel in China before the tourism boom of the post-Mao era. Although the first commercial tours to China were offered by Thomas Cook's company in 1909, political instability in China in much of the first half of the twentieth century hindered such operations. Travel patterns and perceptions developed in this period had far-reaching effects and are still relevant today. This chapter focuses on the background of Western exploration in the eastern half of China in the late 1800s and examines the ways in which Western travelers explored and perceived Chinese landscapes and the implications of such perceptions.

Considerable research has been conducted on Western travel and travel writing in different countries during the "colonial era," especially the eighteenth and nineteenth centuries. One of the best-known references is Pratt's (1992) study of European travel writing on Africa and Latin America in the colonial period, with a strong emphasis on literature, philosophy, and cultural relations. Bishop's (1989) study of English travel writing on Tibet examined how Tibet was transformed into a symbol of romantic idealism, almost religious in nature. Carter (1988) provided a detailed analysis of the evolution of Australian geographic perceptions, often drawing on exploration and travel texts and using a phenomenological approach. Recent geographic work on travel writing appears in a collection of articles on travel perceptions, culture, and history edited by Duncan and Gregory (1999). Portrayals of Africa, Tibet, Egypt, India, and Greece in various travel narratives are examined from postmodern perspectives by different authors in that book. Little research, however, has been conducted on Western travel writing on the eastern half of China, where Han Chinese have traditionally been concentrated. This region was called China proper, classical China, or simply the "eighteen provinces" by Europeans in the nineteenth century. This chapter focuses on this region and is based on the author's recent research on the subject (Wang, 1999, 2000). In both ideas and methodology the author has benefited greatly from these references.

BACKGROUND

Western travelers came to and wrote about China as early as the thirteenth century. Marco Polo, Carpini, Odoric, Rubruck, Mandeville, and Montecorvino all have left accounts of travels in China. Of these only Marco Polo and Odoric reported extensively on China proper. After the sixteenth century, more missionaries came to China from across the ocean, including Pinto and Jesuit priests such as Ricci. Pinto was more an adventurer and his book, *The Travels of Mendes Pinto,* is mainly about pirating and shows a strong religious bias. Jesuit missionaries were preoccupied with promoting Western religion in China, and their writings, such as *The Journals of Mathew Ricci,* dealt with Chinese geography, culture, and political life in the broadest terms.

Interest in Chinese markets, natural resources, and Chinese landscapes was very much a late eighteenth and nineteenth century phenomenon, derived from British influence and the rising popularity of natural science and romanticism. These interests also reflected a much more critical attitude toward Chinese culture. Macartney's mission to Beijing in 1793 included extensive interior travel, and the official account by Staunton (1799) includes detailed descriptions of Chinese scenery, economy, and society. More than 400 plant specimens were collected on this trip. French missionaries Huc and Gabet traveled quite extensively in China in the mid-1800s, but similar to other missionaries their interest was more religious than geographic. In the 1840s and 1850s Robert Fortune collected plant specimens along the coast of Fujian and Zhejiang. These early examples were exceptions rather than the rule, for travel beyond the treaty ports was permitted only after the Tianjin Treaty of 1860, which granted foreigners the right to travel in China. The Taiping Rebellion, however, hindered Western travel in China for a few more years, and travel inside China did not really begin until the 1870s.

Special impetus was given to such travel by the so-called Margary incident when British diplomat Margary was killed while guiding a British expedition from Burma to Yunnan. This led to the Chefoo Convention of 1876, which opened the city of Yichang, Hubei, to foreign trade. Also as a result of the incident and under pressure from British government, the Chinese imperial administration issued proclamations urging local governments to give protection to foreign travelers. Clearly, the British were forerunners in the process, with a longer history of influence in China and a much more strategic sphere of influence: the Yangtze River Valley. The famous French Mekong expedition of 1866, for example, began in Vietnam and ended in Yunnan, with disappointing results (Osborne, 1996). British travelers clearly dominated the scene and produced most of the travel narratives.

ROUTES AND MODES OF TRAVEL

The right to travel was guaranteed by treaties, which proved to be the most important factor in determining routes of travel in China in the late 1800s. Treaties meant privileges; they also meant that Western travelers had to observe formalities, including visiting *yamen* (i.e., government offices), exchanging cards, presents, and salutations with local government officials, and getting permission before moving on. Travelers frequently turned to local Chinese officials for protection and escorts were often provided. Many travelers, however, felt uncomfortable with such arrangements, for official escorts often wanted to follow the shortest route to guide westerners out of their own district as soon as possible; to them westerners meant trouble. This often infringed on the plans of travelers. As a result travelers in general shared a strong dislike of Chinese officials, which was consistent with prevalent attitudes among westerners at the time. Western travelers found that they had to deal with a sophisticated society with a long history and an independent, albeit weakened, government. They had to overcome many physical and cultural barriers, which sometimes challenged their perspectives, giving rise to unique patterns of travel and travel perceptions.

Most Western explorers entered China from the southeast and their travels followed two major routes. One was from the coast, using the early treaty ports, including Guangzhou (Canton), Xiamen, Fuzhou, Shanghai, Tianjin, and so on as launching pads; the other was along the Yangtze River where a number of treaty ports were also established, including Nanjing, Jiujiang, Hankow, Yichang, and later Chongqing. From the coast, travelers followed river valleys such as the Min in Fujian, the Yong in Zhejiang, the Xi, the Bei, and the Dong in Guangdong, the Huangpu in Shanghai, and the Grand Canal in Jiangsu, Anhui, and Shandong. Such travels were confined to southern and eastern provinces as treaty ports were both the starting and ending points of their journeys.

Cumming (1886) explored Hong Kong and from there visited Canton (Guangzhou). From Fuzhou she toured the Min valley and from Shanghai she set out to explore the city of Ningbo and the Yong River. Henry (1886) set out from Canton and explored much of Lingnan, following the courses of the Xi, the Bei, and the Dong. Many, including Cumming, used the Bai River to reach Beijing from Tianjin. Travel in or near treaty ports was easier and more enjoyable. Travelers stayed in European settlements or missionary houses and were accompanied by Europeans on their trips. In the treaty ports they observed Chinese street life and traditional buildings such as temples and houses of wealthy Chinese to which many were invited. From the cities they explored the countryside, emphasizing the picturesque scenery of rural areas. The more they moved away from the coast and treaty ports, however, the more difficult the journey became, especially when water transportation ended.

The Yangtze River served as a line of penetration for English travelers going to western China. Upper Yangtze exploration was a major draw for English diplomats, merchants, explorers, and missionaries in the late 1800s. First the traveler went from Shanghai to Hankow (Hankou) or Yichang, usually aboard modern steamers. After this the Upper Yangtze exploration was made up of two sections. In the first section the traveler left Hankow or Yichang and headed for Chongqing or Chengdu, from where he or she might choose to continue southwest with the second part of the route or simply return to Hankow or Yichang. The second section was from Chongqing or Chengdu to Yunnan and finally Bamo of Burma, a shortcut to British India or Europe. The exploration fever lasted until about 1898 when Chongqing was finally opened to foreign steamers.

With the lack of modern transportation, most travelers used Chinese means of transportation and followed Chinese roads, accompanied by many Chinese, including a "boy" or personal servant, an interpreter, and coolies. Water was the preferred route. Most travelers took steamers from Shanghai to Hankow or Yichang after it became an open port, where they engaged Chinese boats. A contract was signed with the owner of the Chinese boat, and the package usually included the service of Chinese boatmen and a cook. Trackers, i.e., Chinese laborers hauling boats upstream across rapids from riverbanks, were also included, although more usually had to be hired on the way up. The boat was the traveler's home, battleship, and fortress, "a speck of civilization in a country of barbarians," to use the analogy from a traveler in Egypt (Taylor, in Duncan and Gregory, 1999:121); it symbolized Western influence.

For land travels, such as between Chongqing and Chengdu and further into Guizhou and Yunnan, most used Chinese "stages," resting at designated stops on the road. Sedan chair was the most common means of transport, providing both comfort and prestige. One traveler often needed about twenty Chinese laborers on a road trip. Gill (1883) and Mesny hired more than seventy coolies to carry luggage and themselves in sedan chairs. At one point in Sichuan, Hosie's (1897) sedan chair was carried by twelve Chinese to cross a stream. Cumming had sixteen servants and coolies ("human ponies," in her words) on a simple trip to the suburb of Fuzhou. Travelers were sometimes carried on the backs of Chinese when crossing streams or to avoid mud on footpaths between rice fields.

Travelers tended to carry large amounts of luggage, and the most common items, beside food and clothing, included guns and ammunition, alcohol, pens, ink, notebooks, an oil lamp, candles, binoculars, sketching pad, camera, thermometer, barometer, and other supplies. Blakiston (1862) considered weapons and ammunition the most important part of the luggage. Gill was especially heavy laden in his travel to western Sichuan, eastern Tibet, Yunnan, and Burma, carrying 180 candles and cutlery and dining sets. Travelers constantly complained about the poor shape of roads and bad conditions in Chinese inns. Not only were dirt, darkness, and bugs a problem, but the greatest menace came from curious Chinese crowds who surrounded and followed westerners, not leaving until Chinese officials were sent for. For this reason Chinese inns were avoided as much as possible and missionary stations, monasteries, or *yamen* were sought in their place. While in the treaty ports Western travelers associated with a variety of westerners, missionaries were their only allies in the interior. Interactions with Chinese coolies was very limited, for most travelers, unlike missionaries, did not speak Chinese and depended on Chinese interpreters who often spoke pidgin English.

The main interest of Western travelers was in observing Chinese geography, investigating trade opportunities, and, to a limited extent, studying language, people, and social institutions. Observations were made mostly from boats and sedan chairs, sometimes with scientific instruments. When on land, they sought high elevations such as city walls, pagodas, and tall buildings, or they climbed hills and mountains to gain better views. There was little interpersonal communication with native people. Travelers seemed always in a hurry and hated being delayed.

TRAVELERS AND TRAVEL NARRATIVES

Western travelers came from different backgrounds. Many were diplomats who went on official tours of investigation; there were also merchants and independent explorers or travelers. Many missionaries from England and the United States also acted like travelers and left travel accounts. In addition to the British, U.S. and Australian travelers also wrote travel accounts. Although most were men, a few women travelers made outstanding accomplishments. Examples of travel books of the period include those of Blakiston (1862), Gill (1883), Little (1888), Cumming (1886), Henry (1886), Morrison (1902), Hart (1888), Bishop (1899), and Williamson (1870). If travel narratives constitute what has been called "letterpress landscape," to use the term devised by English writer W. M. Thackeray, then this landscape is most developed along coastal China and along the Yangtze Valley because more books were written on these than on any other regions.

For the British, nineteenth-century travel was influenced by several factors. First, territorial interest in the form of establishing spheres of interest was a dominant concern. The significance of gunboat diplomacy was generally recognized and British commercial interest actively promoted. Second, natural science loomed large in the mind of travelers. The main fields of interest were botany, geology, physical geography (topography in particular), and ethnography, which drew many travelers away from the coast and into the interior of China. Third, romantic appreciation of natural landscapes had become well-established in British culture and was represented by ideals of the picturesque and the sublime. Seen in phrases such as "a feast for the eye" and "I'm the monarch of all I survey," these artistic ideals epitomized the pleasures of colonialism, reflecting British power and confidence. They were readily applied to Chinese scenery. Finally, evangelical Protestantism was an aggressive and eager religious influence. A few travelers, such as Morrison and Little, were strong secularists who criticized missionaries. However, most were sympathetic toward religious activities and some missionaries were themselves active travelers. The presence of these influences in the narratives resulted in strong cultural chauvinism and prejudice. They also contradicted one another. When their travel routes went deep into China and first-hand observations were made of Chinese society, a few travelers began to criticize Western stereotypes about China and colonial thinking.

Science and Commerce

Science occupies a prominent place in the travel narratives. Geology, botany, physical geography, and ethnography were the rational justifications for interior exploration of the nineteenth century. These, however, were in close service of commercial interests. There was a preoccupation with steam navigation in the Upper Yangtze among the British in the late 1800s; therefore, travelers devoted considerable space to descriptions of the exact course of the Yangtze, including such data as soundings of the river bed, seasonal changes in the water level, and locations of islands and rocks in the river channel. In addition, geologic knowledge was applied in describing and predicting the existence of coal, gold, silver, and other minerals and in describing salt wells in eastern Sichuan (Hart, 1888). Botany, on the other hand, was used in describing plants and flowers, especially those of economic value, such as the tung oil tree, white wax tree, and mulberry tree. Many geologic and topographic descriptions such as those provided by Margary in Guichow (Guizhou), were also provided from the view of railroad construction (China Consular Office, 1875).

Ethnography was an essential part of Western science in the nineteenth century and an important element in the travel narrative. German explorer Baron Ferdinand von Richthofen and English explorers such as Edward C. Baber, Gill, and Bishop all showed interest in minority tribes in western China, including the Si-fan, the Mantzu, and the Tibetans. Special attention was given to the study of their languages. The isolated and primitive conditions among these ethnic groups enabled Western travelers to approach them both as ideal objects of scientific observation and symbols of freedom and innocence celebrated in romanticism.

Picturesque and Sublime

The picturesque is by far the most dominant landscape ideal in China. It is especially evident in portrayals of coastal regions such as Jiangnan, i.e., the region around Yangtze Delta, and to some extent in agricultural landscapes in other areas. The picturesque is a combination of cultural and natural landscape with a certain degree of irregularity; novelty is essential to this ideal, but so is familiarity. Travelers found the Chinese landscape unique, peculiar, quaint, odd, but most of all charming, like a Chinese landscape painting. In these paintings, the backgrounds were typically made up of mountains, but the foreground of cultural landmarks. The most often used images were the curvy roofs of Chinese buildings, the city wall and its gate towers, pavilions, bridges, memorial arches, tombs in south China, Chinese fishermen on rivers, Chinese boats with unique sails, clusters of bamboo, willow trees, temples half hidden in mountains and woods, pagodas on mountain tops, and other familiar painting themes. Picturesque scenes were also familiar to romantic travelers. The juxtaposition of mountains and rivers, cities and countryside, villages and market towns was not strange to Europeans. The best examples of picturesque scenery come from Cumming's book, in which "picturesque" was a frequently used word. Here is Cumming's (1886) portrayal of the suburb of Fuzhou (Vol. 1:131):

> Each turn of the river is lovely, fringed here and there with clumps of feathery bamboo. Picturesque fir-trees stand out singly or in clusters on prominent headlands; the quaintest of temples and pagodas are perched on perpendicular cliffs; shapely peaks rise above the floating mists, tier above tier, in beautiful groups, and the whole is reflected in the glassy stream, whereon float quaint native boats with their arched sliding covers, great brown sails, bamboo-ribbed, and steered by a gigantic oar astern. The crews are particularly picturesque in stormy weather, when they wear greatcoats of long grass, with capes of the same, and strong bamboo hats, so that each man is not only thatched, but is a moving pillar of grass, supported by two bare legs.

Here images such as "feathery bamboo," "temples and pagodas," and "native boats" are uniquely Chinese. Even people are part of the picture. But for familiarity such scenery is frequently compared with European landscape, including flowers and plants. Again, Cumming (1886) on the suburbs of Fuzhou and Ningbo (Vols. 1:150; 2:76):

> The scenery is becoming more beautiful as we advance, and the villages more picturesque. Some are like Chalets built on piles; others like English farm-houses of the old Sussex type, with cross-beams of black wood, fitted in with white plaster.

> . . . and among the undergrowth, handsome fronds of Solomon's seal greeted us like old friends. So too did rich trails of fragrant honeysuckle, and the snowy blossoms of delicious hawthorn, of two sorts—our own familiar May and a Chinese variety, both blooming in as rich perfection as if in an English lane. No wonder that happy birds sing so joyously! And the cuckoo's note sounded so natural as almost to make us forget how far from home we were.

Here the traveler felt well at home in the Chinese landscape mainly due to the presence of familiar elements. Chinese rural scenery in other areas was also appreciated in picturesque terms. Blakiston (1862), for example, reacted to the rural scenery between Wu-hu and An-qing in similar ways and considered it, like the scenery of Europe, Old World, and thus both strange and familiar (p. 57):

> . . . the beautiful, partially wooded slopes of the mountains reaching down into the highly cultivated lower land; the occasional village; the collection of reed huts gathered on the immediate bank, as if in doubt whether the ground was as safe as the water; the distant pagoda, marking the site of a town approachable only by some canal-like creek; and then, life made apparent by numerous boats with their white cotton wings; the fisherman attending his ingenious dip-net; some coolies trotting along an embankment which raises them above their fellows who are working away in the irrigated paddy-fields below, while two of a more favoured class are being wheeled along a paved pathway in those best of wheelbarrows;—the objects serve to remind one,—the country, of the lake scenery of the Old World,—the river, of the New; but the people, of China, and China only.

The sublime as a symbol of romanticism was born in the late eighteenth century and reached peak popularity in the nineteenth century. It is associated with infinite time and space, with fantasy and thrilling sensations, even terror. English poets of the romantic era sang about wild nature, which was seen as the manifestation of Divine Power. This is mainly applied to mountains and other types of natural scenery. The adjectives used often include "wild," "savage," "vast," "grand," "stupendous," "colossal," "gigantic," "grotesque," "mysterious," and "bewildering." In China the most often described sublime scenery is undoubtedly the Three Gorges, called Yangtze Gorges by Europeans. Mountains in western Sichuan and Tibet are also included in this category. The Yangtze Gorges were the first sublime scenery encountered from the coast and the effect was striking. Blakiston (1862), possibly the first to enter the upper Yangtze, provides the first description of the Yangtze Gorges and was quoted repetitively by later travelers (p. 121):

> . . . but suddenly, as if by magic, we lose the "Son of the Ocean," and in its stead an impetuous current comes rushing towards us out of a long deep cleft in the mountains to the westward. . . . The deep dark appearance of the water shut in from much of the

light of day by the stupendous side-walls of rock, and the distant part of the gorge tinged by the bright atmospheric blue, yet still without end, and only broken by a miniature-looking junk with her spread of white canvas—this view, as it burst so unexpectedly on us as we rounded "Mussulman Point," and shut out I-chang and the plain of Hoo-peh, is one that will never become dimmed in my recollection by the lapse of time.

Little, Hart, and Bishop all viewed the Gorges in similar terms and provided "word paintings" of their own. Bishop (1899) wrote on I-chang (Yichang) Gorge (pp. 109-110):

Streams tumbled over ledges at heights of 1000 feet. There are cliffs of extraordinary honeycombed rock, possibly the remains of the "potholes" of ages since, rock carved by the action of water and weather into shrines with pillared fronts, grottoes with quaint embellishments—gigantic old women gossiping together in big hats—colossal abutments, huge rock needles after the manner of Quiraing . . . higher yet, surmounting rock ramparts 2000 feet high, are irregular battlemented walls of rock, perhaps 20 feet thick, and everywhere above and around are lofty summits sprinkled with pines, on which the snow lay in power only, and "the snow clouds rolling down" added to the sublimity of the scenery.

Rather than being charming and soothing, here the scenery is gloomy and dark, a challenge and object of contemplation. Aside from natural scenery, Chinese trackers and boatmen along the Gorges also became part of the sublime nature, treated like animals much in the tradition of "noble savages" (Blakiston, 1862). Bishop (1899) said of Xin-tan (pp. 123-124):

I never saw such exciting water scenes—the wild rush of the cataract; the great junks hauled up the channel on the north side by 400 men each, hanging trembling in the surges, or, as in one case, from a tow-rope breaking, spinning down the cataract at tremendous speed into frightful perils; while others, after a last tremendous effort, entered into the peace of the upper waters. Then there were big junks with masts lashed on their sides, bounded downwards, and their passage was more exciting than all else. They came broadside on down the smooth slope of water above, then make the leap bow on, fifty, eighty, even a hundred rowers at the oars and yulows, standing facing forwards, and with shrieks and yells pulling for their lives. . . . It is a sublime sight.

Sublime nature was also treated as the opposite of China which was associated with history and man-made nature such as the Chinese garden. Westerners therefore longed for wilderness as an escape from what was Chinese. While in Sichuan, for example, Bishop longed for Tibet where she could escape from the effects of Chinese civilization (Bishop, 1899, p. 337):

> Why should I not go on, I asked myself, and see Tibetans, yaks, and aboriginal tribes, rope bridges, and colossal mountains, and break away from the narrow highways and crowds, and curiosity, and oppressive grooviness of China Proper?

Here the sublime is associated with the wilderness and the ideal frontier. The traveler feels the burden of Chinese civilization in interior Sichuan, and Tibet seems to offer the most convenient escape.

Contradictions and Reflections

Romantic perceptions of landscape are derived from the Western point of view, guaranteed by treaties and obtained from moving boats, sedan chairs, or mountain tops. Because of their entrenchment in colonialism, romantic landscape ideals have several drawbacks. First, visual effects were exaggerated at the expense of social relations and understanding. Cumming, for example, found Chinese smell and speech repelling. When watching Chinese opera, she concentrated on the visual effects only. Even Chinese written language was appreciated as "picturesque." Because they observed China in motion and from the vantage points of colonialism, travelers were often repelled by the "real" China. Close up, travelers found China "ugly" and complained about "dirtiness," "poverty," "darkness," "superstition," and "cruelty" in Chinese life. They were appalled by opium, infanticide, foot binding, and corruption. This undermined their romantic portrayals.

Second, it is useful to compare Western travel writing to Chinese travel descriptions. Chinese travel writing is strongly historical, with details of past experiences behind each landmark or scene. Thus to travel in space means to get in touch with the past as revealed in the landscape. Such cultural facts and their meanings were rarely recognized by Western travelers who appreciated Chinese landscape mainly in European terms. Thus Western travel writing on China is strikingly broad, devoid of historical associations and Chinese place names but rich in generic scientific terms and descriptions of external appearance. China is frequently compared to European places such as Sussex (England), Tirol (Austria), and Switzerland rather than being judged in its own history and value. In the case of the sublime, the fact that there is Chinese art (calligraphy) right in the middle of wild nature areas, such as the Yangtze Gorges, caused considerable ambivalence among Western travelers.

There were many other contradictions in the narratives, such as between romanticism and commercial expansion and between religion and commercialism. Hart (1888) lauded Western commercial advance into China but also lamented the destruction such advances caused to Chinese scenery. Little (1888) reacted similarly to Chinese scenery in Sichuan, praising the beauty of pristine nature while pushing for commercial expansion. Those with religious sentiments tended to criticize commercial expansion just as merchant travelers such as Little disliked missionary efforts. Writers contradicted themselves. Bishop almost despaired at the "poverty" and "corruption" she saw in Sichuan, calling China "hopeless," but toward the end of the book, she praised the Chinese as peaceful and happy, the most "democratic" people in the world. There were also moments of revelation. In a footnote in her book, Cumming (1886) reflected on the positive side of China (Vol. 1: 256):

> I confess that when, on returning to England, I have looked round on the squalid wretchedness and dirt of the densely crowded quarters in which our poor are huddled together ... my thoughts have travelled back to the Chinese street-cooks with positive veneration. And as to the luxurious halfpenny tea-hall, which takes the place of England's gin-palace, there indeed China does excel the barbarians of the West.

In this rare note, the pretensions of colonialism and romanticism are dropped and we witness something genuine and sincere. Travel becomes what it traditionally is, a learning experience based on humility and respect.

IMPLICATIONS

What is the relevance of studying nineteenth century travel in China? Western travelers of the late nineteenth century viewed China largely from a colonial point of view. Their freedom and superior positions were guaranteed by an unequal relationship with China under the treaty system, but they were challenged in such views and conflicts were frequent. Local officials tried to rush them out of their territories; crowds followed them. Curiosity escalated into conflict as Chinese insisted on their right to observe westerners. The Boxer Rebellion of 1900 offers a good example. During the rebellion, according to Glover (1904), when foreigners were attacked, it was often hard to distinguish curious onlookers from rioters. The scholar-official Huang Zun-xian (1848-1905) expressed his resentment toward the presence of Western travelers in a poem titled "Climbing Up Yueyang Tower":

> Majestic mountain pass guards the upper river,
> Eight hundred lakes are swept within view.
> Beware the sun is covered by the head of Qin,
> It is hard to divide the land of Yu.
> Barbarians are clowns since the old,
> How is it that they now stand in the middle of the stream?
> What do the red-haired and blue-eyed know,
> Climbing to the top with binoculars in their hands.

Li Chao Gan Shi Shu (1999, p. 413)

This is not limited to the past or to China, either. Conflicts between natives and tourists have become a fixed feature of contemporary life, often with violent consequences such as in Egypt in 1995 and in the Philippines in 2000.

Tourism reflects cultural values and relationships of political power. Although the People's Republic of China has been a unified country for more than half a century and although nineteenth century technology has been replaced by a newer cyberworld, the status of China as a developing country has not fundamentally changed. With the removal of orthodox Maoism as the dominant ideology and the adoption of open economic policies, more and more westerners are coming into China. The government has approached foreign tourism mainly as an economic activity, so the political and cultural implications have largely been neglected, in sharp contrast to the 1960s and 1970s. As a result, the colonial pattern of Western travelers roaming through the country at will and observing it from superior vantage points is reemerging. Exclusionary foreign hotels occupy strategic locations and more and more scenic spots have remodeled themselves and raised admission fees to cater to foreign tourists, at the expense of local visitors. In the meantime most Western tourists remain sightseers, watching China from a distance, from trains or tour buses. They hurry through the country and leave it with their preconceptions of China reaffirmed rather than newly formed by such tours. Good glimpses of these are obtainable from the writings of Theroux (1988) and Thubron (1987). In light of the colonial experiences and contemporary neo-colonialism in other countries, it is suggested that while promoting foreign tourism, the government must also address the colonial connotations of foreign tourism so that they are controlled and do not become an affront to China as a country and the Chinese people as individuals. Outsiders should be welcomed into China on the grounds of cultural understanding and learning rather than simply satisfying curiosity, for sightseeing is not as innocent as it may seem.

REFERENCES

Bishop, J.F. (1899). *The Yangtze Valley and beyond.* London: John Murray.

Bishop, Peter (1989). *The myth of Shangri-la: Tibet, travel writing, and the western creation of sacred landscape.* London: The Anthlone Press.

Blakiston, T.W. (1862). *Five months on the Yangtsze.* London: John Murray.

Carter, Paul (1988). *The road to Botany Bay.* New York: Knopf.

China Consular Office (1875). *Notes of a journey from Hankow to Ta-li Fu by the late Augustas Margary.* Shanghai: F and Walsh.

Cumming, C.E. Gordon (1886). *Wanderings in China.* Edinburgh: William Blackwool and Sons.

Duncan, James and Derek Gregory (1999). *Writes of passage.* London: Routledge.

Gill, W. (1883). *The river of golden sand* (Condensed). London: John Murray.

Glover, Archibold E. (1904). *A thousand miles of miracles in China*. Glasgow: Pickering and Inglis.

Hart, Virgil C. (1888). *Western China: A journey to the Buddhist center of Omei*. Boston: Ticknor and Company.

Henry, B.C. (1886). *Ling-Nam and interior views of Southern China*. London: S. W. Partridge and Co.

Hosie, A. (1897). *Three years in western China*. London: George Philip and Son.

Li Chao Gan Shi Shu Huai Shi (1999). (Historical and sentimental poems of past dynasties). (In Chinese). Beijing: Hua Xia Press.

Little, Archibold J. (1888). *Through the Yang-tse Gorges*. London: Sampson Low, Marston and Co.

Morrison, G.E. (1902). *An Australian in China*. London: Horace Cox.

Osborne, Milton (1996). *River Road to China: The search for the source of the Mekong River: 1866-73*. New York: Atlantic Monthly Press.

Pratt, Mary L. (1992). *Imperial eyes: Travel writing and transculturation*. New York and London: Routledge.

Staunton, G. (1799). *An authentic account of an embassy to the King of Great Britain to the Emperor of China*. Philadelphia: John Bioren.

Theroux, Paul (1988). *Riding the iron rooster: By train through China*. New York: Putnam's.

Thubron, Colin (1987). *Behind the wall: A journey through China*. New York: The Atlantic Monthly Press.

Wang, Xiaolun (1999). Geographic descriptions in modern Western travel writing on coastal and interior China. Postdoctoral thesis, Fudan University (in Chinese).

Wang, Xiaolun (2000). Route and scenery in Bishop's *The Yangtze Valley and Beyond*. *Historical Geography* (in Chinese) 16: 229-239.

Williamson, A. (1870). *Journeys in north China, Manchuria, and eastern Mongolia*. London: Smith, Elder and Co.

Chapter 4

Chinese Vernacular Heritage As a Tourist Attraction: The Case of Beijing

Ning Wang

INTRODUCTION

The city is a product for residents, tourists, and investors (Ashworth and Voogd 1990). Although a city can be a common product for these three agents, each of them may have various demands and interests as to what that product should be. Sometimes, tensions arise in their rival demands regarding the city product. For example, tourists may demand that a city be a site of heritage and authenticity, with a distinctive identity. However, as will be shown in the following pages, such a tourist demand may come into conflict with local residents' demands for a modernized city to live in. In many aspects, tourists' demands are in congruence with local residents' demands with respect to a city as a product. For example, both of them want the city to be beautiful. However, tensions between a city as a dwelling place and a city as a tourist destination may exist, for local residents may want the city to favor residents rather than tourists. Thus, for a city that aims to develop tourism, urban planning would involve political and social contests between the agents of local residents in favor of

My thanks are due to Dr. Alan Lew for his advice and suggestions. My thanks also go to Beijing Hutong Tour Agency for the information provided.

tourism (including local stakeholders of the tourism industry as well as investors) and the agents of local residents against tourism. Therefore, urban planning in general, and tourism planning in particular, is not merely a scientific process but is also intertwined with social, political, and cultural processes.

Tourism is in a sense identity management, namely, planning and maintaining a desired place identity for both local residents and tourists. What should that identity be? Regarding certain urban elements, such as traditional and vernacular house forms in Beijing, tensions arise in competitions for space. In the case of Beijing, the agents in favor of tourism believe that the city should maintain its traditional identity and preserve vernacular houses. By contrast, the agents in favor of urban modernization believe that vernacular houses are outdated and a waste of land resources and should give way to contemporary architecture; contemporary architecture symbolizes modernization in the city. Although the mass tourism industry does not necessarily have interests in heritage conservation because of a profit-driven and consumptive orientation, the cultural tourism industry does have interests in heritage conservation, in confrontation with the force of urban modernization that keeps destroying local heritage such as vernacular house forms.

This chapter deals with identity management in relation to vernacular architectural heritage as a tourist attraction in Beijing. The central issue is the tension between the preservation of vernacular architecture and urban modernization. As Beijing has rapidly modernized its urbanscape, its vernacular houses have been disappearing. Thus, how to maintain a cultural and touristic identity is a challenge to urban modernization in Beijing. This chapter describes how tourism, in the case of Hutong tourism (Wang 1997), has played a certain role in influencing local residents' and urban planners' attitudes toward the preservation of vernacular architecture. Tourism is a force that has shaped identity management in Beijing.

VERNACULAR ARCHITECTURE AS A SIGN OF IDENTITY

Identity is a widely used term but it is a difficult concept to define (Mol 1976; Rapoport 1981). Nevertheless, various attempts have been made to do just this (for example, Featherstone 1995; Mol 1976;

Morley and Robins 1995; Rapoport 1981). On a basic level, identity refers to certain conditions that make one thing remain itself, not another (see Rapoport 1981). Identity may refer to either the individual (individual or personal identity) (Erikson 1950) or the collectivity (collective identity) (Schlesinger 1987), and the conditions that constitute "identity" can be either objective (languages, symbols, landscapes, etc.) (Lanfant, Allcock, and Bruner 1995) or subjective (belonging, sense of community, self-image, etc.) (Featherstone 1995). Thus, the identity of human beings can be very complicated (Figure 4.1).

Here, objective conditions, or features, do not themselves constitute identity; they constitute the objective aspect of identity only in so far as they function as the *physical markers, indicators, or symbols of identity.* Objective conditions, however, become *signs, symbols, and markers of identity* only when they are locked into a semiotic or communicative process, through which these signs, symbols, and markers are identified as referring to the boundaries of identity by both the members of a group and outsiders. Therefore, the opposite poles of objective and subjective aspects of identity are only analytic constructs; in reality they are merged in a semiotic process, with the objective/physical factors acting as symbols, signifiers, markers, and cues whereby the subjective identity (meanings, sentiments, belonging, collective memory) of a community are conveyed (Figure 4.2).

From a sociological perspective, the identity of a place is not a physical identity. Rather, it is involved in the identification process of

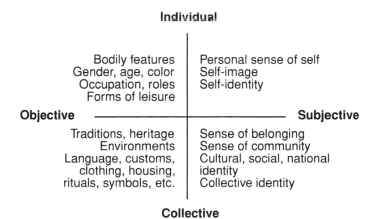

FIGURE 4.1. The Framework of Identity

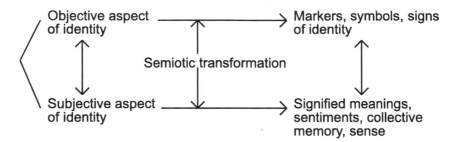

FIGURE 4.2. Semiotic Transformation of Identity Markers

a community at a place. In other words, physical characteristics (physical identity) become the identity of a place only when they are *identified and coded* as the markers, signs, and symbols of the identity of that community. In this way, identity can be communicated, either consciously or unconsciously, by means of markers, cues, indicators, or symbols.

According to Rapoport (1981:14), "there is a major and clear distinction between communicating identity *internally,* i.e., to members of the group or to oneself, and *externally,* i.e., to others, to outsiders." Whereas communicating identity internally is to establish internal cohesion and a sense of togetherness through the process of socialization, communicating identity externally is to "communicate the desired identity to others" (Rapoport 1981:14), which aims to reinforce internal identity. As far as a tourist destination goes, the physical markers or symbols of identity, not the internal feelings and senses of the local identity, catch the attention of the tourists, and hence function to communicate identity to the outsiders. The tourist will stay for only a short period in any given destination, and thus needs recognizable environmental signs to read out local identity.

Various means can be used to communicate identity to outsiders, including both nonenvironmental cues (language, rituals, ways of behavior, etc.) and environmental cues (built environments which include monuments, relics, housing, and townscapes) (Rapoport 1981). The latter constitutes a "nonverbal communication" of identity (Rapoport 1982). As the nonenvironmental cues change in a rapid way, the environmental cues, such as the built environments, the so-called heritage, more convincingly function as the evidence of the past, on which identities are rooted, formed, and sustained. Tourism, as part of cultural industry, is in a sense a form of communicating the desired identity to outsiders by means of both nonenvironmental cues and environmental cues. The environmental cues play a particular role in touristic communication of identity. Among various cultural markers of identity, the house (the aggregation of houses constitutes the townscape or urbanscape) is perhaps the most impressive. In many societies, the vernacular architecture may be one of the most telling environmental clues to identity (Duncan 1981). The form of house is cultural, varying with different cultures, nations, and places (Rapoport 1969). It functions as a sign of cultural identity of a place.

QUADRANGLES AND THE CULTURAL IDENTITY OF BEIJING

That vernacular architecture conveys the cultural identity of a city can be typically exemplified by the case of Beijing. The city of Beijing, it is said, is one of the greatest examples of cultural engineering on the face of the earth, and one of the most magnificent cultural spectacles in the history of civilization (Yan 1993). Beijing is renowned as a well-planned horizontal city. When visiting Beijing in the thirteenth century, Marco Polo was deeply impressed by the checkerboard-like city of Beijing, with its very long, straight streets and its neat order, and he admired it greatly (Wong 1992). The city structure of Beijing was from its inception a product of the absolutist social structure and culture of feudal China.

The history of Beijing dates back to 1045 B.C. (the Zhou Dynasty) at which time it was named Su City and was the capital city of Yan, a small country in that period. After that, from the Qin Dynasty (221-207 B.C.), which unified China for the first time, to the Song Dynasty (960-1279), Beijing did not serve as a capital city. During both the Liao Dynasty (916-1125) and the Jin Dynasty (1115-1234), Beijing first developed as the capital city of northern China, ruled by a succession of smaller minority nations. The urban pattern of Beijing, which shapes today's city, was established in the Yuan Dynasty (1271-1368). The Yuan Dynasty was a feudal empire built by the nomadic Mongolian nation, who defeated the Han majority nation and then ruled China. After the Mongolians moved to Beijing (1260), they found that it had already been ruined by the war of 1215. Therefore, a large-scale reconstruction of Beijing was undertaken (1267-1276).

The planning and construction of the city pattern was deeply shaped by the absolutist power of the emperors, the feudal hierarchical structure of society, and the traditional culture of the Han nation, adopted by the Mongolians, with the emperors' royal palace being located in the "absolute" center of the city. Through this ran a central longitudinal axis, representing the center of the cosmos. The whole city was in fact built around this central axis, with all streets and lanes being arranged longitudinally and latitudinally to it. The imperial kinsmen's and aristocrats' houses were sited close to the east and west sides of the palace. North and south of the palace were the houses of the common folk and merchant class. The urban construction in the Yuan Dynasty laid the foundation for subsequent reconstructions of Beijing in the Ming Dynasty (1368-1644), during which the Forbidden City was built to replace the previous royal palace, in order to drive out the "spirits" of the previous emperor (Li 1993). Hence, the spatial patterns, particularly the street and lane networks of Beijing, were largely laid down in the four centuries of the Yuan and Ming Dynasties. Today's Beijing has been expanded and enlarged, but is still roughly based on the old pattern of central Beijing.

Just as the whole of Beijing had been constructed as a horizontal and square city from the Yuan Dynasty, the houses, as the spatial cell of Beijing, were also built in a rectangular form; the *siheyuan* (i.e., "quadrangle"), a kind of enclosure of buildings. This complex, formed by four houses on the four sides around a courtyard, can be traced back to the Han Dynasty (206 B.C. to 220 C.E.). In the Yuan Dynasty, the invading Mongolian nation completely adopted the housing culture of the Han nation. Of course, the size and design of the quadrangles varied with the status of the occupants, with the Forbidden City representing the biggest and most luxurious quadrangle of all.

There were roughly two kinds of quadrangle. The first type was owned by the imperial kinsmen, high-ranking officials, the aristocrats, or the wealthy. This kind of quadrangle was specially built with imposing features and luxurious decoration, such as beautifully carved and painted roof beams and pillars; these are purely symbolic and aesthetic rather than utilitarian. They contained, at the very least, a front yard and a back yard. This kind of building functioned as a status marker of the upper class and aristocrats. By contrast, the second kind of quadrangle belonged to "ordinary" residents and was simply built on a smaller scale, with small gates, low houses, and containing only one yard. If the Forbidden City and other luxurious quadrangles are the evidence of the history of the emperors and aristocrats, then the ordinary quadrangles bear witness to the history of the "ordinary" people. Various quadrangles constituted a large quadrangle—the city of Beijing was, as a whole, a magnified quadrangle.

"Hutong," a kind of ancient alley or lane, are passageways formed by many closely arranged quadrangles of different sizes. Hutong was a Mongolian term. Its original meaning was "well." Hutong was important for the nomadic people because it implied that there was water for residence and settlement. When the Mongolians ruled China and constructed Beijing in the thirteenth century, they used the term to denote alleys or lanes that lay between many quadrangles (Wong 1992). As the city was designed longitudinally and latitudinally, numerous lanes constituted a checkerboard-like network. Usually, specially built quadrangles all faced to the south for better light. As a result, hutongs running from east to west consist of larger lanes. Between these big hutongs were many smaller ones, going north and south for convenient passage. Before 1949, there were over 3,000 hutongs in Beijing. Up to the present day, the number of hutongs has doubled—over 6,000 now exist (Wong 1992). Recent "Hutong tourism" in Beijing is an itinerary of moving around hutongs to gaze at various quadrangles where local residents live (Wang 1997).

The rise and fall of different dynasties, the success and decline of the empires, the change of societal structures, and the weakening of cultural cohesion all modified the physical and living conditions of quadrangles in Beijing; however, the *physical* structure of the quadrangles has remained roughly the same throughout centuries of history. The *family* structure and the *social* structure in (and between) the quadrangles has, however, changed radically. One of the most obvious changes was that many quadrangles were no longer occupied by one extended family but were shared by several households, partly due to an increase of population. Despite the fact that the wealthy aristocrats still used the luxurious quadrangles as status markers and "conspicuous landscapes," the fact that more and more quadrangles had been increasingly shared not by an extended family but by several households helped to form a sense of community, a vernacular society of "ordinary" people. The quadrangle then became a social unit of a few households forming a neighborhood, or a spatial cell of a community. Thus, a sense of local community was formed and sustained within, and between, quadrangles. The quadrangle became the social space of *folk* society, i.e., a kind of coherent community in which residents and neighbors offered mutual help and warmth. The neighborhood was also extended beyond a single quadrangle to a set of quadrangles, so-called *Jie Fang*. Hutongs (small lanes between quadrangles) functioned as a quasi-public space where children would play, adults would meet to converse, and peddlers, vendors, or hawkers would tout their goods in order to encourage trade with the residents. Most of the quadrangles occupied by "ordinary" households form what Zukin (1992) termed a *vernacular*, a kind of place linked to the powerless, as contrasting to *landscapes*, which are constituted by asymmetrical power (e.g., royal power), such as the Forbidden City and other luxurious quadrangles that were occupied by the wealthy.

The founding of the People's Republic of China in 1949 brought about dramatic changes in the city of Beijing as a whole, and the quadrangles in particular (Li 1993). The city was more comprehensively planned, roads were widened and straightened, and more modern architecture was constructed. In the process, the old city walls were removed. In order to solve the problem of housing for the burgeoning population, many humble houses with simple facilities were built, but not in the form of the quadrangle, during the 1950s. From the 1970s onward, numerous boxlike, featureless, tall apartment buildings were constructed. Within the remaining quadrangles, the tendency toward sharing a quadrangle among a number of households became dominant, due to both the pressure of a shortage of houses and communist egalitarian ideology. Despite several decades of political upheaval and unrest, the communal sense of identity within and between quadrangles has remained. Such an identity is now facing the current triumphal modernization of urban architecture and urbanscape, beginning with the 1978 program of "Reform and Opening Up to the Outside World."

URBAN MODERNIZATION VERSUS VERNACULAR QUADRANGLES

In contemporary Beijing many factors place pressure upon the vitality of the quadrangle. From within, two factors are visible. First, a quadrangle is shared by a number of households (from four or five up to twenty or more households, depending on the size of the quadrangle), causing a feeling of crowdedness. Inside many quadrangles, simple extra rooms are built in order to create more living space; some quadrangles even lost their courtyards due to these added structures. Much worse, there is no private space within the quadrangle. Each family's life is under the scrutiny of others. Once the residents of the quadrangles come to realize the value of privacy, the social value of the quadrangle is devalued. This has already happened in Beijing. Second, as a traditional form of building, the quadrangle lacks many facilities and comforts in comparison with modern apartment buildings, which are better designed and equipped (Wang 1997). For example, many quadrangles do not have central heating or private toilets (instead people use public toilets within the quadrangle or outside the quadrangle). In addition, sound insulation, lighting, and sewage systems are all in relatively poor condition.

From without, two factors challenge the quadrangle. First is the growth of China's urban population. There has been increasing contradiction between the low-profile pattern of the quadrangle and demands for housing due to the dramatic increase in urban residents. Quadrangles worsen the growing urban population's housing situation because they can only supply a very limited number of rooms in relation to a given area of land.

The second factor impacting Beijing's quandrangles is urban modernization. In traditional Beijing, what Zukin calls "landscape" (linked to asymmetrical power) mainly refers to traditional luxurious buildings occupied by emperors, imperial kinsmen, or aristocrats. The Forbidden City and the Summer Palace constitute this grand heritage. Contemporary Beijing's landscape, by contrast, also consists of modern architecture, much of which was started in the 1950s when the so-called ten master buildings were completed (Wang 1997). These buildings were symbols of the socialist modernization which took place at that time. They also reflected the dominant political ideology during this period and were regarded as the architectural symbols of *the achievements of socialist construction.*

From the 1980s onward, a new, accelerating wave of urban modernization has developed in Beijing. Not only the number, but also the height, of the newer buildings has been soaring. In addition to houses and buildings, Beijing's road system has also been modernized; a number of grades of road have been constructed, and three circles of motorway have been developed around Beijing (Li 1993). During this process, old quadrangles in the way of urban modernization have had to "give way" (except in preservation zones, such as in the central city). A British journalist recently observed, "As booming Beijing reaches for the sky, its maze-like old quarters are being swept away" (Tempest 1996:17). The soaring land prices resulting from the economic boom have reinforced this trend. The quadrangles have simply not been able to bear the pressure of the economics of space. Outside the central city (the location of the traditional city of Beijing), Beijing has already been modernized as a landscape of economic growth, and provides a sharp contrast to the old vernacular of ordinary resident areas (Zukin 1992; Wang 1997).

As a result of urban modernization, several identity changes relating to the quadrangle have occurred. Two such changes can be identified here. First, some residents have tended to devalue the quadrangle because of their lack of privacy. Second, urban planners and real estate developers have tended to devalue the quadrangle because of the inefficient use of land. City planners have had to prioritize housing supply within available areas of land for local residents. Thus, highrise buildings have been thought of as more rational and economic uses of land than the quadrangle. This idea is also supported by commercial real estate developers (Wang 1997).

Thus, urban modernization, with the support of both power and capital, tends to establish its dominant position through building its own "landscapes"—contemporary buildings and urbanscapes. As Marx highlighted in *The Communist Manifesto,* under the force of modernization, "all that is solid melts into air." Such a force is now placing the traditional house—the quadrangle—at stake. Can the quadrangle survive the sweep of urban modernization?

TURNING THE QUADRANGLE INTO A TOURIST ATTRACTION

Theoretically, there are justifications for the preservation of the traditional quadrangle: it represents the heritage of Beijing, where the root and the local communal identity of the city lie. Both local "ordinary" residents and city planners are somewhat aware of the cultural significance and implications of the vernacular quadrangle and hutongs. Indeed, some critics have seriously attacked the construction of high-rise buildings in Beijing, because they have destroyed the original style of the city. However, in China's effort to modernize, little space is left for nostalgia. The humble and simple quadrangles and hutongs are overshadowed by the grand heritage landscape of the Forbidden City, the Summer Palace, the Great Wall, the Temple of Heaven, and Tiananmen Square. As a result, although the grand heritage of Beijing has been well preserved because of its worldwide reputation, the heritage of the ordinary quadrangle has not enjoyed the same fate. Many old and deteriorated quadrangles have been demolished in order to build new modern high-rise buildings.

However, a compromise has been made between the preservation of vernacular architecture and urban modernization. In 1993, the municipal government instituted a policy that included the preservation of a number of the quadrangles in three small areas of vernacular housing on the list of Beijing heritage preservation sites. Although the policy was made at a late stage in the city's redevelopment, it has aided the quest for preservation of vernacular heritage. Most of these preserved quadrangles lie in Xicheng Qu and Dongcheng Qu, which are within the city center. In addition, within certain areas of the city stipulations now state that newly constructed houses cannot be higher than two stories. Over 1,000 hutongs, which are beyond the reach of modernization mostly because they are within the preservation areas, are still well preserved in central Beijing (Sun 1995). Beyond these, as much as two-thirds of the city's old residential areas have already been leveled, while much of the rest awaits its turn (Tempest 1996).

Although the preservation of the quadrangle has been part of Beijing's heritage preservation efforts, tourism has been a major factor reinforcing these policies. Indeed, the historical, and hence touristic, value of the quadrangle helped it to survive total destruction under rapid urban modernization. The touristic value of vernacular architectural heritage, therefore, supports the defense of this heritage against the encroachment of urban modernization. In return, the preserved heritage can be turned into touristic capital. For example, a kind of vernacular house tour, known as "hutong tourism," has been offered since 1995 in Beijing (Wang 1997).

Hutong tourism in Beijing has been both a commercial and a cultural project. As a cultural project, it has helped communicate the vernacular identity of Beijing to tourists. Modernization is certainly a force that causes identity change, but the degree and scope of the impact of modernization upon heritage depends upon the action of local agents. The hutong tourism project is a local assertive force that has reduced the negative consequence of modernization upon the vernacular landscape. Hutong tourism is a local action that creates a direct nexus between the local and the global.

In addition to local actors, international tourists who visit the hutong area also exert, unconsciously, their influences in the revaluation of the local cultural identity as exemplified in the quadrangle and the hutong. As far as foreign tourists are concerned, what they like to see most is certainly not an architectural landscape that is similar to their home societies, but one that is different, vernacular, novel, and exotic (Cohen 1972). International tourism powerfully demonstrates that what is mundane and ordinary for local people may be "exotic" and attractive to foreign tourists, as is the quadrangle. Through the international tourist's "visual consumption" (Zukin 1992), the "ordinariness" of the vernacular house and of daily life within the quadrangle and the hutong have been culturally transformed as "extra-ordinariness," and hence as an attraction, itself a cultural product rather than a sheer physical product. Foreign tourists join the process of semiotization that redefines the quadrangle as the symbolic identity of the ordinary Beijing residents.

CONCLUSION

In a modernizing country such as China, identity is often very future oriented. As a result, modernization may become an a priori goal of the whole nation. However, such a drive may put the future existence of certain vernacular architectural heritage, such as the quadrangle in Beijing, at risk. How to rescue and preserve the heritage is indeed a challenge to developing countries that prioritize "hardware" modernization (dynamism) and overlook cultural preservation (conservatism).

Tourism supports the preservation of vernacular architecture, because tourism is a force that commercializes vernacular architecture by turning the architecture into an attraction. Tourism not only makes use of the potential economic and "museumizable" values of vernacular architecture, but also communicates local identity to tourists through treating vernacular architecture as the marker and sign of local community. Thus for a place, tourism is, in reality, a project of identity management. How to maintain and manage a desired identity within the context of rapid and dynamic urban modernization is indeed a major issue that China, along with many developing countries, faces.

There is both a narrow and a broad sense of "museumization" (Relph 1976). The narrow sense is conventional museum making, which is often inauthentic. By contrast, museumization in a broad sense is a form of conservation of an area where traditional and vernacular architecture, ways of life, arts, and customs are prevented from being destroyed, as exemplified in the case of vernacular architecture in Beijing. In the latter case, the realization of authenticity is possible. However, such authenticity is fragile, threatened by the sweeping force of modernization. Thus, cultural conservation and authenticity are made possible only when the cultural identity is felt in crisis and the meaning of heritage is rediscovered within the context of modernization. Although authenticity is constructive in nature, it remains a goal of cultural preservation.

REFERENCES

Ashworth, G. J. and H. Voogd (1990). *Selling the City: Marketing Approaches in Public Sector Urban Planning*. London. Delhaven Press.

Cohen, Erik (1972). Toward a Sociology of International Tourism. *Social Research* 39(1): 164-182.

Duncan, James S. (1981). *Housing and Identity: Cross-Cultural Perspectives*. London: Croom Helm.

Erikson, Erik H. (1950). *Childhood and Society*. Harmondsworth: Penguin (1963).

Featherstone, Mike (1995). *Undoing Culture: Globalisation, Postmodernism and Identity*. London: Sage.

Lanfant, Marie-Francoise, John B. Allcock, and Edward M. Bruner (eds.) (1995). *International Tourism: Identity and Change*. London: Sage.

Li, Deng Ke (1993). *Beijing Dao You Ji Chu* (The foundation of the guides to Beijing). Beijing: Social Science Literature Publishers.

Mol, Hans (1976). *Identity and the Sacred: A Sketch for a New Social-Scientific Theory of Religion*. Oxford: Basil Blackwell.

Morley, David and Kevin Robins (1995). *Space of Identity: Global Media, Electronic Landscapes and Cultural Boundaries*. London: Routledge.

Rapoport, Amos (1969). *House Form and Culture*. Englewood Cliffs, NJ: Prentice-Hall.

Rapoport, Amos (1981). Identity and Environment: A Cross-Cultural Perspective, in James S. Duncan (ed.), *Housing and Identity: Cross-Cultural Perspectives,* pp. 6-35. London: Croom Helm.

Rapoport, Amos (1982). *The Meaning of the Built Environment: A Nonverbal Communication Approach*. London: Sage.

Relph, Edward (1976). *Place and Placelessness*. London: Pion.

Schlesinger, Philip (1987). On National Identity: Some Conceptions and Misconceptions Criticized. *Social Science Information* 26(2): 219-264.

Sun, Yu Bo (1995). Zhan Shi Shen Hou de Wen Hua Di Yun: Beijing Hutong Lu You Dai Lai de Qi Shi (Displaying the depth of the cultural tradition: The inspiration brought about by the Hutong tour in Beijing). *The Economy Reference Daily,* June 17, p. 6.

Tempest, Rone (1996). Horizontal City Loses Its Secret Courtyard Life. *The Guardian,* January 15.

Wang, Ning (1997). Vernacular House As an Attraction: [an] Illustration from Hutong Tourism in Beijing. *Tourism Management* 18(8):573-580.

Wong, Li (1992). *Beijing de Hutong* (Beijing's lanes). Beijing: Beijing Yanshan Publishers.

Yan, Chong Nian (1993). Preface, in *Deng Ke Li: Beijing Dao You Ji Chu* (The foundation of the guides to Beijing), pp. 1-4. Beijing: Social Science Literature Publishers.

Zukin, Sharon (1992). Postmodern Urban Landscapes: Mapping Culture and Power, in Scott Lash and Jonathan Friedman (eds.), *Modernity and Identity,* pp. 221-247. Oxford: Blackwell.

SECTION II:
RESEARCH AND IMPACTS

Chapter 5

Tourism Research in China

Zhang Guangrui

Tourism research in China did not exist until tourism development was encouraged by changes in the central government's policies at the end of the 1970s. This was when the Chinese government began its epoch-making campaign of economic reform and opening to the outside world. China has experienced a dramatic growth in tourism development over the past twenty years and now ranks among the world's top ten international destinations in terms of both international tourist arrivals and tourism revenue (WTO 2000; also see Chapter 2).

However, a large gap still exists between China and other countries on the World Tourism Organization's (WTO) top ten list. WTO forecasts of continuing growth in international visitor arrivals for China, propelling it to one of the top global destination countries in the next twenty years, are very encouraging. On one hand, China is rather excited by these developments, with the central government having designated tourism as one of only a few growth points in the country's latest economic development plans. Most local authorities throughout the country have also announced similar policies. On the other hand, other countries, especially Asian and Pacific countries, are anxious to see how reliable those forecasts are, and how they can best benefit from the projected growth of travel and tourism in the last untapped megamarket in the world today.

As a result of these trends, tourism development in China has been a hot topic both at home and abroad and has been extensively discussed at international and regional conferences, symposia, and in tourism journals. Unfortunately, many of these discussions have occurred among researchers and writers outside of China, while the opinions and findings of Chinese academics have been hardly heard in the outside world. Language barriers and resource constraints have contributed to this problem. In addition, tourism studies were emerging as a distinct field of research in the West just when China was emerging from its period of self-imposed closure and was becoming ready to develop its tourism. This resulted in a large number of people outside of China who now engage in extensive studies of tourism in various forms, whereas the number of well-trained Chinese tourism academics is only now reaching critical numbers and accomplishments. This chapter outlines some aspects of tourism research conducted in China.

TOURISM RESEARCH INSTITUTIONS

The institutions and organizations engaged in tourism research in China can be roughly divided into the following six categories.

Government Agencies

Owing to its diverse nature, tourism is a subject of interest to a number of government agencies. At the present time, the China National Tourism Administration (CNTA) is the leading government body in charge of tourism. It is under the direct control of the State Council, China's top political decision-making body. There is no tourism research institute within the CNTA, although its Department of Policy and Regulations does engage in some specific policy-oriented studies. Many provincial and local governments have similar tourism bureaus that undertake some policy research. Other central government organizations undertake occasional tourism-related applied research through internal institutes, but focus primarily on their own missions. These include the State Planning and Development Commission, the Ministry of Construction, the Ministry of Culture, the State Administration of Environment Protection, and others.

Government-Funded Institutes

Since the reform-open policies of 1978 were implemented, tourism has been considered an economic activity and an important means of earning foreign currency. As a result, many government-funded institutions have taken up tourism research. The Chinese Academy of Social Sciences (CASS), the leading social science research institution in China, set up a special unit in the late 1970s to conduct tourism studies. Within CASS, the Institute of Finance and Trade Economics was the first to conduct tourism research in China. In 2000 a new tourism center was set up in the CASS in response to the central government's call to make tourism one of the cornerstones of the Chinese economy. The Tourism Research Centre (CASSTRC) was sponsored by a private industrial group to undertake independent tourism research. In addition to these core tourism programs, other institutes within CASS have full-time tourism researchers as well, including the Institutes of Economics, Rural Development, Urban Development, History, Nationality, and Sociology.

Since many tourism resources are nature related, the Chinese Academy of Sciences (CAS) has also been extensively involved in tourism research projects, especially within the Institute of Geography. Many ecotourism studies have been conducted by scientists in CAS, and the Chinese Academy of Geology has done some similar research. Another important body, the Economic Development Centre under the State Council, is also engaged in tourism studies in relation to macroeconomic policy formulation.

Institutions of Higher Learning

Tourism research and education are twin brothers emerging from tourism development. Within China's higher education system, tourism research has mostly been undertaken by hotel and tourism schools, such as the Beijing Tourism Institute, or universities with departments or disciplines of tourism and hospitality management or other tourism-related units. According to estimates by CNTA, over 200 universities, educational institutes, and schools are involved in tourism education, training, and research one way or another. On the other hand, independent tourism research institutes hardly exist in any universities. The China Tourism College (also known as the Beijing Second Foreign Languages Institute) has one research institute. Unfortunately, it conducts very little pure research, focusing instead on tourism planning projects, often with a commercial orientation. Recently established tourism centers at several universities have the same orientation. This arises largely because of the low salary earned by academics in China's universities, who are encouraged to undertake consulting work for supplemental pay.

Some higher education institutions have recently started master and doctoral degree studies in tourism. As the degree candidates are required to write a research thesis, this new batch of students, although not many as yet, will help to foster a new research orientation within China's higher education system.

Nongovernmental Organizations

Along with the rapid growth of the tourism economy, new nongovernmental (NGO) tourism associations and societies have also been organized. There are two types of tourism NGOs: the first consists of trade associations, such as the Tourist Hotel Association, the Travel Service Association, the Tourist Vehicles Association, and so on. The other type comprises various academic societies, such as the China Tourism Futurist Society, the Beijing Tourism Society, the Tourism Commission of the China Geographical Society, and the Tourism Education Association. Some of these organizations conduct or coordinate research projects, but more often they organize seminars and conferences on specific themes at which research conducted independently by individuals is presented.

The Industry

Due to the relatively short development history of modern tourism in China, combined with the small size and the diverse and fragmented nature of tourism businesses, the tourism industry itself is not strong. Only one of China's hotel groups (the Jinjiang Hotel Group in Shanghai) has been listed among the world's top 500 hotel groups. Only the largest companies, of which there are very few in China, have the resources to conduct tourism research, and even among those it is rarely done by more than a few people, mainly within their marketing divisions. In addition to the tourism sector, other industries that have recently entered into, or are preparing to enter into, the industry have also been conducting tourism studies. These include securities companies, banks, and large industrial companies. As mentioned previously, a large private industrial group sponsored the new CASS tourism research center, but this is a very rare case in China.

International Organizations

Some overseas organizations have also conducted research into China's tourism. These include the Worldwide Fund for Nature (WWF) China Program, United Nations Development Program (UNDP) China Office, and some independent consulting companies and researchers. However, their findings, like those of the private sector industry, are proprietary and seldom made public.

OUTLINE OF TOURISM RESEARCH DEVELOPMENT

Owing to the fact that most tourism research in China has been done by government or government-funded organizations, the majority of the studies have been confined to the realm of policy development and long-term strategies. So far, China's tourism studies have, generally speaking, gone through the following phases of development.

Introduction: What Is Tourism? (1978-1980)

China was a latecomer on the world tourism stage. For some thirty years after the first travel agency was established, tourism was used solely as a tool of foreign affairs (cf. Chapter 2), and no studies at all were conducted on tourism as a social or economic phenomenon. As the number of visitors was small, the business was tightly controlled by the central government, and hardly any interactions occurred between guests and hosts. As such, it seemed unnecessary to study this matter. Great debates emerged within Chinese society when tourism was first advocated as an economic activity as part of the government's policy to open the country to the outside world in the late 1970s. In fact, by then, tourism was a vague concept to the majority of Chinese, except for a prejudice they held against it, which arose out of ignorance and misunderstanding, as well as antibourgeois Communist values. To win the support of the government officials and the general public, early researchers started to translate foreign language tourism literature into Chinese and wrote papers introducing tourism in a global context. Of course, books and papers that explained the economic benefits of tourism were preferentially selected and introduced at this time in order to support the contention that tourism brought positive economic benefits. This was similar to the emergence of tourism studies in the West a couple of decades earlier when the positive aspects far outweighed the negative. *Tourism: Principles, Practices and Philosophies* (McIntosh and Goeldner 1972) and *Tourism: Past, Present and the Future* by Burkart and Medlik (1981) were the first to be translated into Chinese in these early days.

Action: What to Do (1980-1985)

After considerable debate, the concept of tourism as an economic activity became generally accepted. "What to do?" was typically the next question. Should China follow models from the Western world, or should China follow a path in its tourism development that is more socialist oriented? What kind of tourism should China stress, international or domestic tourism, based on the country's specific conditions? During this period, seminars and conferences were held and numerous academic papers were presented or published on these questions. This helped to chart the course of China's tourism development, including the types of tours that were promoted, the tourism resources that were developed, and the type and forms of tourism administrative structures that were introduced.

Strategies: How to Do It (1985-1990)

With deepening economic reform and further opening of China, tourism development became increasingly important for the central government, particularly in the area of national policy and strategic planning. The first major tourism studies were sponsored by the National Social Science Funds and conducted in 1987 by a working team headed by Professor Sun Shangqing, the former director of the Economic Development Research Centre under the State Council, with researchers from CASS and CNTA. This was the first time in China that the industrial status of tourism was advocated, and a strategy for developing tourism at a rate faster than that of the GDP, under some certain conditions, was pursued. The principles and recommendations that were put forward in the series of reports that emanated from this project were well received and constituted the basis for the subsequent tourism policies in China (Sun 1991, 1992). Tourism was now part of China's centralized national social and economic planning process for the first time.

Planning and Development (1990-1995)

By the end of the 1980s and into the 1990s, China was experiencing countrywide tourism "fever," encouraged by government policies and academic advocacy. Numerous amusement and theme parks, and other man-made tourist attractions were being constructed, regardless of market demand and the availability of resources. The failure of many such attractions (see Chapter 11) taught developers, investors, and governments at all levels a simple yet significant lesson: planning should be conducted before any actual development begins. Hence, many research studies were begun to address the issue of planning and development, from methodology and procedures to various conceptualizations. As a result, many researchers actually began to become heavily involved in planning activities, either master plans for tourism development or physical plans for specific tourist attractions. In the early days, urban planners and geographers took the lead in such planning projects. Later, it seemed that everyone had turned into planning experts overnight and hundreds of institutions, from professional research institutes of both natural and social sciences, to universities and other higher education institutions, to public and private organizations, vied for this business. A host of tourism master plans, both good and not so good, were undertaken. Most of them, however, have not been fully implemented for one reason or another.

Tourism Impacts (1995 Onward)

Tourism has now become one of China's most important industrial sectors, advocated and supported by both central and local governments. Being considered as a new economic growth point, tourism, together with housing and the electronics industries, has been given top priority. Both international (mainly inbound) and domestic travel are encouraged, to earn foreign currency from the former and to stimulate internal consumption for the latter. Consequently, another round of "tourism fever" occurred in the latter 1990s. Tourists can now be found throughout the country both on group inclusive tours (GITs) and as fully independent travelers (FITs). As a result, the concerns of tourism impacts, both positive and negative, have increased and have become the current focus of much attention among researchers, although many applied planning projects continue to take place, as well. Arguments over the costs and benefits of tourism have been launched by many, not only economists, but also by environmentalists, anthropologists, sociologists, geographers, and political scientists. As a consequence, some tourism research is now becoming more closely linked with the contemporary issues and concerns that are studied in the West.

DISSEMINATION OF RESEARCH FINDINGS

Tourism research findings are reported and disseminated in a variety of ways. Major research projects may have their findings published in the form of a monograph, and the grants may (but not always) contain funding for self-publication. Government research institutions prepare reports primarily for related bodies. Not all of these forms of reporting are publicly available. Other ways of sharing research findings include academic journals and conferences.

Academic Journals

In China, tourism researchers may have their papers or research reports published in academic journals, which also provides evidence of their academic achievements. However, specific tourism academic journals are very few in China, unlike in the West where these have proliferated in recent years. The bimonthly *Tourism Tribune,* edited and published by the Beijing Tourism Institute, is the only national academic tourism journal published as of this writing. Learned journals, usually published by universities and other higher education institutes, will occasionally carry tourism papers if their school offers tourism courses (cf. Box 5.1).

The scarcity of academic tourism journals is attributed partly to the financial constraints of the research institutions themselves, and partly to the small number of genuine researchers. Of course, other academic journals in related fields, such as economics, management, urban and regional studies, and environmental science, or internal journals edited by educational institutions, may occasionally carry some tour-

---

**BOX 5.1. Four Major Sources
for Tourism Research Publications in China**

1. *Learned journals of universities and institutes:* Guangxi Nationality Institute (Nanning), Southwest Nationality Institute (Chengdu), Hunan Normal College (Changsha), Fujian Normal College (Fuzhou), Zhanjiang Normal Institute (Zhanjiang), Xiaman University (Xiamen), Huazhong Normal College (Wuhan), Yuzhou University (Chongqing), Yunnan Nationality Institute (Kunming), Guizhou Nationality Institute (Guiyang), Zhongnan Nationality Institute (Wuhan), Northwest University (Xi'an), The Second Beijing Foreign Language Institute (Beijing), Beijing Tourism Institute, Guilin Tourism College (Guilin), Hainan University, among others.
2. *Specific tourism newspapers: China Tourism News* (Beijing), *Tourism Times* (Shanghai), *Jiangnan Tourism* (Wuxi), *Xi'an Tourism News* (Xi'an), *Tourism Culture* (Wuhan), and others.
3. *General economic periodicals and daily newspapers: Economic Daily* (Beijing), *Economic Reference Daily* (Beijing), *Finance & Trade Economics* (Beijing), *Economic Issues* (Kunming), *Business Economy & Management* (Hangzhou), *Economic Geography* (Changsha), *Social Scientist* (Guilin), and so on.
4. *Internal journals or newsletters within government organizations and local agencies:* for example, the China National Tourism Administration (CNTA) and almost all provincial tourism administrations have their own internal tourism periodical.

Source: Compiled from *Tourism Economy* (1999).

---

ism research papers. Thanks to the efforts of the China Renda Social Sciences Information Centre, a collection of tourism research papers published in various journals and newspapers are compiled into a bimonthly periodical titled *Tourism Management* (renamed from *Tourism Economy* in 2000), which now serves as a primary source of tourism research findings. All of these publications are in Chinese and, unfortunately, no foreign language academic tourism journals are yet available in Chinese.

Seminars and Conferences

Government organizations, professional associations, and research institutions sometimes organize regional or national seminars, workshops, and conferences on tourism, often with specific themes. CASS is a particularly noted organizer of nationwide academic symposia on tourism topics. In the 1980s and early 1990s, CASS organized six major national symposia on tourism, either independently or jointly with CNTA and the China Tourism Association. Other tourism academic societies and professional associations also hold annual conferences or workshops, providing an opportunity for the exchange of research findings. The Tourism Commission of the China Geographical Society, for example, meets on an annual basis in conferences separate from the society's main meeting. Although China's tourism development has become one of the focal points of concern for the international investors and researchers, the holding of international or regional tourism meetings in China has been rare, probably because of language barriers, government formalities, or the lack of capable and willing organizers or partners in China for such an event. This may be changing as the IAEST met in Hangzhou in 2000 and the IGU Tourism Study Group met in Guilin in 2001. For similar reasons, plus the issue of financial affordability, attendance by Chinese scholars at overseas tourism symposia and conferences is very limited.

TRENDS AND PROBLEMS

Tourism has become an important service sector in China's economy and a growing part of people's lives, and it is expected to play a more significant role in the country's economic and social development. The central government has paid attention to the development of tourism as an industry. Chinese residents are now encouraged to spend their money and time on travel and tourism, as a way of boosting the economy overall. The granting of three weeklong public holidays (Chinese Spring Festival in February, the National Day in October, and May Day holidays) annually has greatly facilitated the growth of domestic and outbound tourism (cf. Chapter 2). In response to the needs of government administrators and businesses, more educational and academic institutions are undertaking tourism research and study. What is more promising is that many young and energetic scholars from a broad range of disciplines and with foreign experience and language competence are bringing fresh perspectives to tourism research in China, both in terms of methodology and conceptualization. In the meantime, some farsighted entrepreneurs have shown increasing interest in commissioning tourism research.

At the same time, publishers are beginning to introduce Chinese translations of tourism literature, which will better link Chinese researchers with their international counterparts. *Global Tourism: The Next Decade,* edited by William Theobald (1994), now has a Chinese version and is among the many that are now being introduced. Inspired by the open policy of the government, more Chinese tourism research institutions are seeking extensive collaboration and cooperation in tourism education and research with foreign institutions, which will give Chinese research findings more exposure to the world. As a consequence, China's tourism research appears to have bright prospects for the future. However, many problems also remain unsolved in the field of tourism research, and the contradictions between pure academic studies and the industry's interest in the applied practice of administration and operations obviously exist. Some of the long-standing challenges include the following.

Lack of Awareness of the Importance of Research

In general, politicians come to academics only when they are in trouble. In the case of China, very often politicians use academics as "experts" to explain or justify past policies or to find grounds to support their current positions. Tourism is a new phenomenon, yet serious studies of tourism are seldom advocated. Although a good number of educational institutions provide tourism courses and training programs, tourism as an independent discipline has not yet been officially recognized. Some deem that there is not much to learn or study in tourism. In fact, very few specific tourism research organizations exist in China and in-depth investigations and systematic studies are rare.

Lack of Sufficient Information Sources and Means of Exchange

Information is the basis for any research, and Chinese labor under a severe lack of information when they undertake research and analysis. Access to government information is very limited, and very often researchers may only obtain the data they need through personal sources. General surveys are difficult to conduct because of financial constraints and government red tape. Except for the few opportunities to attend seminars and conferences, there are hardly any formal means for information exchange or sharing with other institutions. The absence of effective mechanisms for communication and sharing among the researchers results in duplication and a lack of awareness of important gaps in the study of tourism.

Owing to the language barriers and ignorance of new technologies, the abundant resources of the Internet are not fully exploited. Moreover, most research institutions suffer from tight budgets, which make extensive investigations and field studies out of the question. Probably for the same reason, "cut-and-paste" research is commonplace among some researchers in China.

Lack of Collaboration

Research has long been considered a form of work in which individuals rely upon their own wisdom and knowledge. Many tourism researchers in China have little experience in collaborative research projects. In addition, a clear-cut division of scientific fields of research has been made among the social and natural sciences, which makes the necessary collaboration in multidisciplinary tourism research rather difficult, if not impossible. In fact, in many cases tourism research requires a multidisciplinary approach. For example, ecotourism does not fall into the natural sciences only, but very often involves ethnic cultures and heritage sites. Tourism planning is also rather different from urban planning and needs experts from various fields to work together rather than experts in the single field going alone. Indeed, it is the users who suffer from the impractical plans made due to the lack of a multidisciplinary planning approach.

International collaborative tourism studies in China still remain quite rare. In addition to the language and information barriers, Chinese researchers may be more introverted, having limited knowledge of the outside world, and being more hesitant to contact outsiders. At the same time, outside researchers find it difficult to obtain updated and informative literature and data to support their research proposals and to find appropriate institutions in China to work with.

Lack of Access to International Information

Travel and tourism are not new phenomena; however, their impacts have never been as great and wide on society as today. Travel and tourism is outward in nature; tourists are out of their own "usual habitat" when they travel. Therefore, tourism research should not be confined to certain destinations, divorced from the origin of the tourists. For reasons cited previously, Chinese tourism researchers have limited access to international networks and overseas information. To my limited knowledge, there is no active China member in the World Tourism Organization (WTO), except for a single representative of the CNTA, despite the major importance of China's role in global tourism. Very few individuals or institutes in China join or affiliate themselves to international and regional academic organizations. Numerous international seminars and conferences are now organized by various associations and institutions throughout the world, but participants from China are few and their presentations are even fewer. Among the many papers and articles related to China's tourism development published in international academic journals, those written by mainland Chinese researchers are infrequent. For example, in the first twenty years of articles in the *Annals of Tourism Research,* only some twenty articles related to China and only a fraction of these were written by scholars living in mainland China. Among the 500-plus worldwide subscribers of the popular e-mail discussion list, TRINET (Tourism Research Information Network), not one is actually based in mainland China, except for those from the Hong Kong Special Administrative Region. This is a loss for academic circles both within China and in the rest of the world.

RECOMMENDATIONS

As one of the world's largest countries, China needs the world as much as the world needs China. With growing involvement in the world economy, China will need to seek more collaboration and cooperation with its international counterparts in all fields, and tourism researchers should accordingly do the same. The Internet and other information technology provide more possibilities and opportunities for the realization of this desire. To accelerate this process, the following measures are recommended.

In-Depth and Theoretically Based Tourism Research Should Be Encouraged

Governments should support more comprehensive and pure research projects. Priority should be given to independent research organizations that can provide unbiased and objective analysis. As a precondition, tourism should be treated as an academic discipline. In addition to policies and economic impacts, which have largely come out of economics and management studies, the range of tourism studies should be expanded into other fields, such as sociology and anthropology.

Government, Industry, and Academics Should Cooperate to Support Tourism Research

To enhance the usefulness and effectiveness of tourism research, joint research efforts should be made by the government, industry, and academics. Government at all levels and the tourism industry should make more information and data available to academics on their policies and practices. The government should release policy documents and survey findings for public use regularly, and researchers should be encouraged to conduct systematic surveys and investigations. Again, research findings should be easily shared among all academics and other tourism stakeholders. The government and industry should be encouraged to sponsor academic journals and seminars, serving as forum of exchange of tourism research findings. Researchers should not confine their activities to within their ivory towers. Instead, they should aim at identifying and solving real problems, identifying trends, and forecasting the future, by combining theory with concrete practice.

Necessary Mechanisms Should Be Worked Out for International Tourism Research Collaboration

International exchange programs among researchers should be supported. General dialogue can link China and the rest of the world through TRINET and other Internet discussion lists, especially if someone could provide a clearinghouse with necessary language translation. More international symposiums, particularly those with themes related closely to China, should be held within China, and more grants and sponsorship should be sought to help China's tourism research and to foster collaborative projects. Just as regular sources of information should be available for tourism researchers within China, the same data should be available for international researchers. It is necessary to build up a network for all Chinese-origin researchers throughout the world to conduct extensive research programs on China topics by taking advantage of their language and cultural background.

CONCLUSION

It is worth noting that more and more international institutions are showing increasing interest in tourism development and research in China. For example, in 1999 a survey of tourism research priorities in China was conducted by the Department of Hospitality, Tourism and Property Management, the University of Queensland, Australia on behalf of the Network of Asia-Pacific Education and Training Institutes in Tourism (APETIT) Australian Centre. A good many tourism consulting companies in the West have vied with one another to win bids to prepare tourism master plans in China, with encouragement from the World Tourism Organization and CNTA. Other overseas tourism research and educational institutions have invited researchers from China to participate in research projects related to China. Some leading researchers in China have also been invited to be members of international editorial boards. A British publishing house has been working with the Hong Kong Polytechnic University to publish English translations of selected writings from *Tourism Tribune* on its Web site. These are all just first attempts, and many more innovative activities along these lines will follow in years to come.

Just as many businesspeople believe that China might be the last untapped megamarket for their products and services, China also provides much room and opportunity for tourism researchers. The results of tourism research in such a large, diverse, and emerging country as China are not only beneficial to China's tourism and economic development, but will also benefit the entire world.

REFERENCES

Burkart, A.J. and Medlik, S. (1981). *Tourism: Past, present and future,* Second edition. London: Heinemann.

McIntosh, R.W. and Goeldner, C. (1972). *Tourism principles, practices, and philosophies.* Columbus, Ohio: Grid.

Sun Shangqing, ed. (1991). *Studies of China's tourism economy.* Beijing: People's Publishing House (original in Chinese).

Sun Shangqing, ed. (1992). *Choices towards the 21st century: China's tourism development strategies.* Beijing: People's Publishing House (original in Chinese).

Theobald, William F., ed. (1994). *Global tourism: The next decade.* Boston: Butterworth-Heinemann.

Tourism Economy (1999). Editorial comments (in Chinese), issues 1 to 6. Published by the China Renda (People's University) Social Sciences Information Centre, Beijing.

World Tourism Organization (WTO) (2000). Main tourist destinations 1999. Madrid: WTO.

Chapter 6

Economic Impact of Tourism in China

Xu Gang
Claudia Kruse

China's tourism industry has been flying high since the country launched its "open-door" policy in the late 1970s. From 1978 to 1999, China's inbound tourism receipts recorded an increase of forty-seven-fold, and inbound visitor arrivals forty-fold. Today, travel is a multibillion dollar business in China. In 1999 China earned US$14 billion from inbound tourism, making the country the seventh largest destination in the world in terms of inbound travel receipts (WTO, 2000). Impressive as it is, inbound tourism is only a small part of China's travel business. According to China's National Tourism Administration (CNTA), more than 710 million Chinese took pleasure trips in their own country in 1999, spending a total amount of RMB 283 billion yuan (or US$29 billion).

An industry of this scale is bound to have an impact. This chapter attempts to present a broad account of tourism's contributions to the Chinese economy. The economic impacts of tourism appear pervasive and are hard to measure (Bryden, 1973; de Kadt, 1979; Harrison, 1992; Sinclair, 1998). In this chapter, we confine our discussion to the *direct* effects of tourist spending. "Secondary" effects of tourist spending as well as tourism investment-induced effects are left untouched. This is not a matter of neglect; data do not permit such an analysis. The next three sections examine tourism's economic effects at the national level, followed by a discussion of tourism's impacts on Chinese regional development and tourism's role in poverty alleviation. The chapter closes with a brief discussion of the major challenges ahead.

TOURISM'S EXPORT CONTRIBUTIONS TO THE CHINESE ECONOMY

Tourism is essentially a trading activity. Inbound visitor expenditures represent an infusion of fresh demand from an external source, just like conventional international trading activities such as merchandise export. Figures 6.1 through 6.4 present the basic data on China's travel account and travel's position in the country's overall current account. The picture that emerges from these figures is clear: travel and tourism is an important factor in China's external sector.

From 1978 to 1998, China's inbound tourism earnings increased from US$0.26 billion to US$12.6 billion (Figure 6.1). Together with the US$625 million in passenger fare receipts, inbound tourism injected in 1998 a total of US$13.2 billion directly into the Chinese economy. During this period China's inbound tourism receipts increased at an average rate of 21 percent a year, far outperforming its GNP and merchandise exports (Figure 6.2). Expressed in receipts per visitor for 1999, tourism's export contribution to the Chinese economy is significant, with each international visitor representing an average export value of around US$200 with 30 percent of the receipts going to long-distance transport (within China), 20 percent to retail trade, 14 percent to lodging, 11 percent to food service, 6 percent to entertainment, and 4 percent to local transportation (CNTA, 2000). One striking feature of China's inbound travel earnings structure is

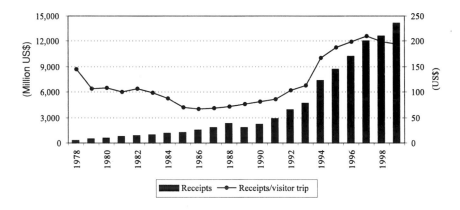

FIGURE 6.1. China: Inbound Travel Receipts, 1978-1999. (*Source:* CNTA, 1986-2000.)

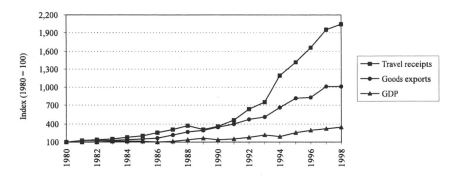

FIGURE 6.2. China: Index of Inbound Travel Receipts, Goods Exports, and GDP, 1980-1998 (1980 = 100). (*Source:* CNTA, 1986-2000; *Statistical Yearbook of China,* 1986-2000.)

the extremely small contribution from Chinese air carriers. The World Tourism Organization (WTO, 1998) reported that worldwide, international fare receipts accounted for about 17 percent of the combined tourism and fare receipts for 1995. This figure for China was a mere 3 percent. This clearly reflects the weak competitiveness of Chinese carriers in the global air transport market.

As a service activity, inbound tourism's role is most pronounced in China's services trade account (Figure 6.3). Three facts are worth mentioning. First, China's inbound tourism has been a service export producing a surplus every year since 1978. Second, inbound tourism has been China's number one services export since 1993. Third, the share of China's total service exports accounting for its inbound tourism has been on a steady rise. By 1998 this share had reached 52 percent, up from 28 percent in 1983, making China's inbound tourism foreign exchange earnings greater than all other service sectors combined.

The ratio of a country's inbound tourism receipts to its merchandise export earnings is another oft-used measure of tourism's export contributions. This ratio should be treated with caution, though, as its numerical value hinges on the host country's merchandise export strength. In the case of China, the ratio of inbound tourism receipts to merchandise export earnings has been rising. By 1998, China's inbound tourism generated an amount of foreign exchange equivalent to around 7 percent of total Chinese merchandise exports (Figure 6.3).

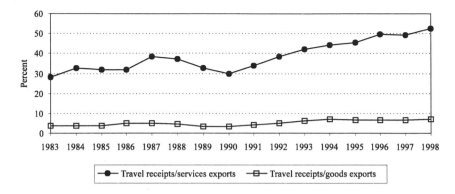

FIGURE 6.3. China: Ratio of Inbound Travel Receipts to Services and Goods Exports, 1983-1998 (percent). (*Source:* IMF, 1991-1999.)

This ratio appears impressive considering that China is a huge country with considerable and growing capability of exporting large amounts of manufactured products.

Putting China's inbound tourism in comparison with its major merchandise export items also tells much about its significance as a foreign exchange earner. Even compared with one-digit Standard International Trade Classification (SITC) categories, inbound tourism appeared among China's leading export sectors (Table 6.1). By the mid-1990s, China's inbound tourism was already able to generate an amount of foreign exchange that not only far exceeded the earnings from various raw material exports combined (SITC 1 + 2 + 4), but also reached a level comparable to those of chemicals (SITC 5) and foodstuffs (SITC 0). By 1998 China's inbound tourism had even overtaken chemicals and foodstuffs to become the country's fourth largest exporter. This rise in ranking of inbound tourism is all the more impressive considering that Chinese merchandise exports had a three-fold increase from 1990 to 1998.

What may appear less expected is the extraordinarily rapid rise in outbound travel by Chinese citizens. In 1983 China spent a mere US$53 million on outbound travel (IMF, 1991). Just fifteen years later this figure already stood at US$9,200 million (IMF, 1999). The immediate effect of this growing outbound traffic is a shrinking surplus on China's travel account. This is not necessarily bad, though. Growing outbound tourism will certainly create new demand for

TABLE 6.1. China: Inbound Travel Receipts in Comparison with One-Digit SITC Export Categories

Millions of U.S. dollars (f.o.b.)	SITC[a]	1978 Absolute	Rank[b]	1980 Absolute	Rank[b]	1985 Absolute	Rank[b]	1990 Absolute	Rank[b]	1995 Absolute	Rank[b]	1998 Absolute	Rank[b]
Primary commodities[c]	0	5,216		9,114		13,828		15,886		21,486		20,600	
Food and live animals	1	2,316	2	2,985	3	3,803	3	6,609	4	9,954	4	10,619	
Beverage and tobacco	1	71		78		105		342		1,369		976	
Crude materials, excl. fuels	2	1,417	3	1,711	5	2,653	6	3,537	8	4,374		3,517	
Mineral fuels, etc.	3	1,345	4	4,280	1	7,132	1	5,237	6	5,335		5,181	
Animal, vegetable oil, and fats	4	67		60		135		161		454		307	
All manufactured goods[d]		4,529		8,798		10,109		34,580		127,277		163,152	
Chemicals	5	234	5	1,120	6	1,358	7	3,730	7	9,094	5	10,316	
Basic manufactures	6	444	6	3,999	2	4,493	2	12,576	2	32,243	2	32,383	3
Machinery and transport equipment	7	332		843	7	772		5,588	5	31,391	3	50,233	2
Misc. manufactured goods	8	3,519	1	2,836	4	3,486	4	12,686	1	54,549	1	70,220	1
Unclassified goods	9	207		207		3,413	5	11,625	3	7		5	

Source: IMF, 1991-1999.
[a] SITC = Standard International Trade Classification
[b] Export categories with a value greater than travel receipts
[c] Primary commodities = SITC 0+1+2+3+4
[d] All manufactured goods = SITC (5+6+7+8) - 68

87

travel services and, hence, generate more business. Overseas travel will also likely help promote China's business integration with the rest of the world. Furthermore, to the extent that overseas travel gives Chinese people greater exposure to other cultures, and that at least part of such exposure is beneficial, then growing Chinese outbound travel should be good for the country's future growth.

THE ECONOMIC CONTRIBUTIONS
OF CHINESE DOMESTIC TOURISM

The recent boom in domestic tourism in China has been spectacular (Table 6.2). Even though CNTA's data probably captures only part of the story, it indicates that China's domestic tourism was larger than its inbound tourism by a factor of ten in terms of visitor arrivals and by a factor of more than two in terms of travel receipts. To be sure, much of China's domestic travel was low spending. In recent years domestic visitors spent, on average, between one-fifth and one-fourth as much as international visitors on a per visitor trip basis, but that does not stop Chinese domestic tourism from having an enormous impact, given the huge numbers of domestic travelers.

The economic impacts of China's domestic tourism are revealed in a variety of areas. First, domestic travel implies transferring expenditures from travelers' origin to destination areas and, hence, has an effect on the interregional distribution of Chinese national income and employment. Case studies show that in a place such as Guilin, nearly one-third of the total local retail sales was generated by domestic visitors (Xu, 1999). In Beidaihe, a seaside resort almost exclusively for domestic visitors, this share reached 70 to 80 percent. Recent evidence suggests that interregional travel is assuming growing importance in China. Traveling to long-haul domestic destinations has become an established trend in the wealthy coastal provinces. As such, the role of domestic tourism in the interregional transfer of Chinese purchasing power looks set to rise in the years to come.

Second, research in China indicates that domestic travel expenditures have been more conducive to the growth of a destination's local economy than inbound visitor expenditures (Gormsen et al., 1991; Huebner, 1997; Xu, 1999). Compared to inbound tourism, domestic tourism is less capital intensive, uses more local inputs, serves far

TABLE 6.2. China's Domestic Tourism, 1985-1999

	Visitors (millions)	Receipts (RMB billion yuan)	Receipts per Visitor (RMB yuan)	Ratio of Domestic to Inbound Tourism		
				Visitor No.	Receipts	Receipts per Visitor
1985	240	8.0	33.3	13.5	2.2	0.16
1986	270	10.6	39.3	11.8	2.0	0.17
1987	290	14.0	48.3	10.8	2.0	0.19
1988	300	18.7	62.3	9.5	2.2	0.24
1989	240	15.0	62.5	9.8	2.1	0.22
1990	280	17.0	60.7	10.2	1.6	0.16
1991	300	20.0	66.7	9.0	1.3	0.15
1992	330	25.0	75.8	8.7	1.1	0.13
1993	398	84.0	211.1	9.6	3.1	0.32
1994	524	102.3	195.2	12.0	1.6	0.14
1995	629	137.5	218.6	13.6	1.9	0.14
1996	640	163.8	255.9	12.5	1.9	0.15
1997	644	211.2	328.0	11.2	2.1	0.19
1998	695	239.1	344.0	10.9	2.3	0.24
1999	719	283.2	393.9	9.9	2.4	0.25

Source: CNTA (1987-2000).

greater numbers of visitors, and, hence, offers a broader basis for local participation.

Third, China's domestic tourism has created plenty of localized business opportunities for small private enterprises. Especially since the blessing was given for individuals to participate in the country's tourism supply in the mid-1980s, a large number of private firms have quickly found their way into this booming business. In many Chinese tourist areas, domestic tourism turned out to be a vital contributing factor to the recent growth of private businesses there.

Fourth, domestic tourism has become an instrument of China's macroeconomic management. A good example of this is the attempt by the Chinese government to absorb purchasing power through domestic travel spending to help ease the prevailing buying panic in the country in the early 1990s (Tang, 1990). Recently, the Chinese government promoted domestic travel to achieve exactly the opposite purpose: to stimulate sluggish consumer demand in the Chinese market (CNTA, 1999).

TOURISM, JOBS, AND GDP

Tourism is often credited with the ability to bring jobs and incomes to the indigenous people of destination areas. However, considerable dispute still exists over the quantity and the nature of the jobs offered to the local people (de Kadt, 1979; Sinclair, 1998). Comprehensive and reliable data on tourism employment in China do not exist. CNTA put the number of the people directly employed in China's international tourism at 1.2 million for 1996 (CNTA, 1997). An estimated 6 million further jobs were indirectly created or supported by tourism for the same year. How CNTA arrived at these numbers is unclear. What seems clear is that the 7.2 million figure reflects no more than a tiny tip of China's tourism employment iceberg. Two factors explain this. First, the number of the jobs directly created by China's domestic tourism was, surprisingly, not included in the previous numbers. Second, even the previous statistic of direct employment in international tourism seems incomplete, as it covered only "designated tourist businesses," which do not represent the entirety of international tourism in China.

Tourism's percentage contribution to GDP is often used to indicate its overall role in the destination's economy. In theory, computing such a percentage makes good sense as all of the effects that tourism generates in an economy ultimately play over to its GDP. However, in virtually all cases where such efforts have been made, *gross* travel receipts, instead of the *value added* by travel and tourism, have been used. This is a problem for China's tourism statistics as well (Figure 6.4). In recent years the ratio of China's gross travel receipts to its GDP was between 4 and 5 percent, with inbound tourism contributing 1 to 2 percent and domestic tourism 3 to 4 percent.

TOURISM AND CHINESE REGIONAL DEVELOPMENT

Up to the mid-1990s, regional objectives were not even mentioned in Chinese tourism policies. In the Chinese context, this resulted in a heavy

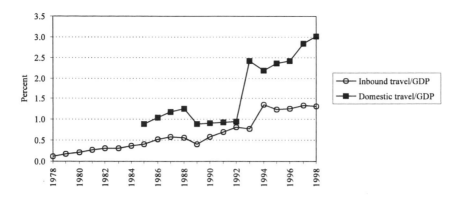

FIGURE 6.4. China: Ratio of Travel Receipts to GDP, 1978-1998. (*Source:* CNTA, 1986-2000; *Statistical Yearbook of China,* 1986-2000.)

policy tilt toward the country's coastal region. Locational advantage, infrastructure investment, and preferential treatment have all favored a high geographic concentration of tourism development activities in China's coastal region (Wen and Tisdell, 1997). At the provincial level, the top five destinations—all coastal provinces—received more than 70 percent of China's total inbound tourism receipts in 1999 (Figure 6.5). It should be noted, though, that smaller numbers of inbound visitors to inland provinces was only part of the explanation to their low levels of tourism revenues. The other factor that worked against the inland provinces was the much lower receipts on a per visitor night basis (CNTA, 1999).

Some evidence suggests that the market dominance of leading Chinese destinations such as Beijing and Guangdong dropped in the 1990s (Figure 6.6), but a large part of this revenue redistribution has apparently gone to other coastal provinces, most prominent among them Jiangsu, Fujian, and Shanghai. Inland provinces, except for Yunnan, gained only marginally.

Things are changing. The Chinese government has been increasingly talking about the need to develop the western part of the country, and tourism has been touted as the way to provide an economic takeoff in poor places. The central government's promises look impressive. As much as RMB 800 million yuan was reportedly earmarked for tourism development in inland provinces for the ninth five-year plan period 2000-2005 (ChinaOnline, 2000). If the Chinese

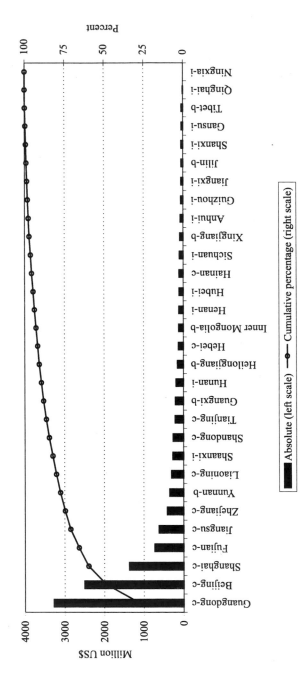

FIGURE 6.5. China: Distribution of Inbound Travel Receipts by Province, 1999. (*Source:* CNTA, 2000. *Note:* c = coastal provinces; b = border provinces; i = inland provinces.)

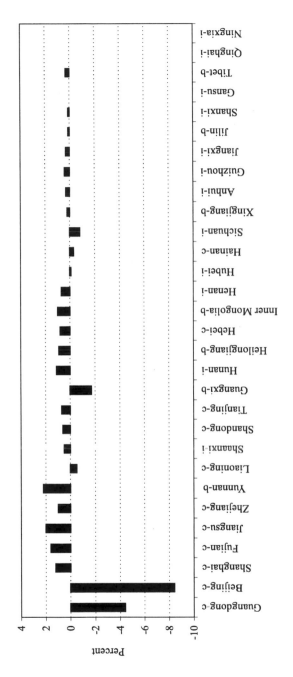

FIGURE 6.6. China: Changes in Percentage Distribution of Inbound Travel Receipts by Province Between 1990 and 1999. (*Source:* CNTA, 2000. *Note:* c = coastal provinces; b = border provinces; i = inland provinces.)

government follows through with these plans, tourism in inland provinces will get a big boost in the near future.

Inland Chinese provinces are facing a range of challenges in their tourism development. The first, and perhaps the biggest, challenge is the lack of infrastructure. Putting in place even a basic tourism infrastructure will require huge investments. Impressive as it may look, the investment promised by the central government can at most meet only a small part of this requirement. Furthermore, unless inland provinces can demonstrate reasonably good prospects for returns on investment, private investors are unlikely to offer much additional support.

The second major challenge that inland provinces face is competition. The competition among Chinese destinations for the country's tourism pie will get ever tougher in coming years. True, growing competition will help Chinese destinations and firms to improve their product, operating efficiency, and service quality, but for the inland provinces, as for all new players entering an already crowded market, competition will be a major hurdle to success. They are currently too weak to stand up to such competition.

The third challenge is competition from overseas destinations, especially those in Southeast Asia. With the recent rapid rise in outbound travel by Chinese citizens, discussed previously, inland Chinese provinces will soon have to compete head-on with overseas destinations for travelers from coastal Chinese provinces. Certain segments of Chinese travelers will go for overseas holidays before visiting other parts of their own country.

The fourth major challenge is ensuring that the local communities of inland destinations benefit from tourism. If anything, past tourism research suggests that, to benefit substantially from visitor expenditures, destinations should do everything possible to use local resources and increase the supply of local products and services. This, by implication, requires that destinations possess the ability to develop a range of local sectors, in addition to tourism. However, if poor places in inland Chinese provinces had the capacity to develop the kind and the level of diversified local economy that allows tourism multiplier effects to work, they would not be as poor as they are.

TOURISM AND POVERTY ALLEVIATION

Growing inequality has become a major concern in postreform China. The income gap between the coast and the interior has been widening, along with the disparities between urban and rural areas. Recent studies have shown that the growth elasticity of income of the lowest quintile of the Chinese population for 1980-1995 was only 0.308, suggesting that the poor did not benefit even half as much from growth as the richer segments of the society did (Lübker, 2000). Despite the fact that China has lifted some 200 million people out of absolute poverty since 1978, the number of poor still amounts to between 65 and 350 million (Cook and White, 1998). Most of the poor live in the interior provinces. Lacking basic infrastructure, these poor regions are typically disconnected from the outside world, while natural resource constraints set considerable limits to employment in agriculture.

The Maoist approach to poverty reduction was characterized by egalitarian income distribution (Kiminami, 1999). This approach failed because under such a system, people had no incentive to be more productive. In the late 1970s a "transfusion-relief" (grant) policy was introduced with only marginal effects, as state-secured supply of minimum necessities left people as recipients rather than active participants. In the mid-1980s, a shift toward "blood-forming" (development-oriented) policies occurred. These policies were expected to be more effective as they brought together public and private players and provided comprehensive input packages. Despite the initial success of such pro-poor policies, China's poverty problem remains abysmal. Mass poverty and growing income gaps could undermine China's social and political stability, which in turn could pose a threat not only to the country's further growth but also to the legitimacy of the Chinese government.

The role of tourism in poverty reduction has gained increasing recognition in China. Most of the poor counties targeted in China's national poverty alleviation plan, "Helping Eighty Million People in Seven Years" (also known as the 8-7 Plan), have announced their intention to develop tourism as a window of opportunity. The 8-7 Plan was initiated in 1994 with the goal of eliminating absolute poverty among 80 million people in rural areas in seven years. Tourism can be built upon assets that may be less desirable for other industries. Many of China's poor areas are adjacent to protected areas with amazing natural scenery and are inhabited by minorities whose cultures and lifestyles are distinct from the Han Chinese. These culture and environment assets can be invaluable for appropriate forms of ecotourism and cultural tourism (Lew, 2001).

In Xinjiang, the government has employed a "food for work" program to carry out environmental protection projects in the Tianshan mountain range ("Forest Tourism," 2000). This area now has a successful forest tourism industry. Within two years about half of the former forest workers had found jobs in tourism, and their average annual income in 1999 amounted to over RMB 10,000 yuan, which was greater than the total earnings of all forest workers. Forest tourism is expected to become the area's leading business in the twenty-first century.

Involving the indigenous people of destination areas is crucial to spreading the benefits of tourism to poor segments of local communities. If local people have a greater say in decision making and planning, they have a better chance to shape the path of development and to receive a fair share of the benefits. If there are adverse impacts on their livelihoods, they have more potential to make claims for compensation. Obviously, a community is not a homogeneous group; intracommunity differences in access to political power and economic credit can be huge. A recent survey revealed that in 72 percent of the 100 Chinese nature reserves that were surveyed, less than one-fifth of the families in local communities benefited from reserve-based tourism (MAB, 1998). Only in one-tenth of the nature reserves did more than 50 percent of the local families gain from tourism. More could be done with household targeting and microfinancing to improve the effectiveness of poverty reduction through tourism. Conventional community-based development approaches need to refocus on individual needs.

Public spending is another way of redistributing the benefits of tourism development. In this respect, Jiuzhaigou in Sichuan Province provides a case in point (LEAD, 1999). Due to its nature-based attractiveness, Jiuzhaigou has become a very popular destination since the mid-1990s. By 1998 tourism had already contributed around 70 percent of Jiuzhaigou county's revenues. The local government revenues from tourism also increased considerably in recent years. As a result, the Jiuzhaigou county government was able to spend 35 percent of its budget on health and education, which benefited the entire local community.

In order to take advantage of tourism's job opportunities, poor households need to develop relevant skills. Such skills are defined by tourism and by the existing social structure. Local people can get involved in tourism in a variety of areas such as food and beverage, accommodation, transport, retailing, sightseeing and entertainment services, and raw material supply. The main inputs needed are credit, management capabilities, and language skills. However, at a more basic level, remote peoples may not be familiar with the concept of a tourist whose travel motive is the pursuit of leisure or education. Understanding the demands and expectations of tourists is essential.

There is tremendous scope for improving employment opportunities through training. Ecotourism is very much a knowledge-based form of nature tourism and, hence, growing ecotourism creates a demand for knowledgeable guides. A recent survey revealed that in the Changbaishan Nature Reserve, about 93 percent of international tourists and 68 percent of domestic visitors wanted environmental interpretation services (UNESCO EABRN, 1997). However, only 17 percent of the 100 nature reserves surveyed had professionally trained guides, while 43 percent had untrained and 40 percent had no guides at all. The survey also showed that the economic potential of souvenir sales remained untapped. With greater attention paid to marketing and skillful production of more varied items, sales can be increased.

Charging admission fees is another way to generate revenues from ecotourism in nature reserves. In the Dinghushan Nature Reserve in Guangdong Province, for example, revenues in the form of entrance fees were estimated at RMB 47 to 100 million yuan (UNESCO EABRN, 1997). In Xishuangbanna Nature Reserve in Yunnan Province and Changbaishan Nature Reserve in Jilin Province, ecotourism has also generated substantial and steady revenues for maintaining the nature reserves (Lindberg et al., 1997).

Possibilities for local involvement in the tourism supply chain can be broadened by training local producers to meet quality standards. With its entry into the World Trade Organization, China must agree to the investment rules set by the GATT agreements. Under these agreements foreign companies must be treated the same as domestic companies and, thus, can no longer be required to have a certain percentage of local content. Therefore, for purposes of poverty reduction, government funding should primarily be devoted to creating income-generating opportunities in domestic tourism. Overall, tourism can be an effective tool of poverty alleviation because it can be developed in areas that may not be suitable for other economic activities and can be more sustainable than resource-extractive industries. As a precondition for any business to start, some infrastructure needs to be in place. If financial and managerial support is targeted at individual households rather than at the county level, the distribution of the benefits from tourism in China will likely be more even.

LOOK TO THE FUTURE: CHALLENGES AND POLICY OPTIONS

Over the past two decades, travel and tourism has evolved from an emerging business to an established and dynamic sector in the Chinese economy. Tourism has already made its economic impacts felt in many parts of the country. Although the huge impact of China's domestic tourism on the country's environment has been an occasional bone of contention between tourism's opponents and advocates, in general tourism's economic effect in China has been considered positive.

China holds great potential for tourism in the years to come, and the future for the Chinese domestic tourism looks particularly good. To the extent that the purchasing behavior of the Chinese is not too different from that observed elsewhere, it is logical to expect China's domestic tourism to continue to grow. The emergence of a Chinese middle class will continue to fuel tourism to new heights.

However, major challenges lie ahead for the Chinese travel industry. To begin with, China's entry into the World Trade Organization will likely present more challenges than opportunities for its travel industry. Even if China does not fully meet its obligations of WTO membership, the opening of the Chinese travel industry is only a matter of time. Also when foreign companies are allowed to fully enter China's travel business in large numbers, the problem of how to survive in this already crowded market will become more real than ever for many Chinese travel companies.

China's postreform experience suggests that in this country people all too often tend to believe that whatever is good for a particular part of the country must, per se, be wonderfully good for all. Anecdotes suggest that tourism has become *the* development fad in China at the time of the millennium. All Chinese provinces, most Chinese cities, and a considerable portion of Chinese towns and villages have been planning to develop tourism in big ways. If the Chinese government fails to get this new tourism "fever" under appropriate control, problems such as overcapacity, overcompetition, and low operating efficiency, which many coastal destinations suffered in the early 1990s, are likely to surface in the not too distant future.

Another issue that deserves more attention in China's tourism in the future is the distribution of economic benefits from tourism. No other statistic in postreform China has a more compelling authority than growth. Growth has become more or less the accepted test of performance and success. China's travel and tourism has not been an exception. For much of the past two decades China pursued what may be called a growth maximization objective in its tourism development. As of this writing, China's tourism policies have remained completely silent on the distribution issue. This neglect will likely be challenged in the future because a broad-based support of the Chinese population is crucial to sustainable tourism development in China.

In addition to the socioeconomic costs of tourism development in China, the recent tourism boom has come at a considerable environmental cost. China needs to take care of its environment, natural and cultural, if the growth of its travel business is to be sustained. Evidence suggests that China's environmental issues are receiving growing attention and some positive actions, however inadequate, have been taken. Evidence also suggests that when it comes to the concept of environmental costs of developing tourism, scholars and practitioners alike often miss the point. It may seem too elementary to argue that what really is relevant in the discussion of tourism and environmental costs is not whether tourism damages the environment; rather, it is whether tourism does more or less damage to the environment *compared* to other options. Traveling through poor Chinese provinces, one gets the impression that much of the environmental degradation has been the result of the lack of development. To the extent that tourism can bring jobs and incomes to a destination, and to the extent that it does comparatively less damage to the environment than other feasible options, then tourism is a good candidate for development. Like it or not, economics are likely to remain more powerful than anything else in China for many years to come.

REFERENCES

Bryden, John M. (1973). *Tourism and development. A case study of the commonwealth Caribbean.* Cambridge, UK: Cambridge University Press.

China National Tourism Administration (CNTA). *Yearbook of China tourism statistics* (1986-2000). Beijing: China's Tourism Press.

ChinaOnline (2000). China to issue US$97 million in tourism bonds. <http:www. ChinaOnline.com>; accessed March 22, 2000.

Cook, Sara and Gordon White (1998). *The changing patterns of poverty in China: Issues for research and policy.* Institute of Development Studies Working Paper 67, Brighton: University of Sussex.

de Kadt, Emanuel (ed.) (1979). *Tourism—passport to development?* Oxford: Oxford University Press.

Forest tourism, a new bright spot in Xinjiang's tourism industry. (2000). *People's Daily,* August 10.

Gormsen, Erdmann, Ralf Hemberger, and Susanne Wagner (1991). Leben von den Fremden—Strukturwandel als Folge des Tourismus. *Das neue China* 18(1) 31-35.

Harrison, David (ed.) (1992). *Tourism and the less developed countries.* London: Belhaven Press.

Huebner, Martin (1997). Der Tourismus und seine Folgen für Regionale Strukturen und soziokulturellen Wandel in China am Beispiel peripherer Regionen. Unpublished PhD thesis. Mainz: University of Mainz.

International Monetary Fund (IMF) (1991). *Balance of payments statistics yearbook.* Washington, DC: IMF.

International Monetary Fund (IMF) (1999). *Balance of payments statistics yearbook.* Washington, DC: IMF.

Kiminami, L.Y. (1999). *A basic analysis of the poverty problem in China.* IDRI Occasional Paper No. 13. Japan: FASID.

Leadership for Environment and Development (LEAD) (1999). Ecotourism in China—A case study from Jiuzhaigou, Sichuan province of China. <http://www. lead.org.cn/Data/Case/en/juizhg.html>; accessed February 23, 2000.

Lew, A.A. (2001). Ecotourism in Asia. In David Weaver, (ed.), *Encyclopedia of ecotourism* (pp. 123-137). London: CAB International.

Lindberg, Kreg, Carmel Goulding, Zhongliang Huang, Jiangming Mo, Ping Wei, and Guohui Kong (1997). Ecotourism in China: Selected issues and challenges. In Martin Oppermann, (ed.), *Pacific Rim tourism* (pp.128-143). Oxon: CAB International.

Lübker, Malte (2000). Growth is good for the poor—sometimes. SOAS MSc thesis.

Man and the Biosphere (MAB) (1998). Analyses and recommendations on ecotourism in China's nature reserves. Research report by Chinese National Committee for Man and the Biosphere, UNESCO. <http:www.cashq.ac.cn/~mab/bb2-11.html>; accessed July 6, 2000.

Sinclair, M. Thea (1998). Tourism and economic development: A survey. *Journal of Development Studies* 34(5):1-51.

Tang, Ruonie (1990). Guonei lüyou (Domestic tourism). In Sun, Shangqing (ed.), *Zhongguo lüyou jingji yanjiu* (Economic studies of Chinese tourism) (pp. 143-181). Beijing: People's Press.

UNESCO EABRN (1997). Conservation and potential for ecotourism development in and around Changbaishan Biosphere Reserve, People's Republic of China, <http:www.cashq.ac.cn/~mab/bb2-12.html>; accessed July 6, 2000.

Wen, Jie and Clem Tisdell (1997). Regional inequality and tourism distribution. *Pacific Tourism Review* 2(1):43-52.

World Tourism Organization (WTO) (1998). *Tourism economic report.* Madrid: WTO.

World Tourism Organization (WTO) (2000). *Main tourist destinations 1999.* Madrid: WTO.

Xu, Gang (1999). *Tourism and local economic development in China.* Surrey: Curzon Press.

Chapter 7

Ecotourism in China's Nature Reserves

Kreg Lindberg
Clem Tisdell
Dayuan Xue

As in other countries, ecotourism has attracted substantial interest in China, particularly among nature reserve managers. The significant number of visitors, both domestic and foreign, has led to positive and negative impacts on the reserves, impacts that are increasingly well understood through recent evaluations by the Chinese National Committee for Man and the Biosphere (China MAB, 1998; Han, 2000). This chapter provides an overview of ecotourism in China, including relevant policy, issues, and trends.

Because there is no universal definition of ecotourism, it is important to clarify the scope of this chapter. As noted by Lindberg and McKercher (1997), most concepts and definitions of ecotourism can be reduced to the following: ecotourism is tourism and recreation that is both nature based and sustainable. As used here, sustainability incorporates environmental, experiential, sociocultural, and economic dimensions, and it implies overall net benefits across dimensions. This concept is consistent with those used in China, including Li and Han's (2000) concept of ecotourism requiring that the four key actors involved—nature reserves, visitors, communities, and practitioners

This chapter draws heavily from work conducted as part of the Chinese National Committee for MAB evaluation of nature reserve policy in China. We would like to thank Professor Nianyong Han and Dr. Wenjun Li for providing documents from that evaluation, as well as Professor Trevor Sofield for his comments.

(businesses)—benefit from tourism (cf. Xing, 1993). In many countries, including China, the sociocultural or community dimension includes ethnic minorities and their cultures, which can be both affected by and a basis for ecotourism.

The focus of this chapter is on visitation at nature reserves in China, which is both more narrow than the conceptual definition just provided (because it is limited to reserves) and more broad (because it includes visitation that may not meet the criterion of sustainability). As noted by Sofield, Li, and Yunhai (1999), visitation at China's nature reserves often would not meet Western views of ecotourism given the very high levels of visitation and the emphasis on generation of financial and economic benefits through infrastructure development. However, the goal of this chapter is not to define ecotourism or evaluate an activity relative to such a definition, but to describe the activity (reserve visitation) that has been the focus of much writing on ecotourism within China. Issues relevant to sustainability and ecotourism objectives are noted in the chapter, and the need for ongoing development of policy and management systems is stressed in order to enhance future achievement of these objectives.

Some of the key issues include (1) lack of clarity in land ownership and management responsibility, which hinders effective ecotourism management and contributes to uncontrolled development; (2) limited government funding, which means reserves depend heavily on revenue from tourism; (3) use of an "open style" protected area management model based on the biosphere reserve concept, which is consistent with the need to generate both revenue for reserves and economic opportunities for local communities; and (4) a larger role in reserve management for local government than is the case in many other countries.

Of necessity, this chapter presents only an overview of issues. Readers interested in further background and recommendations for future policy and management are encouraged to consult the results of the recent evaluation on sustainable management of China's nature reserves, including the reports by Han (2000), Li and Han (2000), and Xue (2000) (cf. Han and Ren, n.d.). Within each of the sections, reference is made to examples from various nature reserves in China, especially Dinghushan and Changbaishan. In addition, the example of Jiuzhaigou is used to illustrate several relevant issues in the context of one particular reserve.

NATURE RESERVES AND ECOTOURISM: CONTEXT AND POLICY ISSUES

Among the first "conservationists" in China were the early Taoist and Buddhist religious orders, many of which sought isolated, mountainous areas to practice principles of harmony with the environment. These traditions meant that areas surrounding religious sites were conserved while other areas in China were cleared for agriculture or other economic activities. This has led to the presence of religious and cultural sites within many of the country's reserves. In more recent times, the number of nature reserves increased from 34 in 1978, accounting for 0.13 percent of the country's area, to 1,146 in 1999, accounting for 8.8 percent of the area. (China does not utilize all six IUCN categories of protected areas, but rather uses the designations of nature reserve, scenic spot, and forest parks; sites designated as nature reserves are the focus of this chapter.) Of these reserves, sixteen have been included in UNESCO's international biosphere reserve network and eighty-three in the China Biosphere Reserve Network (Han, 2000; Li and Han, 2000).

The administrative and management structure of reserves in China is complex. The State Environmental Protection Administration (SEPA) is the administrative authority for nature reserve management and is responsible for formulating legislation, policies, planning, standards, and guidelines for reserve management nationwide, as well as for assessing, supervising, and inspecting the implementation of legislation and policies. However, several other ministries, including the State Forestry Administration, Ministry of Agriculture, State Oceanic Administration, Ministry of Construction, Ministry of Territory Resources, Ministry of Water Conservancy, and State Chinese Medicine Administration, are responsible for on-the-ground management of various categories of reserves, and they can issue regulations and policies for management of reserves under their jurisdictions. (This section is drawn primarily from Xue, 2000, which also contains discussion of relevant legislation and related issues; see also Han, 2000.)

Nature reserves in China are divided into national and local (provincial, municipal, and county) levels. Central government ministries are mainly in charge of national nature reserves, and local governments are in charge of reserves at local levels, but the system sometimes is mixed. As noted by Anon. (1995) and Li and Han (2000), the large number of responsible agencies, with concomitant coordination difficulties, has limited efficient reserve management in China.

The involvement of local government can exacerbate these difficulties, as political interests vary not only across agencies, but also across different levels of government. As in many countries, local government priorities in China may be more "pro-development" than are national priorities when it comes to tourism or other economic activities in reserves. As an example of the role of local government, the Dinghu Tourism Bureau is located within the Dinghushan Biosphere Reserve, but is a unit of Zhaoqing city government. The bureau collects and distributes entrance fees and is responsible for much of the infrastructure development within the reserve. Overlapping responsibilities, and thus potential conflict, arise in part because local governments typically retain the ownership of land in reserves; that is, the agencies that administer the reserves often have no land ownership or land use right. As noted by Tisdell (1999:223) in the context of a different reserve:

> The political system therefore allows for multiple influences on policies pursued by the administration of Xishuangbanna State Nature Reserve [in Yunnan]. Because multiple bodies can have an influence, there is a possibility of conflict between these and such conflict has to be resolved by political means. Lines of command are by no means as hard-and-fast or definite as one might imagine. While this allows the interplay of a variety of social forces, it also provides scope for slackness and inefficiency in the administrative system.

The extent of the communication and coordination challenge is illustrated by cases in which a single area may be designated as a nature reserve by one department and a forest park by another (Li and Han, 2000). Because management goals and functions are different across reserves, this confusion over designation inhibits effective control of tourism development or other activities.

As discussed next in the context of infrastructure management, there is also a lack of enforcement, due in part to financial pressure and the administrative system. Legally, resource development activities such as tourism are not allowed in the core and buffer zones of reserves, but many development activities nonetheless have occurred in these zones.

Li and Han (2000) and Xue (2000) stress that clarification of land ownership and enhanced coordination across agencies will be important steps toward efficient reserve management, both with respect to ecotourism and more generally. Indeed, a single (or at least more concentrated) management authority could (1) provide guiding principles for development to indicate which kinds of resource can be developed, in what mode, under which conditions, and how to allocate the benefits; (2) identify which industries (e.g., tourism, agriculture, forestry, livestock, processing, and commercial business) are suitable for different reserves; (3) identify revenue targets that could reduce pressure for continued development; and (4) implement and enforce environmental management, including EIA procedures, monitoring, and punishment of violations.

Turning to tourism in particular, about 80 percent of China's nature reserves have developed tourism since the early 1990s. Of these, 16 percent have more than 100,000 annual visits. Estimated total annual visitation was approximately 2.5 million in 1995, with annual revenue of approximately US$63 million (China MAB, 1998). Reserve visitation continues to increase rapidly with national economic growth, and at a rate higher than for foreign and domestic tourism generally at the national level. Table 7.1 illustrates recent growth across several reserves.

Despite this recent growth, ecotourism suffers from the same lack of guidance as reserve management generally. Li and Han (2000) observe that no national ecotourism strategy exists, and that such a strategy would be beneficial by addressing issues such as the fundamental concept of ecotourism in reserves, the purposes of ecotourism, the suitability of each reserve for ecotourism, and how best to manage the activity.

THE ROLE OF ECOTOURISM IN RESERVE FINANCE

In most countries, public funds available for the management of national parks and protected areas are limited, and this is particularly true in developing countries such as China (Han and Guo, 1995; Li and Han, 2000). According to World Conservation Monitoring Centre (WCMC) surveys of protected areas in 108 countries, average annual funding (for both infrastructure and maintenance) for developed

TABLE 7.1. Visitation at Selected Reserves (in Thousands)

Reserve	1995	1998
Dinghushan	650	800
Wolong	20	80
Wuyishan	8	20
Fanjingshan	30	100
Shennongjia	5	40
Yancheng	20	40
Jiuzhaigou	150	400
Maolan	20	100
Nanjilie	10	50
Wulingshan	24	60
Dalinor	5	80
Total	**942**	**1,770**

Source: Han (2000).

country areas was US$2,058/km^2, and for developing country areas was US$157/km^2 (James, 1999). In China, national reserves were funded at US$113/km^2 in 1999, which was less than the developing country average (Han, 2000; Li and Han, 2000).

This lack of funding puts pressure on the reserves to find additional sources of revenue, and tourism is one of these sources. Xue (2000) reports that most of China's reserves obtain 20 to 80 percent of their total budget from commercial use of their resources, with one reserve (Jiuzhaigou) being able to finance its whole budget from tourist revenue. Although many countries, especially developing countries, are dependent on tourism for revenue, the dependency appears to be particularly great in China. Canada serves as a developed country comparative example, one in which the Canadian government funds 75 percent of the total national parks budget.

Insofar as tourism generates funding for conservation in China, one can say that it is consistent with ecotourism goals. However, there is also the danger that the reserves can become so dependent on this source of revenue that they sacrifice conservation objectives to maintain or increase it. This incentive not only operates at the reserve level, but also at the individual staff level. The wages of reserve employees in China are relatively low, and tourism receipts provide a means of supplementing employee income (Tisdell, 1999). Thus, from a personal point of view, employees in nature reserves can have an interest in maintaining or increasing revenue from tourist use of the reserve even when this is at the expense of nature conservation (Tisdell, 1999; Wen and Tisdell, 2001).

The example of Changbaishan Biosphere Reserve (CBR) illustrates the contribution of ecotourism to reserve finance. (This section is based on Xue, 1997 and Xue, Cook, and Tisdell, 2000.) Table 7.2 shows the level of funding from the Forestry Department of Jilin Provincial Government (amounts shown in RMB yuan, US$1 = RMB 8.27 yuan).

The amounts shown are supplemented with funding from other governmental sources for activities such as research and forest fire prevention. In 1996, these supplementary funds totaled 0.58 million, leading to a total government appropriation of RMB 2.13 million yuan for the year. However, the cost of managing CBR that year was RMB 11.46 million yuan, which leaves a gap of RMB 9.33 million yuan.

The reserve charges various tourism-related fees. In 1996, fee revenue from domestic visitors was RMB 8.8 million yuan (176,000 visitors × RMB 50 yuan per person). Of this amount, 15 percent went to national government tax, 27 percent to local government, and the rest

TABLE 7.2. Governmental Appropriation to CBR Funding per Year (Million Yuan)

Year	Yuan (millions)
1987	0.85
1988	0.87
1989	0.80
1990	0.77
1991	0.78
1992	0.97
1993	1.14
1994	1.10
1995	1.30
1996	1.55
1997	1.40

Source: Xue, Cook, and Tisdell (2000).

(58 percent or RMB 5.1 million yuan) to the reserve. Fee revenue from international visitors was 18.54 million yuan (71,312 visitors × RMB 260 yuan per person). Of this amount, 15 percent went to national government tax, 42 percent to local government, and the rest (43 percent or RMB 7.97 million yuan) to the reserve. The total reserve gross revenue from tourism was RMB 13.07 million yuan, but miscellaneous costs arising from tourism management are deducted, leaving a net income of RMB 9.23 million yuan. This roughly fills the reserve's gap of RMB 9.33 million yuan.

Naturally, ecotourism-related revenue will vary across reserves. Changbaishan earns approximately 60 percent of its annual budget from tourism, while Jiuzhaigou reserve covers its total budget from this source. The distribution of revenue benefits also varies. As noted by Lindberg et al. (1997), Dinghushan Biosphere Reserve generated an estimated RMB 13.5 million yuan from entrance and related fees in 1995, but only 5 percent of this amount is a direct benefit to the management agency (Dinghushan Biosphere Reserve Arboretum). The majority of reserves receive tourism revenue of about RMB 0.2 to 1.0 million yuan yearly.

Turning to broader economic issues, some members of SEPA have been active in establishing the economic value of biodiversity conservation for providing services (e.g., tourism) and for producing off-site values (e.g., existence values associated with conservation) given the pressure in China to utilize natural resources for material production. Using a travel cost analysis, Xue, Cook, and Tisdell (2000) estimate the consumer surplus of domestic recreation at Changbaishan in 1996 was RMB 34.78 million yuan. The total net economic benefit to Chinese society from visitation at the reserve was thus:

> reserve net revenue of RMB 9.23 million yuan
> + local community net benefit of RMB 27.75 million yuan
> + government net benefit of RMB 47.89 million yuan
> + consumer surplus of RMB 34.78 million yuan
> —————————————————————————————
> RMB 119.65 million yuan

Although a portion of this total (i.e., the consumer surplus) is intangible, such calculations illustrate the value of ecotourism, and thus of reserves, in China and elsewhere.

THE ROLE OF ECOTOURISM
AND LOCAL DEVELOPMENT

Most countries contain a variety of protected area designations that allow various levels of human activity. For example, national parks specifically provide for recreation as well as conservation, while strict nature reserves allow much less human use. However, even national parks can be viewed as a "closed style" designation that places primary emphasis on protection of the environment while limiting human interaction and activity. On the other hand, the biosphere reserve designation can be viewed as "open style," which emphasizes the integration of protection and development (Zhao and Han, 1996).

Biosphere reserves are zoned, multiple-function areas that attempt to integrate conservation with economic development and human interaction with the environment. This is achieved through the integration of a number of central roles including protection, research, monitoring, and sustainable economic development (Batisse, 1986). The zones within a biosphere reserve vary across countries but often include a buffer area allowing sustainable economic activity including tourism development, a core area that is protected with activity generally restricted to scientific and education-based research, and a transition area allowing agricultural activities, settlements, and other uses.

For countries with high population densities and relatively low rates of per capita income, the open-style protected area model is the most realistic. China has chosen the open-style biosphere reserve as the dominant protected area model for the country (State Council, 1994). Thus, the extensive development of commercial tourism enterprises is not surprising, and this has provided significant benefits to local communities, including generation of income and improvement in transport (Han and Guo, 1995). At Dinghushan Biosphere Reserve (DBR), stakeholders believe the reserve has played a positive role in the community, reporting direct benefits from the reserve of increased opportunities for employment, improvement in site facilities, and access to new industries. These beliefs are supported by visitor survey results, which indicate that ecotourism at DBR generates an estimated RMB 47 to 100 million yuan per year in visitor expenditure for the district (Lindberg et al., 1997). Xue (2000) notes that tourism at DBR creates more than 500 jobs for local people.

Xue, Cook, and Tisdell (2000) provide a detailed analysis of economic benefits from Changbaishan Biosphere Reserve. The average visitor is estimated to spend two nights in the reserve, with foreigners generally staying at one of the eight hotels in the entrance area of the reserve and domestic visitors generally staying in one of the many hostels run by local communities. Expenditure associated with this visitation is illustrated in Table 7.3.

Local communities may also benefit as payments made to the national and, especially, the local government can be used to enhance local services. In 1996, CBR generated an estimated RMB 4.10 million yuan for the national government and RMB 10.17 million yuan for the local government through entrance fees. In addition, the net benefit (profit) to the governmental transport sector was estimated at RMB 33.62 million yuan.

As these figures illustrate, tourism at China's nature reserves does contribute to the goal of providing local benefits. This can lead to support not only for tourism, but also for the natural areas with which it is associated (Han and Guo, 1995; Lindberg, Enriquez, and Sproule, 1996). Moreover, with 90 percent of China's tourism receipts being earned in cities and an overwhelming concentration of tourism destinations in coastal regions, ecotourism helps decentralize the tourism industry by dispersing visitors to rural areas (Wen and Tisdell, 1996, 2001).

On the other hand, negative economic or other impacts can jeopardize support for tourism and associated areas. For example, in some areas of China, tourism has led to a reduction in resident access to areas set aside for tourists (Han, 2000; Lindberg et al., 1997; Xue, 2000). In addition, Li and Han (2000) observe that the reserve's monopoly on tourism infrastructure limits the involvement of, and benefits accruing to, local communities. Of the reserves developing tourism, a 1997 survey showed that only 11 percent generate benefits for more than half the local households, and approximately 23 percent do not generate any local economic benefits.

As noted by Xue (2000), benefit allocation is a sensitive issue between reserves and local communities. Some reserves take local government, communities, and farmers into account in resource development. They use the revenue to invest in construction of public facilities for local communities, or help local people by introducing advanced techniques to develop resources in a sustainable way. These reserves

TABLE 7.3. Visitor Expenditure and Net Benefits at Changbaishan Biosphere Reserve

Category	Visitors	Expenditure on Food and Accommodation (Yuan)		Expenditure on Local Products and Souvenirs (Yuan)	
		Per Person	Category Total	Per Person	Category Total
Foreign	71,312	665	47.42 million	200	14.26 million
Domestic	176,000	200	35.20 million	80	14.08 million
	Total		82.62 million		28.34 million
	Net benefit		20.66 million		7.09 million

Source: Xue, Cook, and Tisdell (200C).

experience a peaceful coexistence with local people. On the contrary, some reserves do not promote local benefits, but rather earn money only for themselves.

Relatedly, biosphere reserves are designed not only to provide local benefits, but also to involve local participation as a means of linking conservation and development. Community participation has been stressed in both the biosphere reserve and the tourism literature (Simmons, 1994). At Dinghushan BR, community participation is not as high as desired. This results from various causes, including political structures and traditions, and the significant role played by the local government in de facto reserve management. Although opportunities to enhance community participation exist in many countries, this is particularly true in China, where political norms and complex institutional arrangements hinder high levels of community participation.

INFRASTRUCTURE AND ENVIRONMENTAL MANAGEMENT

Although significant visitor-related infrastructure has been developed in national parks around the world, biosphere reserves specifically allow for, and promote, such development. Moreover, as noted previously, the reserve management agencies depend on tourism and related infrastructure to generate revenue, and this revenue contributes to the agencies' conservation activities. However, the dependence on this revenue is an incentive for reserve management agencies to accept, or even pursue, infrastructure development that exceeds levels viewed as appropriate by some. Such a tendency can be exacerbated by the confusion of land and development rights noted previously. For example, although DBRA officially has the right to control tourism in Dinghushan Biosphere Reserve, the Zhaoqing city government has de facto control over tourism development.

As Li and Han (2000) observe, there is concern about landscape destruction, water pollution, litter, and species reduction in reserves. Wulingyuan Scenic and Historic Interest Area, which was added to the World Heritage List in 1992, provides an extreme example. The area received some 2.8 million tourists in 1999, including 151,000 foreign visitors, and this tourism activity generated 1 billion yuan (Xinhua News Agency, 2000). However, it also has generated serious pollution, with restaurants at one scenic spot (Jinbianxi) discharging 1,500 tons of sewage daily. The UNESCO World Heritage Centre is now advising on a RMB 300 million yuan relocation program to move numerous hotels and restaurants, as well as 9,000 local residents.

Other sites experience lower levels of visitation and development, but pollution remains an issue. In Dinghushan Biosphere Reserve, Kong et al. (1993) found that the high level of visitation and the increasing use of motorized transport, with 130,000 to 140,000 vehicles entering DBR each year, have generated negative impacts on air and water quality, as well as soil condition. A recent survey of China's nature reserves found that 22 percent of the reserves were so damaged that they failed to meet their conservation targets, 11 percent were degraded by tourism, and 61 percent had constructed tourist facilities that clashed or failed to harmonize with their natural landscapes.

To some degree, these negative impacts are due to the lack of resources, combined with preexisting trail networks and external control of development. Few natural areas, particularly in developing countries, have the human and financial resources to implement comprehensive visitor management strategies. At Dinghushan BR, the trail network stems from centuries of access to temples in the area, while in other countries the network might stem from fire control roads, trails to historic scenic or recreation areas, and so on.

However, the financial and other pressures to develop tourism may have even greater impact. Spatially, Chinese nature reserves are split into core, buffer, and experimental zones. In principle, people are allowed to enter the core zones solely for scientific research and with approval by the relevant management authority. Tourism development is banned in buffer zones, but is allowed in a controlled manner in experimental zones. Detailed plans must be approved for the various activities in such zones. Despite these regulations, almost every reserve has in fact developed tourism to some degree in buffer and experimental zones in order to generate revenue.

In principle, the industry should impose self-regulation to ensure that development does not destroy the experience sought by visitors. Such a principle is supported by responses to a visitor survey conducted in Dinghushan BR (Lindberg et al., 1997). For example, when asked how important "to view scenery in the reserve" was as a motivation for the visit, 46 percent of the respondents selected 4 or 5 on a

5-point scale where 1 = Not Important and 5 = Extremely Important. Similarly, 58 percent of respondents said they would support or strongly support restrictions on the construction of hotels and other buildings in the reserve.

Moreover, self-regulation may provide important economic benefits to current tourism businesses in Dinghushan BR. Many businesses reported declining sales in the mid-1990s, with entrance fee increases or a general economic slowdown being blamed. However, the decline also may be due in part to growth in the number of businesses and the limited diversity of products sold. Future growth in the number of businesses may generate further downward pressure on sales per business, such that existing businesses have a natural self-interest to restrict such growth. Despite these considerations, further increases in infrastructure have been proposed, and restrictions on the number of businesses appear unlikely.

Another issue in the context of infrastructure development is that the relevant authorities often have unrealistic expectations about the commercial viability of ecotourism. Political decisions by government officials with limited experience in commerce play an important role, and market assessment is often limited. In some cases, this has led to substantial losses, which can result in less funding being available for nature conservation (Tisdell, 1995). Thus, when ecotourism development fails economically, nature conservation can be negatively impacted. Parks agencies in many countries lack commercial expertise, and therefore at times pursue projects that may not be commercially viable. However, the government in China generally plays a larger role than in other countries, and the financial discipline of the private sector is weaker, such that there is a greater likelihood of unrealistic expectations.

A potentially countervailing force is a tendency to allocate funding to hire new staff rather than to capital (e.g., infrastructure) development. As Tisdell (1999) noted, this may be due to pressure from local government, and may also be a political strategy—it is more difficult to reduce government funding if doing so would lead to dismissing staff rather than postponing capital works.

With respect to environmental monitoring, the 1997 survey found that only 16 percent of reserves in China had regular environmental monitoring, and 46 percent of reserves never monitored the environment. Li and Han (2000) stress the importance of an effective monitoring system, one that includes the following:

- *Reporting system*. Management agencies should request economic activity reports from each reserve, and require that some projects be subject to an approval procedure.
- *EIA system*. Development projects should be subject to environmental impact assessment (EIA) and environmental monitoring programs in order to minimize environmental damage.
- *Inspection system*. Management agencies should conduct field inspections of the economic activities in reserves, and correct harmful practices where necessary.
- *Monitoring system*. Nongovernmental organizations, journalists, conservation experts, local communities, and the public should be allowed to monitor the reserve's activities.

SEPA requires EIAs for tourism development, but this requirement is not always followed. For example, Sofield, Li, and Yunhai (1999) report that Huangshan Scenic Area contains seven hotels with more than 3,000 beds, three cable cars totaling more than 12 km in length, and two reservoirs constructed across alpine streams to provide water for the hotels, yet all occurred without an EIA.

STAFFING ISSUES

Staffing difficulties are common in natural area management, and China is no exception. Han and Guo (1995) note that poor working conditions impact staffing, while Li and Han (2000) note that the knowledge level of reserve managers is improving but remains low. The 1997 survey indicated that only 16 percent of staff members at national reserves had higher education (undergraduate degrees or higher), but this was an improvement from 9 percent in 1992.

Aside from the issue of training level, there is also the issue of training focus. As discussed in Lindberg et al. (1997), the global tendency is for protected area staff to be trained in the natural sciences, particularly biology or ecology, and staff at China's reserves are no exception. However, the challenges reserve managers face often are social and political rather than simply ecological and technical. Protected area visitation has a technical ecological component (e.g., the environmental impact of ecotourism), but it also has a significant social and political component, and that component requires skills in those areas.

The tendency of protected area staff to have an ecological orientation and, to a lesser degree, a research orientation leads to several outcomes. First, planning and management tend to focus on the natural environment rather than the human environment, and on visitation in particular. For example, although tourism-related planning has been pursued in some Chinese reserves (Tisdell, 1996), it appears uncommon. Second, it often is difficult for staff to work effectively with tourism professionals, who typically have very different training, priorities, and personalities. As a result, developing the trust and personal relationships that contribute to effective cooperation is difficult. Third, staff often find it difficult to work effectively with local communities. Although some reserves in China have actively developed symbiotic relationships with local communities (Tan, 1996), achieving such harmony is a challenge for reserves in China and internationally.

Both the ecotourism and the biosphere reserve concepts stress the importance of the natural *and* social environments, as well as the importance of developing effective and symbiotic cooperation among protected areas, local communities, and tourism businesses. However, this is a challenge around the world, and to achieve these goals it will be necessary to broaden the skills and interests of existing reserve staff and/or to hire new staff with these skills.

THE VISITOR EXPERIENCE AND INTERPRETATION

Li and Han (2000) observe that there is little monitoring of visitors, including visitor numbers or the visitor experience. Lindberg et al. (1997) describe one of the few visitor survey efforts in China reported in the Western literature. Results from other surveys are reported in Wen and Tisdell (2001) and Xue, Cook, and Tisdell (2000). Results suggested that many Dinghushan BR visitors are motivated by the opportunity to view scenery in the reserve, as well as to learn about nature. These motivations lead to support for restricting activities, including infrastructure development, that might threaten natural features. Nonetheless, observation of visitor behavior in DBR suggests that these responses should be interpreted cautiously and with due regard to the cultural context. For example, littering in the reserve is tolerated more than would be the case in many Western areas. As noted by Hashimoto (2000; cf. Petersen, 1995), the Chinese image of natural landscapes is nurtured by cultural sources such as poems and paintings. One respondent in his survey of Chinese travel industry professionals remarked, "even if a famous attraction of natural landscaping is suffering from environmental degradation, in the Chinese tourists' minds, the place is still as beautiful as described in the poem" (Hashimoto, 2000:132).

Moreover, cross-cultural evaluations of human relationships with the natural environment suggest that, relative to Western cultures, Eastern cultures tend to favor human manipulation of nature in order to enhance its appeal, in contrast to preservation of nature in a pristine state (Kellert, 1996; Sofield, Li, and Yunhai, 1999). Thus, Chinese visitors may be more tolerant of human changes to nature reserves than would be true of visitors in many Western reserves.

Although little empirical research has been conducted on cross-cultural motivations and desired experiences in ecotourism settings, observation and discussion with researchers and reserve managers in many countries suggest that substantial cross-cultural differences exist. The example of litter suggests that perceptions of depreciation and environmental degradation caused by other visitors varies across cultures. Similarly, perceptions of crowding may vary across cultures. Lindberg and colleagues (1997) note that of the 242 respondents who reported that they saw at least 200 other people during their visit to Dinghushan BR, fewer than 25 percent selected the number five or higher on a scale of one to nine, with one being "not at all crowded" to nine being "extremely crowded." The reserve is located within two hours of a city of six million people, and it is unlikely that visitors expect a wilderness experience. Nonetheless, the level of crowding in the reserve probably is much more tolerable to Chinese visitors than to Western visitors.

Of course, variability exists within cultures, with certain individuals and groups in Chinese society being more sensitive than others to environmental degradation and crowding. For example, Xing (1993) reports high levels of visitation at Wuyishan, Changbaishan, and Huangshan (with the latter having more than 10,000 visitors per day during peak periods) and observes that such visitation levels, and associated infrastructure, may devalue the natural beauty of the reserves.

Two other issues are of interest. First, Dinghushan BR and many other reserves in China offer not just natural attractions, but also religious and cultural attractions. In precommunist times, leisure travel consisted primarily of pilgrimages to Buddhist or Taoist temples (Qiao, 1995). On-site observations indicate that religious pilgrimage is still a key component of tourism activity at Dinghushan, particularly for older visitors. Of the seven motivations presented on the visitor survey, "to have a spiritual experience" was reported as the least important, but this result may be due to underrepresentation of older visitors in the survey sample. (Many older visitors refused to participate in the survey.)

Second, although most Dinghushan visitors travel in groups, "to do something with friends or family" was not highly rated as a motivation. However, this may be explained by recent research on leisure and values in China, which indicates that family is not a preferred context for participation in leisure activities (Freysinger and Chen, 1993).

Reserve managers around the world must cater to visitors with differing motivations and desired experiences. In the Dinghushan context, an example is the challenge of managing general temple visitors whose behavior may conflict with the desired experience of visitors who go to the temple for religious purposes. In countries where cross-cultural differences are great, which often is the case for developed country ecotourists visiting sites in developing countries, this challenge is exacerbated. Currently, most reserves in China cater to domestic visitors, but this issue must be considered if international visitation is pursued.

Li and Han (2000) stress that environmental education (through guides, visitor centers, signs, brochures, etc.) can raise the environmental consciousness of visitors, but has not been well developed in China (cf. Lindberg et al., 1997; Tisdell, 1996). The 1997 survey indicates that 40 percent of the reserves with tourism have no guide service, and most of the guides that do exist lack basic environmental knowledge. Only 17 percent of the reserves have specially trained guides. Lack of funding and the difficulty of attracting to remote areas the qualified staff to develop and present interpretive material are common limitations to effective interpretive programs in many countries, including China. Last, several more practical visitor management issues require attention. For example, the 1997 survey found that only 12 percent of reserves had designated first aid persons, 18 percent had emergency response plans, and 22 percent had established emergency evacuation routes for visitors.

THE EXAMPLE OF JIUZHAIGOU BIOSPHERE RESERVE, SICHUAN PROVINCE

Jiuzhaigou Biosphere Reserve illustrates several aspects of ecotourism in China (Han and Guan, n.d.). The area was previously used for plantation forestry, but was designated as a nature reserve in 1978, a world heritage site in 1992, and a biosphere reserve in 1997. There are 222 households in nine villages, with a population of 1,021 living in the reserve.

With its beautiful landscape and local (Tibetan) culture, Jiuzhaigou has attracted visitors since the early 1980s. However, numbers have increased significantly, especially after the construction of a new road from Chengdu in 1997; there were 181,000 visitors in that year, rising to 580,000 in 1999. This visitation has generated substantial revenue, with annual entrance fee revenue amounting to RMB 46.88 million yuan in 1999. This equals nearly one-quarter of the total government allocation for the country's 926 nature reserves in 1998. The tax paid by the reserve to the county government also increased from RMB 2.780 million yuan in 1997 to RMB 11.486 million yuan in 1999, and now represents about 80 percent of the total annual taxes collected by the county government.

Tourism at the reserve has also generated significant benefits for local residents. The annual local income per capita was RMB 2,000 yuan in 1995, rising to RMB 10,000 yuan in 1999. This income is six times the average of the farmers in Sichuan Province and is entirely due to tourism.

The economic benefits have also brought ecological gains. Agricultural land within the reserve has been completely returned to forest regeneration because local people no longer need to rely on farming. Wastewater treatment plants have been built in villages, as have high-quality waste control toilets at some sites in the reserve. A visitor center was established, with the nearly RMB 30 million yuan cost being covered by the reserve. The more than 400 buses and cars used to transport visitors into the reserve have been replaced by 180 natural gas "green" buses.

These gains have been achieved by involving local residents. Residents benefit through ecotourism operation such as a cultural village showing local customs, family hotels, restaurants, horse and yak riding, cultural performance, handicraft shops, and so on. In addition, the new "green" bus company was established through stock sharing, which brought the interests of the owners of old buses together when dealing with the sensitive issue of establishing a new system. Moreover, one-third of the reserve staff, ranging from the reserve directors to tour guides to cleaners, comes from local communities; this helps the management team balance conservation and local needs.

Nonetheless, problems remain and need to be addressed in the future, such as overcrowding, traffic jams and noise, rapid town growth, and environmental problems outside the reserve, as well as the need to strengthen tour guide training. Visitor numbers are expected to continue to increase, as an airport will be built near the reserve in 2002. Management will need to keep pace with the growth and will need to rely increasingly on sound scientific research and monitoring, as well as strengthened coordination with the various interest groups.

SUMMARY

Few, if any, sites around the world fully achieve the ideals of ecotourism. The issues and challenges presented here face reserve managers in many countries. However, some features of ecotourism in China stand out. First, and perhaps most important, the lack of clarity in land ownership and management responsibility hinders coordinated and effective reserve management, including management of ecotourism. This contributes to uncontrolled tourism development. Second, this lack of clarity hinders expanded government funding of reserves, which means reserves depend heavily on revenue from tourism, which is a disincentive to controlling development.

Third, in accordance with its population and economic development context, China is pursuing an open-style protected area management model based on the biosphere reserve concept. This model is consistent with the need to generate both revenue for reserves and economic opportunities for local communities. However, economic activities, including tourism development, have exceeded regulatory guidelines established within the Chinese biosphere reserve model. Fourth, local government, which also plays an industry function, has a larger role in reserve management in China than in many other countries. Although this role facilitates tourism development, it may jeopardize conservation objectives.

In short, ecotourism in China involves greater levels of visitation and infrastructure development than one typically finds in other countries. The desirability of this depends on the objectives of the various stakeholders. There have been strong calls for clarifying the legal and policy framework, as well as implementing it effectively (e.g., Han, 2000; Xue, 2000). The process of doing so can facilitate understanding and consensus building with respect to diverse stakeholder objectives, and can help ensure that ecotourism goals are achieved in China.

From a research perspective, the recent evaluation of reserve management, which includes but goes well beyond ecotourism, illustrates the role of researchers in understanding and informing policy and practice. Nonetheless, continued research is important, not only within the broad policy arena, but also with respect to more focused topics such as the economic (e.g., local community) and ecological impacts of ecotourism, as well as further exploration of the visitor experience.

REFERENCES

Anonymous (1995). Proposals for strengthening management of nature reserves in China. *China's biosphere reserves—Special English issue*. Beijing: Chinese National Committee for Man and the Biosphere Program.

Batisse, M. (1986). Developing and focussing the biosphere concept. *Nature and Resources* 22(3): 1-10.

Chinese National Committee for Man and the Biosphere Programme [China MAB] (1998). *Nature reserves and ecotourism*. Beijing: Science and Technology Press of China (in Chinese).

Freysinger, V.J. and T. Chen (1993). Leisure and family in China: The impact of culture. *World Leisure and Travel* 35(3): 22-24.

Han, N. (2000). *Analysis and suggestions on management policies for China's nature reserves*. Report for Chinese National Committee for Man and the Biosphere.

Han, N. and Y. Guan (n.d.). Ecotourism practice in Jiuzhaigou Biosphere Reserve of China. Mimeograph.

Han, N. and Z. Guo (1995). An investigation into the current situation of China's nature reserves. *China's biosphere reserves—Special English issue*. Beijing: Chinese National Committee for Man and the Biosphere Program.

Han, N. and Z. Ren (n.d.). Ecotourism in China's nature reserves: An opportunity and challenges. Mimeograph.

Hashimoto, A. (2000). Environmental perception and sense of responsibility of the tourism industry in mainland China, Taiwan, and Japan. *Journal of Sustainable Tourism* 8(2): 131-146.

James, A.N. (1999). Institutional constraints to protected area funding. *Parks* 9(2): 15-25.

Kellert, S.R. (1996). *The value of life: Biological diversity and human society*. Washington, DC: Island Press.

Kong, G., C. Liang, H. Wu, and Z. Huang (1993). *Dinghushan Biosphere Reserve: Ecological research history and perspective*. Beijing: Science Press.

Li, W. and N. Han (2000). *Ecotourism management in China's nature reserves: Situation, issues and countermeasures*. Report for Chinese National Committee for Man and the Biosphere.

Lindberg, K., J. Enriquez, and K. Sproule (1996). Ecotourism questioned: Case studies from Belize. *Annals of Tourism Research* 23(3): 543-562.

Lindberg, K., C. Goulding, Z. Huang, J. Mo, P. Wei, and G. Kong (1997). Ecotourism in China: Selected issues and challenges. In M. Oppermann (Ed.), *Pacific Rim Tourism* (pp. 128-143). London: CAB International.

Lindberg, K. and B. McKercher (1997). Ecotourism: A critical overview. *Pacific Tourism Review* 1(1): 65-79.

Petersen, Y.Y. (1995). The Chinese landscape as a tourist attraction: Image and reality. In A. Lew and L. Yu (Eds.), *Tourism in China: Geographic, political and economic perspectives* (pp. 141-154). Boulder, CO: Westview Press.

Qiao, Y. (1995). Domestic tourism in China: Policies and developments. In A. Lew and L. Yu (Eds.), *Tourism in China: Geographic, political and economic perspectives* (pp. 121-130). Boulder, CO: Westview Press.

Simmons, D. (1994). Community participation in tourism planning. *Tourism Management* 15(2): 98-108.

Sofield, T.H.B., F.M.S. Li, and K. Yunhai (1999). *An ecotourism strategy for nature reserves in southwest Yunnan*. Report for the Sino-Dutch Forest Conservation and Community Development Project. Australia: Cooperative Research Centre for Sustainable Tourism, Gold Coast.

State Council (1994). *Regulations of the People's Republic of China on nature reserves: Order of the State Council of the PR China No. 167*.

Tan, W. (1996). Ten great achievements in ten years' struggle. *China's biosphere reserves—Special English issue*. Beijing: Chinese National Committee for Man and the Biosphere Program.

Tisdell, C.A. (1995). Investment in ecotourism: Assessing its economics. *Tourism Economics* 1(4): 375-387.

Tisdell, C. (1996). Ecotourism, economics, and the environment: Observations from China. *Journal of Travel Research* 34(4): 11-19.

Tisdell, C.A. (1999). *Biodiversity, conservation and sustainable development: Principles and practices with Asian examples.* Cheltenham, UK: Edward Elgar.

Wen, J. and C. Tisdell (1996). Spatial distribution of tourism in China: Economic and other influences. *Tourism Economics* 2(3): 235-250.

Wen, J. and C.A. Tisdell, (2001). *Tourism and China's development.* Singapore: World Scientific.

Xing, W. (1993). The increasing impact of tourism on protected areas in China. *Contours* 6(3-4): 38-43.

Xinhua News Agency (2000). Restoration of Wulingyuan Scenic and Historic Interest Area. Press Release, June 20.

Xue, D. (1997). *Economic valuation of biodiversity: A case study on Changbai Mountain Biosphere Reserve in northeast China.* Beijing: China Environmental Science Press.

Xue, D. (2000). Resources management within nature reserves in China. *Economics, ecology and environment.* Working Paper No. 51, Department of Economics, The University of Queensland, Brisbane.

Xue, D., A. Cook, and C. Tisdell (2000). Biodiversity and the tourism values of Changbai Mountain Biosphere Reserve, China: A travel cost approach. *Tourism Economics* 5(4): 335-357.

Zhao, Z. and N. Han (1996). Open management strategy: Biosphere reserves in China. *China's biosphere reserves—Special English issue.* Beijing: Chinese National Committee for Man and the Biosphere Program.

SECTION III:
INDUSTRY AND DEVELOPMENT

Chapter 8

Critical Issues in China's Hotel Industry

Lawrence Yu

After two decades of rapid hotel development since the late 1970s, China has emerged as a country with an adequately established hotel industry. The growth of China's hotel industry during this period has been analyzed by several previous studies (Yu 1992; Zhang 1995; Yu 1998; Xu 1999). The spontaneous growth in the late 1970s, the joint venture and cooperative development in the 1980s, and the private ownership and stock ownership development in the 1990s have all demonstrated the growth and change of China's hotel industry during the past two decades. The hotel supply caught up with travel demand in the upscale and luxury market segments, and now hotel operators are facing the challenge of improving service quality and intense competition among both domestic and international hotel operators. To stay above the competition, hotel operators need to offer travelers a focused choice with superb service. Therefore, they have been seeking managers with a good management track record to run their lodging businesses. On the other hand, professional hotel companies have realized that a great potential exists for consolidation and brand development in the Chinese hotel industry, as most Chinese hotels are nonbranded. These factors have stimulated the development of professional hotel management companies in China. The emergence of the Chinese hotel groups that own and manage hotels both at home and abroad began to make an impact on the global hospitality industry.

At the same time, global hotel corporations are also jockeying for positions in the Chinese lodging market to enhance their brand development and expand global sales because China is projected by the World Tourism Organization to be the top tourism destination in the world by 2020 ("Travel to Surge" 1997). As a member of the World

Trade Organization, China will open its market for global competition and the hospitality industry will experience rapid globalization and competition.

This study attempts to analyze some critical development issues confronting the Chinese hospitality industry in the new millennium. It analyzes consolidation and specialization in China and examines market penetration by international hotel corporations. It analyzes hotel financial performance in selected tourism destinations, and compares the performance results to those of destination cities in the region. The analysis of these critical issues reveals current hotel development in China and identifies challenges for future development.

CHINA'S HOTEL INDUSTRY

China witnessed a rapid growth of hotel development in 1999. By the end of 1999, 7,035 hotels were qualified by the China National Tourism Administration (CNTA) to accommodate international visitors, an increase of 17.8 percent over 1998. These hotels represent highly diversified and complex ownership and business structures (Table 8.1). As Table 8.1 illustrates, 64.12 percent of the total hotel inventory in China was owned by the state in 1999. Private ownership

TABLE 8.1. Hotel Ownership in China, 1999

Ownership	Hotels	Rooms	Occupancy (%)	Revenue (Billion Yuan)
State owned	4,512	543,146	51.45	37.44
Collectively owned	1,003	85,284	50.41	6.20
Privately owned	174	12,910	52.14	0.87
Alliance	223	57,282	62.42	8.49
Stock ownership	404	50,635	53.39	4.70
Foreign ownership	472	90,841	57.46	17.60
Hong Kong, Macao, and Taiwan ownership	247	49,332	58.40	9.28
Total	7,035	889,430	53.41	84.58

Source: CNTA (2000) p. 92.

by Chinese hoteliers was only 2.47 percent in this period. International investors solely or jointly owned 6.71 percent of Chinese hotels in 1999, while Hong Kong, Macao, and Taiwan developers owned 3.5 percent. It is interesting to note that a new category of hotel ownership was included in this report: publicly traded hotel companies. In 1999, 404 hotels were listed that are now traded in the Chinese stock markets. This new category reflects the current economic reform in China, as many companies have gone public to raise capital for business development. The Jin Jiang Tower Co., Ltd., which is discussed in the following section, is a good example of a hotel company that is listed in the Shanghai Stock Exchange. However, one must realize that the publicly traded hotel companies are still owned by the state.

The star-rated hotels increased from 3,428 hotels in 1998 to 3,856 hotels in 1999. The breakdown of the hotels in the five-star categories and the nonstar-rated hotel category is described in Table 8.2. Of the 7,035 hotels in China that are qualified for receiving international tourists, 54.81 percent are rated by the five-star system developed by CNTA. Most of the star-rated hotels are concentrated in the three-star and two-star categories, and only 385 hotels are in the one-star category. Hotels with higher star ratings generated higher room occupancy rates in 1999. It is reported that 3,179 hotels did not participate in the star rating evaluation program in China.

TABLE 8.2. Star-Rated Hotels in China, 1999

Star Rating	Hotels	Rooms	Occupancy (%)	Revenue (Billion Yuan)
Five-star	77	36,160	61.41	10.59
Four-star	204	66,689	58.96	12.40
Three-star	1,292	206,905	55.43	21.05
Two-star	1,898	187,899	50.76	9.66
One-star	385	27,241	46.14	0.94
Nonstar hotels	3,179	364,536	51.96	29.94
Total	7,035	889,430	53.41	84.58

Source: CNTA (2000) p. 92.

CONSOLIDATION AND BRAND DEVELOPMENT

As the hospitality industry matures, Chinese hoteliers have realized that they must offer guests a more focused choice of products and services. Hotel management experience in the United States and Europe has demonstrated that branded hotels have gradually outperformed independent properties in the past twenty years, and it is the brand rather than the company owning the hotel that matters (Sangster 2000; Frabotta 2000; Prasad and Dev 2000). Global hotel brand development has now been strategically planned in Europe and Latin America by international companies (Alisan 2000; Cruz 2000b; Sangster 2000). Amid the rapid hotel development and diversified hotel ownership in China, there exists great potential for hotel companies to consolidate and brand hotel portfolios and operations. Some Chinese hotel companies have capitalized on these opportunities to develop hotel brand and management contract companies.

Hotel magazine, the official journal of the International Hotel and Restaurant Association, conducts an annual survey of global hotel corporations to determine the size of hotel organizations by the number of rooms and hotels they own, manage, franchise, or lease in each year. The journal then publishes its ranking of the top 325 global hotel corporations in each July issue. In 1999, three Chinese hotel management companies were listed (Table 8.3). The Shanghai-based Jin Jiang Hotel Group, China's largest state-owned hotel corporation, ranked fifty-first in the world in 1999, moving up from ninety-seventh place in 1998. It showed an impressive increase of 61 percent in hotel room count. The newly established Beijing Kingdom International Hotels was ranked the eighty-fourth largest hotel company in the world with a total of 10,076 rooms. The Gloria International Hotels was ranked 219 on the top 325 global hotel list.

TABLE 8.3. Chinese Hotel Companies on the Top 325 Global Hotel List, 1999

Company	Rank 99/98	Rooms 99/98	Hotels 99/98
Shanghai Jin Jiang Hotel Group	51/97	13,744/8,375	50/29
Beijing Kingdom Int'l Hotels	84/–	10,076/–	34/–
Gloria International Hotels	219/211	3,228/3,233	10/10

Source: Cruz (2000c), 52, 58.

Table 8.4 illustrates the Hong Kong-based hotel corporations that were included in the top 325 global hotels in 1999. Comparing the Hong Kong-based companies with the Chinese hotel companies, most Hong Kong-based hotel companies showed flat growth between 1998 and 1999. Three Hong Kong companies even reduced their hotel portfolio holdings during 1999. Clearly, the travel markets in Hong Kong and Asia continued to stabilize and recover gradually from the Asian financial crisis in 1997, and the hospitality companies primarily focused their strategies on rebuilding the market rather than expansion. However, the two Chinese hotel companies, Jin Jiang Hotel Group and Kingdom International Hotels, demonstrated phenomenal growth in 1999.

The emergence of the large hotel management groups in China indicates clearly an industry trend of consolidation and specialization in China. This trend reflects that the Chinese hotel companies have prioritized and implemented their strategy to develop professional management services and enhance brand recognition in the Chinese market. As illustrated in Table 8.1, hotel ownership in China is very complex and diversified. Most hotels are owned or jointly owned by government agencies at various administrative levels, such as the Department of Culture, Department of Sports, and so forth. However, since these government agencies do not have expertise in running profitable lodging operations, they have to find professional manage-

TABLE 8.4. Hong Kong-Based Hotel Companies Ranked Among the Top 325 Global Hotels, 1999

Hotel Company	Rank 99/98	Rooms 99/98	Hotels 99/98
Shangri La Hotels & Resorts	11/11	19,202/18,455	37/36
Century International Hotels	157/151	5,332/5,293	20/19
Mandarin Oriental Hotel Group	163/153	5,177/5,210	12/13
Great Eagle Hotels International	188/181	4,063/4,062	7/7
Zenith Hotels International	212/174	3,448/4,353	9/13
Peninsula Group	238/248	2,974/2,974	8/8
Park Lane Hotels International	246/248	2,800/2,800	5/5
Marco Polo Hotels	251/219	2,732/3,112	7/8

Source: Cruz (2000c), 66.

ment companies to manage the properties profitably for them. There-fore, market demand for professional management services has been answered by the establishment of hotel groups specialized in provid-ing standard service procedures and institutionalizing quality man-agement and guest services.

Furthermore, because of the highly fragmented hotel market re-sulting from the complex ownership structures, most Chinese hotels are not branded except for hotels owned, managed, or franchised by international hotel companies. This market situation creates a great opportunity for consolidation and brand development in the Chinese lodging market. Chinese hotel groups have thus capitalized on these demands and opportunities to offer branded products and profes-sional management services.

The Jin Jiang Hotel Group has a highly diversified portfolio of business operations. Its business operations include hotel investment and operations, property management, amusement parks, passenger transportation, trade, real estate, and financial investment. Its main hotel business consists of two companies: Jin Jiang International Management Corporation (JJIMC) and Jin Jiang Tower Co., Ltd. JJIMC provides professional management services for both hotels and commercial properties, such as office buildings and apartments. Its business also encompasses the training and delivery of manage-rial, technical, and service staff for hotels, apartments, and office buildings domestically and globally. The company's mission is to de-liver superior management services to its clients by creating a combi-nation of elegant hotel ambiance and personalized services. JJIMC has a total asset of ¥7.1 billion and a total of over ¥10.9 billion assets under its management (JJIHC 2000). The company wholly owns seven hotels in Shanghai, including such landmark hotels as Jin Jiang Hotel and Peace Hotel by the waterfront in Shanghai. Geographically, JJIMC has three subsidiaries, which cover northern China, southwestern China, and the scenic Hunagshan area in Anhui Province.

Jin Jiang Tower Co., Ltd. is listed in the Shanghai Stock Exchange and is the first hotel company to issue shares to overseas investors (B shares). It has total assets of ¥1.68 billion and shareholder equity of ¥1.52 billion (JJIHC 2000). The company also operates a chain of mid-scale hotels under the brand of Jin Jiang Inn. This type of accom-modation targets domestic tourists and business travelers by offering single rooms, double rooms, and suites with air-conditioning, bathroom, TV, and phone amenities. Each property has a restaurant that features local cuisine. The hotels provide typing, fax, photocopying, city tours, and airline ticket services to the guests. The company projects increasing future demand for such mid-scale lodging facilities for both domestic and international tourists in China.

The Gloria International Hotels is a hotel development and management company. Established in 1992, it is a wholly owned subsidiary of Top Glory Company, Ltd., the investment arm of China National Cereals, Oils, and Foodstuffs Import and Export Corporations. The goal of Gloria International Hotels is to establish a network of mid-range hotels throughout China, and to introduce and develop international service and management standards throughout its system hotels. Unlike the Jin Jiang Hotel Group, Gloria International Hotels is determined to develop and manage its own brand in both domestic and overseas markets, and maintain full ownership and management control of all properties in China. Table 8.5 illustrates the three types of hotel products under the Gloria brand that are owned and operated by Gloria International Hotels. Table 8.5 reveals that Gloria International Hotels' properties are primarily situated in northern China while the resort properties are located in southern China. Its future strategic development is to expand aggressively to southern China and central China along the Yangtze River (GIH 2000).

Jianguo International Hotels Limited, formed in early 1999, is a partnership between Beijing Tourism Group Company and Jianguo Hotel Beijing (JIH 2002). It offers three hotel brands that serve both business and leisure travelers: Jianguo Grand, Jianguo, and Jianguo Garden. Jianguo International Hotels is also aggressively expanding its operations in overseas markets. Its affiliate companies already

TABLE 8.5. Hotel Brands by Gloria International Hotels

Brand Name	Number of Properties	Location
Gloria Plaza Hotels	5	Beijing, Dalian, Nanchang, Shengyang, Suzhou
Gloria Inns	3	Harbin, Shengyang, Qindao
Gloria Resort	2	Sanya in Hainan Province

Source: Gloria International Hotels Web site, <www.gloriahotels.com>, 2000.

own hotels in Honolulu and San Francisco, and will buy a hotel in Los Angeles. The U.S. lodging market is targeted by Jianguo International Hotels as the primary market target for its international expansion ("Better Days Ahead in Asia" 1999).

The rapid growth of Chinese hotel development and management companies demonstrates that the pace of consolidation has picked up speed in China's hotel industry. This trend will only accelerate as the full implications of China's membership in the World Trade Organization are realized. When China opens its door for global competition as a member of the World Trade Organization, Chinese hospitality enterprises will face formidable competition from well-capitalized and well-managed global hotel companies. Thus Chinese hotel companies have realized the great importance of strategically positioning themselves in the Chinese lodging market by consolidating and branding their operations. These companies want to establish a strong corporate identity and improve operations and services by international standards.

At present, these Chinese hotel companies are still in an early stage of development and are relatively small in capitalization and hotel portfolio size as compared to their global counterparts. For instance, *Hotels* magazine top-ranked global giant Bass Hotels and Resorts has a portfolio of 2,886 hotels under nine brands in ninety-eight countries, whereas the largest Chinese hotel group, Jin Jiang Hotel Group, has a portfolio of fifty hotels in China. However, future potential growth is promising for well-managed hotel companies in China.

DEVELOPMENT STRATEGY
BY GLOBAL HOTEL COMPANIES

China is considered an attractive market for hotel development by major international hotel corporations since China is projected by the World Tourism Organization to be the top tourism destination in the world by 2020 (Cruz 2000a; Selwitz 2000). Many early hotel market entrants to China, such as Holiday Inn, Sheraton, Hilton, Hyatt, Nikko, etc., have well established themselves in primary destination cities. Other international hotel companies have identified niche markets for developing hotel operations through acquisition, conversion, and strategic alliance in the primary and secondary markets. Table 8.6 describes some current hotel development projects by international

TABLE 8.6. Hotel Projects Currently Under Development by Global Hotel Companies

Hotel Company	Planned Construction Period	Hotels	Rooms
Bass Hotels & Resorts	1999-2001	7	2,205
Asia World/Taipei	1999-2001	1	2,000
Best Western International	1999-2001	8	1,720
Marriott International	1999-2001	4	1,520
Accor Asia Pacific	1999-2001	4	1,420

Source: Cruz (1999), 46-58.

hotel companies in China. Four of the top ten global hotel giants, Bass, Best Western, Marriott, and Accor, are strategically developing new hotel projects in China.

Marriott International is a late entrant to the Chinese hotel market. After acquiring New World/Renaissance Hotels and Resorts in 1997, Marriott International had its first exposure in China through the New World brand. Marriott International signed an agreement with New World Development Company, Ltd. to jointly develop new hotels to be operated or franchised by Marriott International. Marriott is currently developing its Courtyard brand with New World in China. This brand targets domestic and regional business and leisure travelers who need quality accommodations at reasonable prices. Because Marriott International is a new entrant to the Chinese market, it has developed a cobranding strategy with the New World brand since its name is more familiar to the Chinese consumers. Therefore, Marriott Courtyard Hotels will be named New World Country by Marriott for the initial years of operation. Once Marriott is more established, the hotel will be renamed Courtyard by Marriott (Durbin 1999). This creative marketing strategy can enhance the Marriott brand in the Chinese hotel market.

ANALYSIS OF HOTEL FINANCIAL PERFORMANCE

The hotel industry in China is still recovering from the Asian financial crisis in late 1997 ("Accommodation" 1998), and the oversupply of lodging properties in the upscale segment in certain destinations has significantly impacted hotel financial performance. The total revenue generated by China's lodging industry was recorded at ¥84.58 billion in 1999, an increase of 6 percent over that of 1998. However, when the operation performance of some selected destinations is closely examined, one will find that major tourism destination cities such as Beijing and Shanghai did not perform well in 1999. Table 8.7 shows hotel performance of three major tourism destination cities in China in 1999 and the performance results of the major tourism cities in the region as a comparison. As Table 8.7 illustrates, hotel occupancy in Beijing showed an increase of 4.9 percent in 1999 over 1998, but the average daily rate and revenue per available room continued to slide in double-digit figures. In Shanghai, all the operation performance indicators recorded further decline in 1999 as compared to 1998. The decrease of average daily rate (ADR) and revenue per available room (RevPar) in Shanghai were even greater than those in Beijing. Xian saw a slight decrease in room occupancy rate, a flat ADR performance, and an increase of 9.9 percent in RevPar in 1999.

If one compares the hotel operation performance of these three Chinese cities to other major tourist cities in the region, such as Bangkok, Hong Kong, Seoul, and Taipei, one will find that hotel operations in Beijing and Shanghai were outperformed by their counterparts in the region. Such unsatisfactory performance can be mainly attributed to two factors, namely, the lingering effect of the Asian financial crisis and the intense competition due to the oversupply of hotels in these destinations. First, the Asian financial crisis had a ma-

TABLE 8.7. Hotel Performance in Selected Asian Destinations, 1999

City	Occupancy (%)	Change from 1998 (%)	ADR (US$)	Change from 1998 (%)	RevPar (US$)	Change from 1998 (%)
Beijing	56.0	2.14	65.76	−17.7	46.45	−13.4
Shanghai	55.5	−2.52	76.65	−22.4	48.16	−24.7
Xian	60.1	−0.49	36.13	0.1	21.67	9.9
Bangkok	64.3	4.40	57.15	12.7	36.78	17.2
Hong Kong	75.6	5.90	120.52	−12.6	91.77	−6.4
Seoul	82.0	0.10	126.34	0.2	103.80	0.3
Taipei	75.9	−2.70	122.10	1.2	92.57	−1.8

Source: CNTA (2000), 99, 101, 111; Cruz (2000a), 62.

jor negative impact on hotel operations in China beginning in 1997. The major indicators of occupancies and revenues were all down in 1998 (CNTA 1999). By 1999, the market was stabilized as the economy in many southeast Asian countries began to improve. However, the hotel market needed more time to recover and rebuild its business for future growth. Therefore, the lingering effect of the financial crisis continued to affect hotel performance in 1999. Second, poor performance in Beijing and Shanghai was strongly affected by the oversupply of hotel properties. In 1999, thirty-four new hotels were open for business in Beijing and contributed to an increase of 9.1 percent to the city's total hotel inventory. In Shanghai, hotel capacity more than doubled in 1999, growing from 136 properties in 1998 to 286 hotels in 1999. These new properties created great pricing pressure on hotel operations in Shanghai in 1999. However, six hotels were taken out of the market in Xian in 1999, resulting in a reduction of the city's hotel capacity by 19.35 percent. Clearly, hotel performance in Beijing and Shanghai suffered from the building glut in 1999.

CONCLUSION

The hotel industry in China has experienced rapid growth in the past two decades. As the industry matures, it faces new challenges for sustained development and growth. Critical issues include consolidation and brand development by the emergence of large management contract companies, globalization strategy by international hotel companies, and hotel financial performance. The consolidation trend began in the 1990s and it has now gathered great momentum in China with the establishment of several large professional management contract companies. The growth of Jin Jiang, Kingdom, Gloria, and Jianguo has demonstrated that these Chinese hotel management companies have capitalized on the market opportunity of consolidation to rapidly develop their business. Market demand for professional management and brand enhancement will continue to stimulate future growth and more establishments of large hotel organizations in China.

International hotel companies are also aggressively jockeying for market position in China by strategically selecting niche markets. Global sales expansion and brand recognition are the prime motivations for international hotel companies to develop new hotel projects.

Identifying a niche market in a strategic location will be the key to future operation success since the upscale market segment is quite crowded in major destination cities. Creative marketing strategy has been developed to capture market share in China, such as the co-branding strategy between New World and Marriott International. The development and competition generated by international hotel chains will enhance the operation standards and quality service in the Chinese lodging industry.

The overbuilding of upscale hotels continued to hurt the financial performance of hotels in the top tourism destinations in 1999. The doubling of hotel capacity in Shanghai in 1999 had a major impact on the financial performance of the city's hospitality industry. It is believed that many hotels in China lose money every year. Market glut in certain destinations will continue to pressure hotels' financial performance, and money-losing properties will face possible liquidation or acquisition as the government owners may not be able or willing to continue to support failing operations. Effective marketing and cost-cutting measures are needed to run profitable operations in the highly competitive hotel market in China.

China's hotel industry faces great prospects and challenges in the new millennium. China is now one of the top tourism destinations in the world, and increasing travel volume will generate demand for lodging products and services. The hotel industry can offer a wide range of products and services to international tourists. International hotel companies will continue to identify niche markets for development and compete with Chinese hotel companies for the international and domestic tourist markets. The majority of unbranded hotels in China provide a great opportunity for Chinese and international hotel companies to consolidate and develop branded chain operations. The consolidation will intensify if the oversupply problem persists in China's hotel market. This is because competition will continue to pressure operating profits, and the hotels that lose money will eventually be acquired by successful ones or go out of business. Furthermore, China's recent membership in the World Trade Organization will gradually increase global competition in business operations. The hospitality industry will thus face tough competition from well-established global hotel companies. Such competitive pressure will enhance management efficiency in hotel operations in China and eliminate the ones who cannot compete.

REFERENCES

"Accommodation: Asia-Pacific's 1997 Hotel Results" (1998). *Travel and Tourism Intelligence* May: 21-22.

Alisan, Patricia (2000). "Latin America Becomes Hot Spot for Brands." *Hotel and Motel Management*, 214(16): 58, 60.

"Better Days Ahead in Asia" (1999). *Hotels*, 33(4): 43-46.

China National Tourism Administration (CNTA) (1999). *China Tourism: Annual Report 1998*. Beijing: China Tourism Press.

China National Tourism Administration (CNTA) (2000). *The Yearbook of China Tourism Statistics*. Beijing: China Travel and Tourism Press.

Cruz, Tony D. (1999). "Better Day Ahead?" *Hotels*, 3(4): 46-58.

Cruz, Tony D. (2000a). "Asia: Clean Bill of Health?" *Hotels*, 34(1): 52-62.

Cruz, Tony D. (2000b). "Forecast 2000: Strong and Steady." *Hotels*, 34(1): 46-50.

Cruz, Tony D. (2000c). "Hotels' 325." *Hotels*, 34(7): 66.

Durbin, Bridget (1999). "Marketing Plan for Developing Courtyard by Marriott in China." In Yu, Larry (Ed.), *The International Hospitality Business: Management and Operations* (pp. 319-324). Binghamton, NY: The Haworth Hospitality Press.

Frabotta, David 2000. "Brands Gain Global Clout." *Hotel and Motel Management*, 215(9): 1, 12.

Gloria International Hotels (GIH) (2000). Web site at <http://www.gloriahotels.com>, accessed May 2002.

Jianguo International Hotels (JIH) (2002). Company Web site at <http://www.jianguohotels.com.cn>, accessed May 20, 2002.

Jin Jiang International Hotel Group (JJIHC) (2000). Web site at <http://www.china-jinjiang.com>.

Prasad, Keshav and Chekitan S. Dev (2000). "Managing Hotel Brand Equity." *Cornell Hotel and Restaurant Administration Quarterly*, 41(3): 22-31.

Sangster, Andrew (2000). "The Impact of Branding on the UK Hotel Industry." *Travel and Tourism Analyst*, No. 2, pp. 65-82.

Selwitz, Robert (2000). "Development Opportunities in Asia Abound." *Hotel and Motel Management*, 214(16): 62, 64.

"Travel to Surge in the 21st Century" (1997). *WTO News*, November 5, pp. 1-2.

Xu, Gang (1999). *Tourism and Local Economic Development in China: Case Studies of Guilin, Suzhou and Beidaihe*. Surrey, UK: Curzon Press, pp. 131-137.

Yu, Larry (1992). "China's Hotel Development and Structures." *International Journal of Hospitality Management*, 11(2): 99-110.

Yu, Larry (1998). "China's Hotel Industry: Prospects and Challenges." *Journal of Vacation Marketing*, 4(2): 36-51.

Zhang, Guangrui (1995). "China's Tourism Since 1978: Policies, Experiences, and Lessons Learned." In Alan A. Lew and Lawrence Yu, eds., *Tourism in China: Geographic, Political, and Economic Perspectives* (pp. 3-17). Boulder, CO: Westview.

Chapter 9

Travel Agencies in China
at the Turn of the Millennium

Qian Wei

As the world enters a new millennium, China is emerging as a major player in regional and global tourism, in terms of both inbound and outbound tourism. According to World Tourism Organization (WTO) statistics for 1999, China ranked fifth in international arrivals with 27 million, an increase of 8 percent over 1998. In its 2020 Vision report, the WTO forecast that China would be the number one tourism destination and the fourth ranked tourist-generating country in the world by 2020, with 137 million international visitor arrivals and 100 million outbound tourists. The China National Tourism Administration (CNTA) announced that 1999 saw its visitor arrivals, including visitors from Taiwan, Hong Kong, and Macao, reaching a record of 72.8 million and international tourism receipts of US$14.1 billion (CNTA, 2000a). Despite the differences in the way the WTO and CNTA compile their statistics, one can conclude that tourism growth in China has been spectacular. Based on CNTA statistics, during the twenty-year period from 1978 to 1998, China's visitor arrivals increased at an annual average rate of 22 percent and its international tourism receipts at 23 percent (Qian, 1999a). Along with this growth in arrivals, China has seen a fast increase in the number of travel agencies (Table 9.1) and their revenues (Table 9.2).

Although the country has seen encouraging growth of its tourism industry and a steady expansion in the number of travel agencies in recent years, many of the stories in newspapers and magazines about them have been negative. Examples have included reports of deteriorating service, cutthroat competition, decreasing profit, and an increasing number of travel agencies operating unprofitably. In aca-

TABLE 9.1. Number of Travel Agencies in China, 1987-1999

Year	Number of Travel Agencies	Change over Previous Year (%)
1987	1,245	—
1988	1,573	12.6
1989	1,617	10.3
1990	1,603	−1.0
1991	1,561	−2.6
1992	2,595	66.2
1993	3,238	24.8
1994	4,382	35.3
1995[a]	3,826	−12.7
1996	4,954	29.5
1997	5,732	15.7
1998	6,222	11.0
1999	7,326	17.7

Source: CNTA (2000c)

[a]The decrease in 1995 was partly due to a change in the way agencies were categorized, with the three categories reduced to two—namely, international and domestic travel agencies—but largely due to a new CNTA-initiated system in travel agency administration—namely, the travel agency service quality cash deposit system. In 1995 alone, 1,402 Category 3 travel agencies, 114 Category 2, and 5 Category 1 had their licenses rescinded for failing to deposit the required amount of cash (CNTA, 1998b).

demic journals, too, papers prepared by scholars, researchers, or industry experts have examined problems with travel agencies and how they can be rectified. China Youth Travel Service's (CYTS) president, Jiang Jianning, in an interview reported in the *Tourism Tribune* (China's leading tourism research journal), indicated that undesirable price-cutting practices have become so rampant in the newly emerging but chaotic tourism market in China that nobody, not even the most authoritative persons, could play a decisive role in bringing about the radical reforms that are needed. As the president of one of the largest travel agencies in China, he did not know what would be the proper strategic plan for the development of China's tourism industry (Jiang, 1999). The situation faced by China's travel

TABLE 9.2. Total Revenue of China's International Travel Services, 1991-1999

Year	Yuan (Billions)
1991	5.9
1992	10.2
1993	13.1
1994	14.8
1995	17.2
1996	20.2
1997	28.1
1998	29.7
1999	38.7

Source: CNTA (1998a); CNTA (1999d); CNTA (2000c).

agencies appears bleak. How China's travel agencies have fared, what difficulties they have encountered, and how they have been able to surmount those challenges are some of the questions and issues that this chapter addresses.

OVERVIEW OF THE DEVELOPMENT OF CHINA'S TRAVEL AGENCIES

China's first travel agency was established in 1923 when the Bank of China set up a small, separate department in its Shanghai head-quarters to handle travel as a business. Four years later, in 1927, the China Travel Service (CTS) was formally launched. The growth of the travel services was slow, however, with just a few hundred travelers using CTS each year until the outbreak of World War II, when such travel came to a halt. In November 1949, shortly after the People's Republic of China was founded, CTS resumed its operations with the reopening of the Shenzhen branch to serve visitors arriving by land from Hong Kong. In 1954, China International Travel Service (CITS) was launched with eight branches located in various cities throughout the country. For over twenty years, however, its highly limited services were considered part of an effort called "People's Diplomacy" (Lew, 1987). The travel service was not a business, still less an industry (Qian, 1999b).

China began to open its door to the outside world in 1979, following the historic meeting of the Central Committee of the Communist Party of China at the end of 1978 at which it launched the "open door policy." The post-1979 development of China's travel agencies can be broadly divided into three stages. The first was from 1979 to 1986 when inbound travel business was largely dominated by CTS, which focused on tour groups of overseas Chinese and compatriots from Hong Kong and Macao, and its counterpart, the China International Travel Service (CITS), which took care of foreign inbound travel. The travel business was essentially a monopoly in which demand far exceeded supply. This resulted in huge net profits, reaching as high as 67 percent for one major travel agency (CNTA, 1998a).

The second stage of China's travel agency development started in 1988 when the travel business monopoly came to an end as the number of Category One travel agencies (those authorized to engage in international inbound tourism) increased from seventeen in 1987 to forty-four in 1988. This stage was primarily characterized by growing demand and supply, with a controlled yet rapid increase in the number of travel agencies. By the early 1990s, increasing competition and an overextension of company resources resulted in almost all travel agencies suffering from lagging market demand, increasing financial debt, and increasing complaints from travelers. Hardly anybody was happy, least of all big travel agencies at the national and provincial levels that were under the rigid control of the government and unable to compete on price. Consumer complaints flooded in, which embarrassed the government.

There was an urgent need to reform, which came in 1992, marking the beginning of the third stage. This also marked a major transition stage in the central government's move from a planned to a socialist market economy. CNTA took a major role in regulating travel agency activities through a variety of legal and administrative measures. The licensing of travel agencies began in 1993, followed by a travel agency service quality cash deposit system, which was introduced in 1995. That same year saw the establishment of a tourism quality supervision network at various government levels. More important, in 1996, the Travel Agency Management Regulations Act, China's first tourism-related law, was signed by Premier Li Peng. These efforts played a positive role in bringing order to the somewhat chaotic tourism industry.

Unfortunately, many entrepreneurs soon found ways to circumvent the new regulations. The so-called *chengbao* system was used to allow individuals to subcontract with larger travel agencies and operate outside the regulatory system while using the name of the larger agency (which was regulated).

This was done by individual staff members (mostly departmental managers) who would reach an agreement with the general manager of a travel agency to meet a profit quota and who would then be given full charge of the operation and management of their departments. According to CNTA's Department of Management, the *chengbao* system was a type of unregulated privatization and, therefore, CNTA opposed it (CNTA, 1998a). What actually happened under the *chengbao* system was that a travel agency was split into a number of smaller agencies and the departmental managers were allowed to use the name of a travel agency, an intangible property, to pursue their short-term interests. Very often huge personal profits were made while any losses or debts were passed on to the agency. No legal restrictions had been imposed on this practice and if there was any loss, the departmental manager simply quit without having to pay the debt, leaving it to the travel agency. Many travel agencies that practiced the *chengbao* system were on the verge of bankruptcy after three or four years. According to Wang (1998), director of the Tourism Research Center at the Shanghai Social Sciences Academy, the *chengbao* by individuals, a practice which was far from being standardized, was one of the root causes of unfair competition in the Chinese marketplace.

CHINA'S TRAVEL AGENCIES TODAY

Despite the problems previously experienced, especially under the *chengbao* system, to understand properly how China's travel agencies are faring today, it is necessary to examine them from both positive and negative perspectives. On the positive side, the scope and volume of business for China's travel agencies has expanded dramatically. Throughout the 1980s, inbound tourism was emphasized to the neglect of domestic tourism and the exclusion of outbound tourism, both of which were largely discouraged by the central government

(Lew, 1987). However, as economic conditions improved and government regulations were relaxed, the demand for domestic tourism and outbound tourism mounted and many travel agencies, seeing a chance to make money, became involved in both inbound and outbound travel, whether they were authorized or not to engage in either of these markets. It was under these circumstances that, in 1997, CNTA adopted a three-prong policy of vigorously promoting inbound tourism, actively developing domestic tourism, and increasing outbound tourism at a controlled and steady pace (CNTA, 1998a). Travel agencies had an important role to play in all three of these areas, although less so with domestic travel (Tables 9.3, 9.4, and 9.5).

Satisfaction with the service quality of China's travel agencies has been monitored closely so that China's tourism industry will continue to grow in a healthy manner. In this regard, CNTA's efforts deserve credit. Tour guide licensing and a national tour guide qualifying examination were introduced in 1989. An annual review of all travel agencies was initiated in 1991, which served partly to screen out those agencies that were poorly operated and managed. Starting in 1995 every travel agency had to make a substantial cash deposit as a guarantee of service quality. By 1997 approximately 2,000 travel agencies had their business certificates revoked for failure to make this deposit. Despite the revocation of these licenses, the number of travel agencies continued to grow. A service quality supervision network was also set up involving the CNTA and local tourism administrations (CNTA, 1998a), which played a positive role in improving

TABLE 9.3. Travel Agency Involvement in Domestic Tourism in China, 1994-1999

Year	Domestic Tourist Arrivals (Millions)	Serviced by Travel Agencies (Millions)	% Serviced by Travel Agencies
1994	524	20	3.8
1995	629	19	3.0
1996	639	25	3.9
1997	259	15	5.9
1998	250	21	8.5
1999	719	—	—

Source: CNTA (2000c).

TABLE 9.4. Travel Agency Involvement in China's Outbound Tourism, 1993-1998

Year	Outbound Tourists Serviced by Travel Agencies (Thousands)	% of all Outbound Tourists	% Change from Previous Year
1993[a]	723.6	19.3	–
1994	1,098.4	29.4	51.8
1995	1,259.9	27.9	14.7
1996	1,640.0	32.4	30.2
1997[b]	1,430.7	26.9	−12.8
1998	1,810.9	21.5	26.6
1999[c]	2,352.4	–	30.0

Source: Ministry of Public Security (1999).
[a]Travel agencies were allowed to service outbound leisure travelers for the first time starting in 1993.
[b]The reduction in 1997 was due to the Asian financial crisis beginning in 1997.
[c]The figures for 1999 are taken from *Report on the Annual Review of Travel Agency Business for 1999* (CNTA, 2000b). That report says that revenues from outbound tourism in 1999 made up 14.30 percent of the total tourism revenues, but it does not give the percentage required in this table.

service quality and protecting customers' rights. With the continuous development and refinement of these regulations, it comes as no surprise that most overseas visitors have enjoyed their travel experience in China. A report of a comprehensive sample survey of 41,360 overseas tourists, including 14,490 compatriots and 26,870 foreign tourists, provided evidence to support this conclusion, with 85 percent of the respondents rating tour service quality as "acceptable," "pretty good," or "very satisfying" (CNTA, 1999c). The rates were even higher for hotels, with 95 percent rating them as "pretty good" or "very satisfying."

Qian et al. (2000) conducted a survey with the help of national and local tourism administrations and travel agencies in major tourist destinations, including the cities of Beijing, Shanghai, Xi'an and Wuxi, and the provinces/autonomous regions of Shandong, Anhui, Fujian, Zhejiang, Guangxi, and Xinjiang (Table 9.6). In all, tourists from the United States, Britain, Canada, Australia, New Zealand, Germany, France, Japan, and Pakistan completed 214 usable questionnaires.

TABLE 9.5. Travel Agency Involvement in China's Inbound Tourism, 1994-1999

Year	Foreign Tourist Arrivals[a] (Millions)	Serviced by Travel Agencies (Millions)	% Serviced by Travel Agencies*
1994	43.68	2.91	6.7
1995	20.03	3.05	15.2
1996	22.76	2.77	12.3
1997	23.77	3.04	12.8
1998	25.07	2.90	11.6
1999	27.04	2.28	8.4

Source: CNTA (2000c).
[a]Includes day excursionists and excludes compatriots from Hong Kong, Macao, and Taiwan.
*The reason for the small percentage of travel agency-serviced tourist arrivals compared to the total number of arrivals is the significant increase in Fully Independent Travelers (FITs) and business travelers in the 1990s who often did not use travel agency services. In Beijing, Shanghai, and some other metropolises, numbers of FITs have long surpassed group inclusive tourists (GITs). Another important reason is the existence of a large number of organizations (governmental, business, and others) that take care of their own visitors and for which no statistics are available.

Most of the respondents were either satisfied or very satisfied with their tour guide services. Knowledge of the destination and trustworthiness and courtesy were the highest rated qualities of the guides. There were, however, some ratings for which dissatisfied and very dissatisfied combined exceeded 10 percent of responses. Qualities that had the highest levels of dissatisfaction included the guides' ability to solve problems quickly and their flexibility in addressing special needs and interests of the tourists. All in all, however, the service quality provided by the Chinese tour guides for overseas visitors was regarded as good, although with room for improvement. In particular, China's tour guides could develop more skills in providing personalized service or individual attention to visitor interests and needs.

The situation with domestic tourism may be somewhat different based on a small survey of 100 Chinese tourists by Guo (2000) (Table 9.7). The results are far more mixed than were the evaluations by overseas visitors. The highest evaluations were for knowledge, clar-

TABLE 9.6. Quality of Service Offered by Chinese Tour Guides to Overseas Tourists

Service Items	Level of Satisfaction (N = 214)					
The Guide...	Very Satisfied (5) (%)	Satisfied (4) (%)	Unsure or Mixed (3) (%)	Dissat- isfied (2) (%)	Very Dissatisfied (1) (%)	Mean Score (5 to 1)
Knows his or her city well	63	28	9	0	0	4.53
Is trustworthy and dependable	66	21	9	4	0	4.49
Is courteous and professional	61	28	7	2	2	4.45
Is good-natured	52	31	13	2	2	4.29
Knows China well	45	44	88	4	0	4.29
Treats everyone fairly	56	28	6	8	2	4.29
Loves his or her job	56	23	16	4	2	4.27
Explains things clearly	47	39	10	0	4	4.26
Knows how to communicate with us	50	33	13	0	4	4.26
Is ready to go an extra mile to help us	52	31	7	4	6	4.19
Provides timely help when we have problems	50	30	12	2	6	4.16
Is cooperative with other service per- sonnel	52	25	12	7	4	4.14
Can quickly solve problems	54	20	12	10	4	4.11
Respects our special requests	50	27	12	4	7	4.09
Is humorous	47	21	23	9	0	4.06
Is sensitive to our needs and wants, and tries to satisfy them	45	30	12	6	7	4.00
Is knowledgeable about history, ge- ography, culture, and flora and fauna	45	27	16	6	6	3.99
Shows an interest in learning about us	40	28	24	6	2	3.99
I feel comfortable interacting with the guide	41	26	22	10	2	3.93

Source: Qian et al. (2000).

ity, fairness, and ethics. The lowest evaluations were for personal service and liveliness of presentations. These findings were similar to those of overseas visitors. Where the two groups differ is in the range of positive and negative evaluations. Domestic tourists were far more critical of the guides they had, with positive evaluations ranging from 33 to 73 percent and negative evaluations ranging from 15 to 30 percent. This pattern is not surprising as domestic tourists in most countries

TABLE 9.7. A Survey of Tour Guide Performance for Domestic Tours (N = 100)

Service Area and Item	Evaluation of Guide (N = 100)					
	High (5) (%)	Moderate (4) (%)	Unsure or Mixed (3) (%)	Moderately Low (2) (%)	Low (1) (%)	Mean Score (5 to 1)
Work Attitude						
Fairness in treatment	21	49	20	6	4	3.77
Professional ethics	20	43	22	8	7	3.61
Sense of responsibility	18	43	23	10	6	3.57
Enthusiasm for work	19	35	29	14	3	3.53
Willingness to cooperate	11	47	27	8	7	3.47
Willingness to help tourists	14	39	24	16	7	3.37
Personalized service	11	22	37	19	11	3.03
Professional Skills						
Liveliness of language	20	40	22	20	8	3.74
Clarity in explanation	18	50	22	3	7	3.69
Ability to communicate with tourists	21	30	33	13	3	3.53
Humor of language	18	40	20	13	9	3.45
Flexibility in expressions	17	33	33	11	6	3.44
Ability to deal with emergencies	16	30	37	11	6	3.39
Professional Knowledge						
Knowledge about places of interest	35	38	18	7	2	3.97
Knowledge about the city	24	41	20	9	6	3.68
Knowledge about Chinese history and culture	10	32	37	20	1	3.3
Knowledge about modern China	7	39	31	16	7	3.23
General knowledge	6	38	34	14	8	3.2

Source: Guo (2000).

have higher expectations of guides due to their greater knowledge of the destinations visited. This is further exacerbated by the lower level of education and training that most domestic guides receive in comparison to guides who serve overseas visitors. More often than not, tour guides catering to overseas tourists are college or university graduates who, besides being fluent in a foreign language, have had far more specialized training than their domestic counterparts, many of whom have only completed secondary school. The problem of guide flexibility and responsiveness to tourist wishes could be a reflection of the high volume and steep competition that travel agencies in China face, making deviations from set itineraries difficult.

In addition to service quality, travel agencies have worked with CNTA to develop new tourism products. Some newly developed travel routes have been very popular with foreign tourists and compatriot Chinese. Examples include the Best of China tour, which takes the visitor to Beijing, Xi'an, Guilin, Shanghai, and Guangzhou; the Silk Road tour; the Yangtze River tour; and the Tibetan tour. Some festivals have been attracting large numbers of overseas visitors, including the Confucian Culture Festival in Qufu (Shandong Province); the Kite Festival in Weifang (Shandong); and the Ice and Snow Festival in Harbin (Heilongjiang Province). Since 1992, CNTA has focused its annual promotion on one theme, such as Heritage in 1994 and Ecotourism in 1999.

This strategy has been highly successful in diversifying China's tourism products. Travel agencies, especially the larger ones such as the CITS Head Office, CITS Beijing, Shanghai, Yunnan, and Suzhou branches, deserve credit for helping to implement CNTA's annual themed promotions. Many spared no effort to market and sell new travel routes and events with the latter numbering in the hundreds. As a result, China's image as a tourist destination is gradually changing to one of more than just a few historic or beautiful places, and the western part of the country, rich in ethnic culture and ideal for adventure tourism, is attracting an increasing number of overseas visitors.

Some of China's travel agencies have developed a presence in cyberspace on the World Wide Web. Most, however, have yet to take full advantage and use of e-business. The head office branch of CITS, still one of the largest travel agencies in China, began a joint venture with a Hong Kong partner in launching its Web site, and by 1999 over half of the head office's business was conducted online. China Youth Travel Service (CYTS) Corporation, Ltd., another well-established travel agency dating back to the 1970s, decided in early 2000 to invest 100 million yuan (US$12.05 million) to develop its e-business.

In 1997, the Shanghai-based Spring International Tours (SIT), the country's largest domestic tour operator at that time, began to develop computer network for marketing purposes (Zhang, 2000). Now domestic Chinese travelers can book, change, or cancel a tour at any of its nearly 200 branches located throughout the country within a matter of minutes. However, payment transactions are still made in cash, and Internet transactions have yet to be introduced. By 1999, SIT handled 400,000 domestic tourists and achieved revenues of RMB 640 million yuan with RMB 60 million yuan in e-business—a small but growing percentage. The increased use of computers and chartered flights have considerably improved SIT's efficiency and reduced its prices. To encourage online business at its branch agencies, SIT adopted a policy to allow 80 percent of the profit made through online business to be kept by the agency. This farsighted development strategy is sure to attract other agencies to follow and could facilitate the consolidation of China's travel agencies by having more smaller operators become affiliated with larger agencies that have the technology to facilitate e-commerce.

One other area in which China's travel agencies have been successful is in the degree of personnel training that they have been involved in. An army of professionals, namely managers, marketing and sales people, tour guides, and ground operating personnel, has come to the fore in the past twenty years. In 1997, when there were nearly 5,000 travel agencies, managerial staff numbered some 10,000 and there were about 40,000 to 50,000 tour guides (CNTA, 1998a). By 1999 there were a total of 108,800 staff working in the 7,326 travel agencies throughout the country. The size of this workforce is not small and the staff will help to facilitate the development of China's tourism industry and make China one of the top players in the world the world level in terms of tourism revenues, job opportunities, and tax revenues, a goal that CNTA has set for itself over the next twenty years (He, 2000; CNTA, 1999a, 2000a).

MAJOR PROBLEMS FACED BY CHINA'S TRAVEL AGENCIES TODAY

Despite considerable efforts at reform, the number one problem facing China's travel agencies today is still a chaotic market where unfair competition, or more specifically, an intractable price war, has disrupted the tourism industry in general and adversely affected the profitability of the travel agency sector in particular. According to Jiang (1999, p. 19), president of CYTS, "At the moment, our prices cannot be made any lower because of the raging price war among ourselves." He also accused some travel agency general managers of "caring nothing about reputation, brand and business intangibles. All they know is how to undercut the competitors through lower prices."

In fact, prices are often cut simply to take a group of tourists from another travel agency. Some overseas tour operators (although clearly not most of them) have taken advantage of this competition by "fishing in the muddied waters" of China's travel industry, enabling them to obtain rock-bottom wholesale prices to maximize their profits. Competition for inbound tourism has been so fierce that in some areas, notably Guilin, "zero quoted rates" are offered by some Chinese agencies. This means that a group of tourists could fly in to Guilin basically for the cost of airfare only, while staying in the city for two to three nights free of charge for sightseeing, accommodation, and meals. These tourists (mostly from Hong Kong and Asian countries) will see some of the scenic sights of the area, but spend most of their time being taken from one shop to another, as it is through the commissions from shopping that the travel agencies and tour guides derive their income. This practice is an open secret among some of the small- and medium-sized travel agencies, and it is especially hurtful to agencies that refuse to follow this practice as their wholesale prices are higher.

In the rush to enlarge or maintain market share, many travel agencies have had to compete in the price war. This is the primary reason that profits have been dropping for many travel agencies in recent years (Table 9.8). In its "Communique on China's Tourism Statistics for 1998," CNTA (1999b) disclosed that although the business volume and scope of China's travel agencies increased in 1998, they handled fewer tourists and made less profit (Table 9.9). Despite the overall decline in profits, international travel services experienced a slight increase in profit. According to Du (2000) that may be attributed to three factors. First, international marketing and sales efforts had been intensified. Second, outbound tourism was (and still is) monopolized by several large tour operators. Third, as a result of their excellent performance in previous years, 280 of the best domestic travel agencies were authorized to engage in international tourism.

TABLE 9.8. Losses by China's International Travel Services, 1991-1996

Indicator/Year	1991	1992	1993	1994	1995	1996	1997	1998	1999
Number of businesses with losses	61	77	81	136	256	286	111	407	219
Percentage of businesses with losses	9	10	10	16	21	28	11.2	31	17.4
Number of businesses losing 1,000-10,000 yuan	26	38	50	75	86	110	93	381	191
Number of businesses losing more than 10,000 yuan	3	6	14	33	59	59	111	407	219
Average Profit Rate (%)	6.7	6.5	6.2	4.9	3.4	3.4	2.5	2.4	2.4

Source: CNTA (1998a,b, 1999a, 2000d).

TABLE 9.9. Profits and Rates of Profit for China's Travel Agencies in 1998

Type of Travel Agency	Total Revenue (Million RMB Yuan)	Percentage Change Over Previous Year	Profit Rate (%)
International	756	6.3	3.5
Domestic	58	− 82.0	0.7
Total	814	− 21.0	2.7

Source: CNTA (1999d).

Many of the largest tour operators have consistently shown a profit, including the CITS Head Office (Beijing), CITS Shanghai, the CTS Head Office (Beijing), CYTS, and the Beijing Overseas Travel Corporation. The CITS Head Office, in particular, made a record profit of 100 million yuan in 1999.

In spite of the cutthroat competition, low profitability, and ongoing losses within the travel agency sector, very few Chinese travel agencies have declared bankruptcy. Therein lies the dilemma and crux of the matter. Almost all the travel agencies in China are state-owned and protected, in one way or another, from bankruptcy. Every one of them has a parent organization, which ranges from a tourism administration, to a government-owned company, to a "mass organization" such as the trade union, to the Communist Youth League and the Women's Federation, to a ministry of the central government. For example, in 1993 more than thirty ministry-affiliated travel agencies were established with CNTA's approval (CNTA, 1998a). The last thing these parent organizations want is their affiliated travel agency to be declared bankrupt, and they can always find the funds or excuses to keep them afloat.

In addition to the profitability problem, the second major concern currently faced by China's travel agencies is that the industry is highly fragmented with most agencies being small, financially weak, and not efficient (CNTA, 1998a). According to Cai (1999), "The majority of travel agencies in China do not have a clear idea of what their division of labor is, or what their strategy is in terms of positioning, or what their own strengths are. Therefore, all they can do is to do whatever they happen to be able to do, with no idea of what is to come, nor the capability to develop new products" (p. 11). To bring the point home, a rough comparison has been made between the nearly 5,000 travel agencies in China in 1996 and the travel-related business of American Express in 1996 (CNTA, 1998a). The total revenue of all of China's travel agencies in 1996 was 20 billion yuan while that of the travel-related business of American Express reached US$8 billion, which was equivalent to 64 billion yuan.

These circumstances have led to a call for greater consolidation of China's travel agencies. CNTA was one of the first to call for consolidation. In his speech at the National Conference on Tourism, CNTA Chairman He (1998) used four Chinese characters to describe China's travel agencies in his call for travel agency consolidation: *xiao* (small in size), *san* (fragmented in marketing), *ruo* (weak in strength), and *cha* (low in efficiency). However, nobody knows exactly how to implement this consolidation. Trying to be the first, the Beijing Municipal Tourism Administration (BMTA) merged the major state-owned travel businesses under its jurisdiction, including travel agencies, hotels, and bus companies, into the Beijing Tourism Group (BTG). This move was criticized by some, including Wei Xiaoan, then the director of CNTA's Department of Management, as not conforming to the objective laws of tourism management and operation, because it was driven more by government than by market. However, seeing things in their own way, administrators in some other provinces (such as Zhejiang) and cities (such as Suzhou and Xi'an) lost no time in following Beijing's example and set up their own tourism groups encompassing travel agencies, hotels, and bus companies. Mostly regional in nature, these groups are quite different from some of the well-known and famous private hospitality and travel groups commonly seen in developed, capitalist economies (such as Thomas Cook and American Express). Recently, the BMTA restructured the BTG system and established a number of separate subgroups along distinct business lines. For instance, CITS Beijing, Beijing China Travel Service, and Beijing Overseas Tourism Co., Ltd. were merged into a new BTG International Travel and Tours. As well, the major state-owned hotels under BMTA's jurisdiction have been combined to form the Beijing Capital Tourism Co., Ltd., a company that went public in May 2000 on the Shanghai Stock Exchange.

A number of scholars and researchers, as well as industry people, have come forward with their own ideas on the subject of travel agency consolidation. Du Jiang (2000), of the China Tourism Institute, commented that

> [f]or many years, the travel agency trade in China has followed a system of horizontal division of labor, characterized by fragmented markets with every travel agency doing everything from sales and marketing to handling tours. Little effort has been made to differentiate channels of marketing with some specialized in wholesale and some in retail. Nor has any effort been made to develop specialized and customized products. As a result, travel agencies can only compete on a low level, i.e., on price, which has resulted in the chaotic situation of the trade as well as the market. (p. 3)

Together with some other academicians, Du has been calling for large tour operators to consolidate, for medium-sized travel agencies to specialize in developing and marketing specialty tour products, and for small operators to focus on retailing. Wei Xiaoan (cited in CNTA, 1998a: 41) described this as "a pyramid whose top is the consolidated tour operators; the middle part is the specialized medium-sized travel agencies, and the bottom part is the large number of retailers affiliated with one or another tour operator." In a study of development trends of the travel agency trade in the United States, Zhaoping Liu (1999) noted that the large tour operators have, in recent years, been able to steadily enhance their size and efficiency. Accordingly, many travel agents in small agencies have either been forced by the pressure of competition to join a network of large operators, or form themselves into alliances in order to survive. Wei Liu indicates that market competition is beginning to force travel agencies in China to seek alliances. A good example of this is Shanghai Comfort International Travel Service (SCITS). Since it joined the CITS network, the country's largest network of travel agencies, SCITS has been handling CITS tour groups in Shanghai (Wei Liu, 1999). As a result, its business has been thriving and in 1997 it handled 72 percent more overseas tourists than in 1996, ranking it number two among the forty international clientele travel agencies in Shanghai.

Considering the chaotic situation China's travel agency trade finds itself in, it is not difficult to see the wisdom of Dai's (1999) comment:

> The primary reason why improper competition exists in the travel agency trade lies in improper government regulations resulting in market failure. Add to this are the inherent special features of the travel agency trade, and you are face to face with an unwholesome situation where repeated prohibitions from the government fail to work. To remedy the situation, it is paramount for the government to relax its regulations. (p. 47)

Dai's suggestion will probably be considered too academic and radical to be taken seriously by CNTA or other government tourism administrators. This is because China's tourism industry has long been considered an important "government-led" industry, and this policy has reinforced regulatory involvement by the government. Hence many municipalities, provinces, and autonomous regions have embraced tourism as a "pillar" or "core" industry and in China much of the success of the industry is seen as the result of government involvement and support. Even though central government policies have encouraged privately owned travel businesses as a supplement to the public sector since at least 1997, private travel agencies are still few and far between. This situation might change should China join the World Trade Organization, which would require further deregulation of the tourism industry.

CONCLUSION AND RECOMMENDATIONS

China will continue to draw a steady and increasing number of overseas tourists attracted to its history, culture, scenic beauty, and last but not least, its people with their infinite variety of ethnic customs, music, and dance. As China's tourism industry continues to grow, so will the travel agency trade. This growth will not be smooth amid the chaos that currently exists. The reason is that one of the oldest civilizations in the world is undergoing enormous structural change. It is encouraging that about 85 percent of overseas visitors indicated that their trip to China was good and offered fairly good value (Table 9.6). On the other hand, reform of China's enterprise system is only at its initial stages, with only some travel agencies turning into joint stock limited companies and shareholding companies. Private travel agencies are still practically nonexistent and the privatization of travel agencies is still very much taboo. Many joint venture travel agencies are hoping that they will help reduce unfair competition, the way joint venture hotels have helped China in the fair competition of the hotel industry.

In late 1998, CNTA and the Ministry of Foreign Trade and Economic Cooperation jointly announced a temporary set of rules on the starting and operation of joint venture travel agencies in China. However, most major overseas tour operators do not seem very enthusiastic about it and, to date, only a few have been set up. One is a joint service for foreign individual visitors launched by American Express and CITS Head Office. Another is a joint venture between the Japan Travel Bureau (JTB) and China International Trust and Investment Company's (CITIC) International Tours. Both of these joint ventures are currently operating on a small scale. Under these circumstances, no radical changes in China's enterprise system are envisioned. With less qualified travel agencies continuing to stay in the market, the somewhat chaotic situation may remain as is for some time to come. All this may begin to change when China formally enters the World Trade Organization and is forced to implement a truly open market.

One of CNTA's successful guiding principles has been that China's tourism industry should be government led. Applied to the travel agency trade, this principle has undoubtedly reaped some apparent results in outbound tourism as well as for inbound and domestic tourism. It is worthwhile for CNTA to continue its efforts to regulate the travel agency trade at the national level. However, Chen (1999), a senior researcher with the Beijing Municipal Tourism Administration, has pointed out that the concept of a "government-led tourism industry" is sometimes interpreted as rationalizing irrational interference and an improper zeal for investment [in attraction development]. What is needed is for CNTA (and other levels of tourism administration) to distinguish what they can and should do and what they cannot and should not do, leaving the latter to the power of market forces. Responsibilities already assumed by CNTA and other government tourism agencies include:

- helping the National People's Congress, the national legislative body, to stipulate a comprehensive law on travel and tourism (although this has yet to be adopted);
- working with the State Council, i.e., the central government, to formulate statutes and regulations, aimed at facilitating growth of the travel agency trade; and enforcing the tourism laws, statutes, and regulations;
- supervising the quality of service offered by travel agencies, rewarding the best and punishing the worst, and helping ensure the rights of the consumers; and
- helping train professionals, managers in particular, for the travel agencies.

Attention should be drawn to a big difference between the hotel industry and the travel agency trade in China. Hotel managers generally have far more opportunities for training and skill development than travel agency managers do, although many of the latter are college graduates while most of the former are not. Many seminars are offered and conducted for hotel managers every year by the China Hotel Association and its local branches, universities and colleges with a hotel management department, and tourism research centers in Beijing, Shanghai, and other cities. In addition to national or local trade papers on tourism, hotel managers can also benefit from reading hotel magazines. A small number of hotel managers have even been sent abroad by CNTA to study hotel management. Joint venture hotels have also literally served as the best schools for technology transfer and the training of Chinese hotel managers.

Most travel agency managers do not benefit from any of these types of opportunities and joint venture agencies are very small in number. There are no travel agency trade magazines or papers and seldom do travel agency managers go to seminars held for their benefit. Only a few training courses have been sponsored by the China Travel Agency Association (CTAA) and its local branches, universities and colleges, and research centers. Consequently, most Chinese travel agency managers learn primarily through their own private practice and experience. Although a large number of managers do learn, have learned a lot, and have developed a high degree of professionalism, educational and training opportunities are limited for them. That being the case, the vast difference that exists in the satisfaction ratings of overseas tourists between hotel and travel agency service (cited previously) comes as no surprise.

It is, therefore, highly recommended that seminars sponsored by CTAA, colleges, research centers, or overseas organizations should be held regularly and widely for travel agency managers so that they can keep up to date on world travel trends and keep pace with technological advances. More important, they need to learn how to compete in a market economy through fair means and "thrive on chaos," as management guru Tom Peters (1991) puts it. Emphasis should be put on managers being open, honest, and able and for their travel agencies to be "learning organizations." In addition, a special magazine should be published for travel agency managers to keep them continually abreast of industry trends. Training and enhancing the quality of the travel agency managers will provide the best hope for the development of a progressive and prosperous travel agency trade in China.

REFERENCES

Cai, Jiacheng (1999). The System Structure of China's Travel Agencies and Its Trends of Change. *Tourism Tribune,* No. 6, pp. 9-13 (original in Chinese).

Chen, Weiming (1999). My Understanding of the Administrative Management Behavior and Characteristics in China's Tourism Industry. *Tourism Tribune,* No. 4, pp. 14-17 (original in Chinese).

China National Tourism Administration (CNTA) (1998a). *Report on the Development of the Travel Agency Trade in China: An Analysis of Market Competition and Management Strategies.* Beijing: CNTA, Department of Management (original in Chinese).

China National Tourism Administration (CNTA) (1998b). *The Yearbook of China Tourism Statistics 1998, Supplement,* pp. 8, 102. Beijing: China Tourism Press (original in Chinese).

China National Tourism Administration (CNTA) (1999a). *Basic Principles for the Development of China's Tourism Industry in the Tenth Five-Year Plan Period.* An informal publication, p.16 (original in Chinese).

China National Tourism Administration (CNTA) (1999b). Communiqué on China Tourism Statistics for 1998, May 31, 1999. In *The Yearbook of China Tourism*

Statistics 1999 (Editor-in-chief, Chang Zhenguo), pp. 207-213 (original in Chinese).

China National Tourism Administration (CNTA) (1999c). Report on a Systematic Analysis of Overseas Tourists Sample Survey for 1998. In *The Yearbook of China Tourism* (Editor-in-chief, Chang Zhenguo). Beijing: China Tourism Press, pp. 236-239 (original in Chinese).

China National Tourism Administration (CNTA) (1999d). Report on the Annual Review of Travel Agency Business for 1998. In *The Yearbook of China Tourism 1999* (Editor-in-chief, Chang Zhenguo). Beijing: China Tourism Press, pp. 228-230 (original in Chinese).

China National Tourism Administration (CNTA) (2000a). Managing the Travel Agency Trade: The Present Situation and the Tasks. *Tourism Survey and Study,* April, p. 15 (original in Chinese).

China National Tourism Administration (CNTA) (2000b). Report on the Annual Review of Travel Agency Business for 1999, pp. 5-6. A CNTA document, not published (original in Chinese).

China National Tourism Administration (CNTA) (2000c). *The Yearbook of China Tourism Statistics 2000.* Beijing: China Tourism Press (original in Chinese).

China National Tourism Administration (CNTA) (2000d). *The Yearbook of China Tourism Statistics 2000, Supplement,* pp. 20, 114. Beijing: China Tourism Press (original in Chinese).

Dai, Bin (1999). On Government Regulations and the Unfair Competition in the Travel Agency Trade. *Journal of Guilin Institute of Tourism,* Vol. 10, No. 1, pp. 46-48 (original in Chinese).

Du, Jiang (2000). An Analysis of the Status Quo and Development Trends of China's Travel Agency Trade. *Journal of Beijing Second Foreign Language Institute,* January, pp. 1-12 (original in Chinese).

Guo, Jin (2000). A Survey of the Performance of Tour Guides for Domestic Tourists. Unpublished graduation paper, English Department. Beijing: China Tourism Institute.

He, Guangwei (1998). CNTA Chairman's Address at the National Conference on Tourism, March. Beijing: *China Tourism News,* March 28 (original in Chinese).

He, Guangwei (2000). CNTA Chairman's Address at the National Conference on Travel Trade Management, April 14, 2000. *Tourism Survey and Study,* May, pp. 4-11 (original in Chinese).

Jiang, Jianning (1999). Effect a Change in Concept, Submit Our Staff to Rigorous Training So As to Meet New Challenges—An Interview with the Correspondent of *Tourism Tribune. Tourism Tribune,* July, pp. 18-21 (original in Chinese).

Lew, A.A. (1987). The History, Policies and Social Impact of International Tourism in the People's Republic of China. *Asian Profile,* Vol. 15, No. 2, pp. 117-128.

Liu, Wei (1999). Thoughts on Development Strategies for Guangzhi Tours of Guangzhou. *Tourism Tribune,* January, pp. 36-38 (original in Chinese).

Liu, Zhaoping (1999). A Study of the Latest Trends of Travel Agencies in the U.S.—And What It Teaches China's Travel Agency Trade. *Tourism Tribune,* May, pp. 27-31 (original in Chinese).

Ministry of Public Security (1999). *Statistics on China's Outbound Travel.* Beijing: Department of Exit and Entry Administration (original in Chinese).

Peters, Tom (1991). *Thriving on Chaos: Handbook for a Management Revolution.* Harper Trade. New York: Knopf.

Qian, Wei (1999a). China's Tourism and Professionalism. *Asia Pacific Journal of Tourism Research,* Vol. 4, No. 1, pp. 22-29.

Qian, Wei (1999b). China Tourism 2010—New Role for a New Millennium. In Heung, V., Ap, J., and Wong, K.F. (eds.), *Proceedings of the Fifth Annual Conference of Asia-Pacific Tourism Association, Hong Kong,* August, pp. 17-30 Hong Kong: The Hong Kong Polytechnic University.

Qian, Wei, Cai, Liping, and Hu Bo (2000). Your Comments Matter—An Overseas Visitor Survey. Unpublished survey, Beijing Tourism Institute, China, and Purdue University, United States.

Wang, Dawu (1998). What Is the Root Cause of the Unfair Competition in the Travel Agency Trade? *Tourism Tribune,* March, pp. 32-34 (original in Chinese).

Zhang, Xiuzhi (2000). E-Travel—A New Trend in Travel Industry. A Collection of Speeches at the Seminar on E-travel sponsored by the Shanghai Spring International Tours in Beijing on April 27 (unpublished conference paper).

Chapter 10

China's Tourist Transportation: Air, Land, and Water

Barry Mak

China is situated in the Far East, far from the major tourist-generating regions of North America and Western Europe. Getting to China, therefore, is a major long-haul consideration for most travelers, even those from other Asian countries, such as those in Southeast Asia and even Japan. Air transportation is the crucial link to almost all of China's major international market regions, although land transportation plays a significant role for many emerging markets in getting to China and for travel within China. Water transportation also has a complex, although more limited, role to play in China's transportation system.

Transportation is an integral part of the tourism industry and is one of the most important factors that contribute to tourism development (Middleton, 1988; Page, 1999) and, according to Pearce (1982), is a key component of the tourist experience. Since the People's Republic of China started to develop its modern tourism industry in 1978, major efforts have been made to improve the country's international and domestic transportation system. Travel to and within China is now much easier than before, although challenges still remain.

China's total international tourist arrivals in 1999 reached 72.8 million (CNTA, 2000). The number of foreigners (which excludes Hong Kong, Taiwan, and Macao citizens) accounted for 11.6 percent, or 8.4 million (Table 10.1). The most common mode of access into China was by foot (68 percent) via border crossings. This data includes the compatriot market from Hong Kong, Macao, and Taiwan, many of whom take trains or buses from Hong Kong and Macao to the border, cross the border by foot, then take another train or bus to

TABLE 10.1. Visitor Arrivals by Mode of Transport, 1999

	Sea	Air	Rail	Motor	Foot	Total
All Visitors	3,814,253	6,626,545	1,015,717	11,918,211	49,420,868	72,795,594
Percentage	5.2	9.1	1.4	16.4	67.9	100
Foreigners	1,130,214	4,493,958	400,324	1,146,973	1,260,827	8,432,296
Percentage	13.4	53.3	4.7	13.6	15	100

Source: CNTA (2000), 24, 35.

their destinations in southern China. This practice is cheaper than purchasing a through train or air ticket, and is the major reason for the high percentage of entry by foot. Long-haul foreign travelers mainly use air transportation, with the percentage of air transport arrivals, which accounts for 9 percent of China's total arrivals, over 50 percent of foreign arrivals. China has one of the longest land borders of any country in the world, and foot crossings along this border, from Russia, Central Asia, and Southeast Asia, account for most of the 15 percent of foreign travelers who enter the country by foot. Rail arrivals are mostly from Hong Kong and foreign sea arrivals come primarily from cruise and ferry ships out of Hong Kong and a smaller number from long-haul international cruise sailings.

Long-distance transportation in 1999 accounted for 33 percent of all international visitor expenditures in China (totaling US$14 billion), while local transportation was an additional 3 percent (CNTA, 2000). For the foreign visitor market segment, these numbers were slightly less for long-distance expenditures (30 percent of US$14 billion in 1999), and slightly more (4 percent) for local transportation.

Despite major physical expansion, China's transportation system has continually faced problems of inefficient usage of carrying units (i.e., aircraft, vessels, coaches, and trains), poor management, lack of maintenance, inadequate and even backward facilities, and safety problems. Much of the problem occurs because demand continually outstrips supply. The central government's Tenth Five-Year Plan (FYP, for 2000-2005) has put these issues in the spotlight by focusing on improvements on infrastructure, particularly transportation, as a national priority. Premier Zhu Rongi even declared that China's development emphasis in the first half of the 21st century will be on the modernization of the country's transportation ("The Tenth Five-Year-Plan," 2001). The Tenth FYP allocated RMB 2,000 billion yuan for infrastructure each year, half of which is earmarked for western China (Chen, 2001). Both road and water transportation will be developed, with the target of 1.6 million kilometers of new roads (including 25,000 km of highways) by 2005 ("China Changes Its Transportation Structure," 2001). Some 80 major projects in the more distant western parts of China will create 350,000 km of roads in the remote regions.

AIR TRANSPORTATION

China's aviation industry has been a focal point of transport development in recent years. Although air transportation has some way to go to match the standards found in most developed countries, improvements made in the 1990s indicate a prosperous future. The demand for air travel is tremendous and in 1999 China's air transport ranked sixth in the world in terms of passenger traffic ("China Civil Air Passenger Volume," 2000).

After 1949, China had only one airline for over thirty years, the Civil Aviation Administration of China (CAAC), which was also responsible for aviation licensing and regulation, making it the country's supreme aviation body. The functions of CAAC included: (1) certification for air traffic control; (2) management of, and procurement for, airport operations; and (3) operation of the national carrier airline. In 1984, Gu Mu, a member of the State Council who was also in charge of the country's modernization program, announced that CAAC would cease to exist as a combined airline and civil aviation body (Mak, 1989). This administrative reorganization arose as the CAAC came under increasing attack for its tradition of poor service and rude staff. These structural reforms were initiated in September 1984 and completed by June 30, 1988 (Yu and Lew, 1997). The national airline was divided into six nonprivatized regional airline companies: Air China (Beijing and the new national carrier), China Eastern (Shanghai), China Southern (Guangzhou), China Northwest (Xi'an), China Southwest (Chengdu), and China Northern (Shenyang). The aim of this breakup was to increase competition and separate government regulatory functions from commercial operations. Airports were also to operate separately from the airlines and the regulatory authority. In September 1985, the Chinese State Council issued regulations confirming

CAAC's role as a regulatory agency with jurisdiction over civilian air operations. CAAC would continue to regulate and license pilots, approve flight plans and routes, set airfares, oversee airports, and approve aircraft and equipment purchases.

The new airlines were allowed to operate regionally within China, as well as on some international routes. They were allowed to borrow at home and overseas in order to finance fleet expansion. In addition, local government organizations were permitted to set up airlines and establish airline joint ventures with foreign companies. As of 2001, foreign investors held shares in China Eastern, China Southern, and Hainan Airlines (Chang, 2001). These are smaller airlines that mostly act as feeders to larger airlines and operate charter flights. In 1988 seventeen regional and local airlines had been approved by CAAC to operate passenger and/or cargo routes (Chen, 2000); and by 1999 that number had grown to thirty-four (CAAC, 2000).

Despite its rapid growth, China's airline industry remains tightly regulated. China Southern Airlines, for example, was required to pay compensation to its competitors for violating CAAC pricing regulations when it signed a secret deal with a Hainan travel agency, which allowed discounts of up to 70 percent on chartered flights between Chengdu and Haikou (Li, 2001). The discounted prices were much lower than those approved by CAAC. In January 2001, CAAC threatened the Chinese airlines with flight cancellations if they offered unapproved discounts. Other examples of recent CAAC efforts to control prices included permission for airlines to raise fares by up to 20 percent to help offset higher fuel prices in October 2000 and in allowing a 1 percent lowering of airfares in February 2001. A Hong Kong analyst commented that the price adjustments were another form of price regulation (Ng and Reuters, 2001). The CAAC still has a bit of a planned-economy mentality, which is at odds with China's growing market-based economy.

Globalization is a major force for change in China's airline industry. To increase its competitiveness in the international market, China Eastern Airlines, for example, is seeking to improve its safety and management and derive economies of scale by forming strategic alliances with international counterparts ("Magnetic Levitation Airway," 2001). Meanwhile, Air China began seven code-shared flights with U.S.-based Northwest in February 2001, and China Eastern and China Southern airlines have code-share arrangements with airlines in the United States, France, and Korea (Chang, 2001; "China Civil Air Passenger Volume," 2001). By April 2001, the number of weekly flights between China and the United States was twice that of a year earlier (Zhang, Liu, and Wang, 2001) due to the signing of bilateral agreements between the U.S. and Chinese governments.

Presently, foreign companies can have a maximum 35 percent ownership stake in a Chinese airline. As China's accession to the World Trade Organization (WTO) looms, the percentage will be increased. Bao Peide, deputy head of the CAAC, indicated the target is to increase this up to 49 percent (Ng, Barling, and Lo, 2002). This will be required under the General Agreement on Service Trade, which is part of the WTO agreement that will allow foreign airlines to participate in joint ventures in aviation engineering, sales and marketing, computerized reservation systems (CRS), and investment in air transportation (Chang, 2001). This will further integrate China's airline industry internationally.

In addition to the industry's increasing global ties, greater consolidation is likely among the many airlines that now operate within China. As of 1999, six major airlines served the country and selected international routes. Another sixteen smaller civil airlines owned by local government or state-owned enterprises operated on a regional scale (CAAC 2000). As the major airlines expand their influence over time, they are likely to incorporate many of the smaller airlines.

International, Regional, and Domestic Air Transport

China's airline industry enjoyed the highest growth rate among all transport modes since the open door policy was initiated in 1978. Over a twenty-year period from 1978 to 1998, air transport increased by 911 percent in total route miles, while roads increased 43 percent and rail only 19 percent (Guo, 1999). Chinese airlines carried a record of 67.2 million passengers in 2000, a twenty-eight-fold increase on the 2.3 million passengers carried in 1978 ("Steady Growth of China's Civil Aviation," 2001; CAAC, 2000). These large increases were mostly because air travel was very limited in 1978, when only 70 domestic and international air routes were regularly flown compared to the 1,115 scheduled routes (including the 150 international routes) flown regularly in 1999 (CAAC, 2000; Guo, 1999).

In 1980, China had eighteen international routes to fourteen countries. New routes have been added frequently and there are regular international flights from Beijing, Shanghai, and Guangzhou to destinations in the United States, Europe, the Middle East, and Asia. Foreign airlines also operate routes to China under bilateral agreements, the number of which has increased dramatically in the last decade. In 1999 Chinese carriers transported 6.3 million passengers on international routes operating to sixty-two cities in thirty-three countries (CAAC, 2000) (Table 10.2). In the other direction, major airlines now flying into China include United Airlines, Northwest Airlines, Japan Airlines, All Nippon Airways, Thai International Airways, Korean Air, Singapore Airlines, British Airways, Lufthansa, and Dragon Airlines. There were 488 passenger flight services (excluding those from Hong Kong and Macao) operated by foreign airlines to and from China in 1999 (CAAC, 2000) and foreign airlines see China as a great potential market. According to *Takungpao Daily News* ("Lufthansa

TABLE 10.2. Route Services and Cities of Air Transportation, 1950-1999

Year	Total	Domestic		Regional		International	
		Routes	**Cities**	**Routes**	**Cities**	**Routes**	**Cities**
1950	7	7	8	0	0	0	0
1955	16	15	17	0	1	1	1
1960	17	12	27	0	5	5	5
1965	57	51	50	0	5	6	5
1970	71	67	65	0	4	4	4
1975	135	128	80	0	10	7	10
1980	180	159	78	3	15	18	14
1985	267	233	82	7	21	27	18
1990	437	385	94	8	32	44	24
1995	797	694	133	18	51	85	31
1996	876	757	134	21	56	98	33
1997	967	851	135	7	11	109	31
1998	1,120	983	135	8	10	131	34
1999	1,115	987	132	22	23	128	33

Source: CAAC (2000), 37.

Airlines," 2001), China is a major air transport destination for the German-based Lufthansa Airlines in the Asia Pacific region.

Hong Kong has been an important gateway for China, serving as a crucial transit point for foreign tourists entering and departing China. It is also a major center of international and regional aviation in Asia with over 3,000 flights per week providing services to some 120 destinations worldwide (Economic Services Bureau, 2001; CAAC, 2000). The regional route services between Hong Kong and mainland Chinese cities still serve as the primary connection between much of China and the outside world. Some forty cities are linked to Hong Kong through 285 weekly scheduled flights and additional non-scheduled services. One of the newest routes, initiated in June 2001, connected Hong Kong to Urumqi, the capital of Xinjiang Province in western China ("Direct Flight," 2001). Previously, travelers to Urumqi had to transfer several times to get there. Some tourists, especially from Taiwan, have increasingly used Macau International Airport as a transit point to mainland China. In 1999, there were sixty-four passenger flight services between Macao and China (CAAC, 2000).

Most travel by foreign visitors between the major cities in China is by air. By 1999 China had 983 domestic routes to 132 cities compared with 159 routes to 78 cities in 1980 (CAAC, 2000). Although the increase in serviced routes has been very rapid, air transportation still plays an insignificant role in domestic transportation (0.5 percent of all domestic trips), especially when compared with road transportation (91 percent of domestic trips). In the 1980s, flights in China were almost always full, mainly with government officials, People's Liberation Army personnel, and foreign tour groups. However, by the 1990s, the situation changed and quite a large number of seats on planes were empty due to a dramatic increase in supply. In the year 2000 only ten Chinese airlines had more than 60 percent passenger load factor performance ("Steady Growth of China's Civil Aviation," 2001). Nevertheless, in China the rate of growth for air transport has been faster than for any other mode of transport.

Aircraft, Airport, and Aviation Facilities

In addition to the opening of new routes, China's aviation industry has upgraded its aircraft and airport facilities. In the 1980s CAAC modernized its fleet by buying more Western-made planes to replace its older fleet of Tridents and Soviet-made Il-14s and Il-62s. This has continued into the 1990s as China's airlines spent more than US$5 billion to buy foreign-made wide-body passenger aircraft to meet the demands of rising international and domestic traffic. By the end of 1999, China's airlines operated 510 aircraft, mainly new-generation Boeing 737s, 747s, 757s, 767s, and 777s (totaling 269); McDonald Douglas MD82s, MD90s, and MD11s (totaling 55); and Airbus A300s, A310s, A320s, A321s, and A340s (totaling 84). In an analysis of future aircraft demand, the China Aviation System Engineering Research Institute projected that from 2001 to 2009, the country's civil aircraft will need to increase from 520 to 911, and by 2019 the number will go up to 1,730 ("China Aircraft Market Forecast," 2001). Similarly, the Boeing Corporation projects China will need 1,400 new aircraft in the next two decades.

CAAC has improved existing airport facilities and enlarged some airports in order to cope with the rapid changes in China's air travel since 1978. In 1999 a second airport in Shanghai (Pudong Airport) was opened and the new terminal building was built at the Capital Airport in Beijing (Guo, 1999). Construction was started in 2000 on a new airport in Guangzhou to replace Baiyun Airport ("Guangzhou's New Airport Runway Design Approved," 2001). The new airport will be opened in October 2003 ("Guangzhou's New Airport Will Open in 2003," 2001) and connected to the city by underground rail transport. It will also be the first airport in China to have two independently operating runways, although Beijing Capital Airport currently has two runways. In the future the new Guangzhou airport will have the capacity to accommodate four runways.

During the 1990s, new airports were built in Shanghai, Haikou, Nanchong, Hangzhou, Shenzhen, Kunming, Guilin, Zhuhai, Wuhan, Jinan, Yantai, and Xishuanbanna, and existing airports were expanded at Xi'an, Chongqing, Changsha, Shenyang, Xiamen, Changchun, Qingdao, Ningbo, Jinan, Chengdu, Urumqi, Harbin, Kunming, Lanzhou, Luoyang, Beihai, Mexian, and Dalian (Chen, 2000). In Yunnan Province alone, ten airports were either being upgraded or were under construction in 2001 (He, 2001). The ongoing improvement of China's airports provides better geographical access and increases the overall carrying capacity of the country's air transport system. For example, by the end of 1999, twenty-two of the country's 142 airports could accommodate Boeing 747s (CAAC, 2000) compared with only eight of the total ninety airports in 1986 (Mak, 1989).

Air traffic control and management in China has also greatly improved. The Air Traffic Management Department of China was established in 1987 to assume responsibility for all domestic aviation movements. Reform of the air traffic control (ATC) network was needed to help advance China's civil aviation. The old system, based on Soviet models of the 1950s, was no longer suited to modern conditions and hindered development of the industry. CAAC upgraded its ground navigation facilities and new radar systems were introduced in the major airports, while instrument landing systems were installed in over half of the civilian airports. New air traffic control systems have also been introduced for civil aviation. For example, in January 2001 the Beijing air traffic control center started using a radar control system to manage flight movements ("Beijing Implements Radar Control," 2001). A new nationwide civil aviation ATC system is planned and CAAC will invest RMB 2 billion yuan to modernize and develop three air traffic control centers, to be located in Beijing, Shanghai, and Guangzhou ("CAAC Will Develop Three Air Traffic Control Centers," 2001).

CAAC only started to use computers for seat reservations in 1983, and then only for international flights. Today, computerized reservation systems (CRS) are available for almost all air services. The CRS used by China's airlines involves cooperation agreements with ten international CRS companies (Chang, 2001), and since January 2001 all airline tickets issued in China are now done so through automated ticketing machines ("Goodbye to CAAC Manual Tickets," 2001). With the new millennium, manual ticketing in China has become a thing of the past.

INTERNATIONAL TOURIST LAND AND WATER TRANSPORTATION

International Coach Services

In addition to air travel, transportation between China and other countries takes place via railways, ships, and roads, although none of these is very well developed. The Northwest China Highway in Xinjiang Province links China with Pakistan and was rebuilt and re-opened in the 1990s (Mak, 1989). In northeastern China, coach services were started in November 2000 between Harbin and Ussuriysk, Russia, and between Jiemuchi (Heilongjiang Province) and Birobidzhan in Russia in January 2001 ("Chinese-Russian Border Transportation," 2001). Other international land crossings exist on China's borders with Nepal, Vietnam, and North Korea. Cross-border bus services between Hong Kong and Guangdong Province were introduced in 1981 and more than 190 bus routes connect Hong Kong to Guangdong and Fujian provinces ("Seventy-Eight Coach Companies Operate," 2001).

International Railways

International railway services in China are not like the railway system in Europe. This is partly because of the physical barriers of mountains, deserts, and seas, and partly due to the unstable political relationship in the past between China and some of its neighboring countries, such as Vietnam and Russia. The vast and largely under-developed land mass of central and western China has been a challenge for the country's rail network. Differences in types of rail systems and varying levels of economic development further complicate China's international railway connections (Mak, 1989). As of 2001 only three countries were connected to China by railway: Russia (all the way to Moscow), Mongolia (to Ulan Bator), and North Korea (to Pyongyang). China can be reached by rail from Europe through Moscow and Ulan Bator. The most direct railway route from London to Hong Kong passes through Paris, Berlin, Warsaw, Moscow, Irkutsk, and Ulan Bator before entering China. Most of this trip takes place on the well-known Trans-Siberian Railway (Mak, 1989). However, there is a proposal to build a new cross-Asia railway connection to southern Europe ("Ten Nations' Understanding," 1999). It would run from China's Yunnan Province through Myanmar (Burma), India, Bangladesh, Pakistan, Iran, and Turkey, entering Europe through Bulgaria. If completed, this 11,705 km railway would be the longest in the world. All nations involved agreed to the idea of the project during the four-day meeting organized by the Economic and Social Committee of Asia and the Pacific of United Nations. However, there are political problems to resolve such as the unstable relationship between India and Pakistan, and technical problems such as different track systems. The completion date of this gigantic project is still unknown.

In early 2001, another rail project proposal was put forward by ASEAN to develop the US$2.5 billion Pan-Asian railway, which will go from Singapore to Kuala Lumpur, Malaysia and then proceed to Bangkok, the Mekong River basin, Yunnan Province, China then onward to Europe. The project would take five years to complete if it is developed ("Pan-Asian Railway in Yunnan," 2001).

Regionally, Guangzhou in China is linked to the Hong Kong Special Administrative Region (SAR) by railway. Guangzhou is one of the top three visitor destinations in China and frequent rail services connect it to the neighboring Hong Kong SAR. The Kowloon-Canton Railway Corporation (KCRC) provides eleven conveniently scheduled round-trip express trains between Hong Kong and Guangzhou on a daily basis ("Eleven Pairs of Direct Trains," 1999). In addition, as many as forty trains per hour run in both directions in the daily morning and evening peak commuter periods between Hong Kong and the Lo Wu border (Kowloon-Canton Railway Corporation, 2001b). In 1998, the total number of cross-border passengers carried by KCRC was 65 million (Kowloon-Canton Railway Corporation, 2001a). After crossing the border on foot, passengers can board coaches, rails, or taxis taking them to various destinations in China. Most of the people making these crossings are not tourists, but workers who live on one side of the border and make daily commutes.

International Sea Transportation

High-speed hovercraft services are provided between Hong Kong and many coastal destinations in Guangdong Province. They mostly accommodate the demand from the compatriot and overseas Chinese markets from Hong Kong, Taiwan, and Southeast Asia. These regional water service routes include destinations such as Guangzhou, Zhongshan, Shekou, Zhuhai, Zhaoqing, and Jianmen (China International Travel Service Hong Kong, 2001). Since 1985, journeys by sea have also been available from Hong Kong to Xiamen in Fujian Province and Shanghai. These journeys take twelve and sixty hours, respectively (China International Travel Service Hong Kong, 2001). Although ferry services between Hong Kong and China have expanded considerably in the 1990s, the China-Hong Kong Pier, which opened in Hong Kong in November 1988, needs expansion and renovation.

In addition to Hong Kong, there are scheduled passenger ferry services from Shanghai to Kobe and Osaka in Japan, and from Dalian in China to Inchon in Korea. Moreover, many world cruise liners now feature shore excursions in northeast China as highlights of their regional and transworld voyages. From Hong Kong, the Asia-based Star Cruises line makes weekly calls on Haikou and Sanya (Hainan Province) and Xiamen (Fujian Province). A regular cruise service also started on April 13, 2001, between Haikou, Hainan Island and Halong Bay, Vietnam ("Regular Cruise Services," 2001).

DOMESTIC TOURIST SURFACE TRANSPORTATION

The construction of new railways and roads to better link and integrate the western regions of China with the eastern coastal areas has been the focus of domestic transport development in recent years. Most foreign visitors travel by air for lengthy trips within China, and use rail or coach for shorter trips. Domestic travelers mostly use rail and coach services when they travel within China.

Domestic Railways

China's rail network comes under the administration of the Ministry of Railways, which is divided geographically into several railway bureaus. Railways are the major means of transportation in China between all major cities and tourist centers, accounting for 85 percent of the country's total medium- and long-haul transportation ("China Developing a Series," 1999). However, in terms of overall passenger traffic in China, dependence on the railways has declined from 32 percent in 1978 to 15 percent in 1988, and it dropped further to 7 percent by 1998 (Guo, 1999). In 1998, 936 million passengers were carried on the rail system in China compared to 1,027 million in 1995. One of the major reasons for the drop in passenger numbers has been the rapid development of China's road transport, which has replaced rail as the major mode of passenger travel.

In 1949 there were just 21,800 km of railway line in China, but by the end of 1998 the network was extended to 57,600 km, of which 13,000 km (or 8 percent) was electrified (Guo, 1999). With the exception of Tibet, every province and region is connected to the rail system. More than 75 percent of the new rail lines added since 1949 have been built to the west of the north-south Beijing–Guangzhou artery that roughly bisects China's population. The population is more dispersed in western China and long rail lines are required to serve settlements that are few and far between. The first major expansion of the railway system toward the west took place in the 1952-1962 period when the important Trans-Xinjiang railway was built from Lanzhou to Urumqi, the capital of Xinjiang. Progress in the 1960s was slow but picked up again in the 1970s (see Table 10.3). During the 1978-1998 period, China invested billions of yuan in railway construction, extending the total length of the railway system by 9,000 km, doubling 12,043 km of track and electrifying 12,000 km of track, twelve times the total length of electric railway lines built before 1978.

Construction of new lines are still in progress, with the major project of 2001 being the Qinghai-Tibet line, which will be the first to connect Tibet to China's rail system ("Qinghai-Tibet Railway Costs 20 Billion," 2001). The central government has approved the construction of this 1,118 km railway between Gemuermu, Qinghai and Lhasa, Tibet, which will be the highest railway in the world. The Ministry of Railways is conscious of the negative impacts of rail de-

TABLE 10.3. Railway Transportation in China, 1952-1998

	Mileage (1,000 km)	Electrification (1,000 km)
1952	22.9	0.0
1962	34.6	0.1
1975	46.0	0.7
1978	48.6	1.0
1980	49.9	1.7
1985	52.1	4.2
1990	53.4	6.9
1995	54.6	9.7
1998	57.6	13.0

Source: People's Republic of China Yearbook (1999), 15-4: Length of Transportation Routes, <http://www.stats.gov.cn/yearbook/1999o04c.htm>; accessed January 23, 2001.

velopment on the ecology of the region that this line will pass through and has stated that efforts have been taken to minimize its impacts ("Qinghai-Tibet Railway Will Not Destroy the Ecology," 2001). Furthermore, the Chinese government has budgeted RMB100 billion yuan for additional railways in western China ("Railway Development in Western China," 2001).

In eastern China more of the focus has been on upgrading existing rail lines. However, the system that serves the eastern half of the country remains heavily burdened. The technological levels of the service, including traction, rolling stock, signaling, and telecommunications has mostly been upgraded and improved. The development of new feeder lines, double tracking, and electrification has also been quick but still it has not been able to meet increasing demand. Funds have also been targeted for eight information technology projects that focus on operational safety and management information systems to enhance railway efficiency and service quality ("China Rail Builds," 2001).

China's Ministry of Railways has plans to further improve the present situation with emphasis placed on electrification, double tracking, and extension of the network to western China. This, however, is expensive. For example, the electrification of the Harbin to Dalian railway, originally built in 1989, was estimated to cost RMB10 billion ("Electrification of Harbin-Dalian Railway," 1999). A German consortium, Transrapid, has a commercial contract to build a high-speed magnetic levitation railway in Shanghai with trains that would be able to reach a speed of 500 km per hour (Reuters, 2001). This 30 km rail line is scheduled for completion at the end of 2003 and will enable passengers to travel from the Shanghai Pudong Airport into central Shanghai in less than ten minutes (Agence France-Presse, 2001a). Consideration is also being given to building a 1,300 km high-speed train line to connect Beijing and Shanghai ("Fastest Passenger Train Unveiled," 1999), and there are plans to construct a light rail system radiating from Guangzhou to surrounding cities, such as Foshan, Panyu, and Shunde ("Lintingyang Bridge," 2001).

China has been building electric locomotives since 1958 ("Fastest Passenger Train Unveiled," 1999) and the country's fastest locally made passenger train, which can operate at up to 200 km per hour, made its debut in October 1999, operating between Guangzhou and Shenzhen in southern China ("New Train on the Rails," 1999).

In terms of passenger service, designated credit cards can now be used to buy rail tickets from automatic vending machines at Beijing's main train station ("Fastest Passenger Train Unveiled," 1999) and a second-generation electronic ticketing system has been launched in China's major cities ("Outstanding Performance of Shenzhen Rail," 2001). However, the pace of automation is still slow and the dissemination of information about the range of available transportation services is poor, often leaving passengers confused over what is available.

Domestic Road Transportation

Road transport is the major means of travel in China and in 1999 it accounted for 91 percent of the total passenger traffic in China ("Road Ranks Number One," 1999). By the end of 1998, China had more than one million passenger vehicles, including taxis and coaches, 126,300 coach routes, and 7,355 coach passenger terminals. Official figures put the length of the national highway at 1.27 million km, but 7 percent of this road system is still unpaved (Guo, 1999) and a good number of the paved roads are of poor quality. The average annual increment of new roads built has been 26,420 km, although in 1998 there were 52,100 km of new road construction. Congestion in many of the larger cities has eased as newer road-building efforts have been concentrated on the development of intracity motorways and intercity links. Road construction grew the fastest in the 1995-2000 period when China expanded its network from 1.16 million km to 1.4 million km and the country's road density increased from 12.05 km per 100 km² to 14.6 km per 100 km².

For economic purposes, funding for road improvements at the national level has tended to focus on motorways leading to major ports. Rural areas have been expected to improve their road systems largely on their own with support from government subsidies. Local authorities must find their own funding and often resort to collecting road tolls to help fund a project. Accessibility for the rural areas has a major role to play in the potential economic and tourism development of such areas. With the exception of the developed tourist areas, road travel in rural areas remains difficult, especially in western China, but the situation will soon change as the central government has announced plans to build 350,000 km of road in the west, at a cost of 700 to 800 billion yuan ("Investment of 800 Billion," 2001).

China started building expressways in 1988 and most of the expressway network has been concentrated in the heavily populated eastern coastal areas (Zhou, 2000). They serve as trunk lines radiating from important large and small economic zones and regions. The expressways have also provided a major alternative to rail travel. They provide access to the ports, service interprovincial routes, and provide access to some of the more remote areas of China.

One interesting development has been the Guangzhou-Shenzhen-Zhuhai highway (Mak, 1989). This thirty-year joint venture project between Hopewell China Development and the Guangdong Provincial Highway Construction Company is expected to promote economic development and tourism throughout the Pearl River Delta area. Expressways in China are projected to grow to 35,000 km by 2010 (Zhou, 2000), and include fourteen new highways in western China, including two linking China proper with Tibet (Beijing Homeway, 2000). One of these roads will link Dandong in northeast China's Liaoning Province with Lhasa, the capital of Tibet, and the other will link Chengdu, the capital of Sichuan Province, with Zhangmu in Tibet. The completion of these fourteen main traffic arteries should provide a modern highway network serving most of western China by 2030. Three highways have already been constructed linking eastern China with Tibet, but most of the roads in western China remain inadequate in number and are of poor quality. For example, western China's 7.8 km of highways per 100 km^2 is half the national average.

Long-distance bus coach services have grown with the development of the motorway system in China. There are many intercity bus services and although foreigner visitors are permitted to use them, few do except where air and rail services are not available, such as in Tibet. This low usage of long-distance coach services is due to a number of factors such as the lack of time foreign travelers have during their trip, the generally poor road conditions, poor condition of the buses, and the services provided. For wealthier domestic travelers, luxury coach tours have become trendy on the newly built motorways. There were 216,000 cross-provincial bus routes in operation in 1998 in China ("Road Ranks Number One," 1999) and the intercity bus services compete directly with rail and air services for domestic passengers. The Beijing-Shanghai Expressway, which opened to traffic in December 2000, has greatly eased access and congestion between China's two most important northern cities. This toll road also links the two cities to Tianjin and the provinces of Jiangsu, Shandong, and Hebei. The long-distance (1,262 km) bus service takes sixteen hours between Beijing and Shanghai and costs RMB 525 yuan ("Long-Distance Coach Services," 2001) and a car can now travel between the two cities in thirteen hours. It even costs less than a train ride if three people share a car with each paying RMB 178 yuan for the trip (Zhou, 2000). In comparison, a hard berth train ticket and airfare between Beijing and Shanghai cost 518 and 1,030 yuan, respectively (China Travel Net, 2002; Ng, 2001).

There were 13.19 million vehicles on China's roads for passenger use in 1998 compared to 1.35 million in 1978 (Guo, 1999). Demand for more vehicles, especially cars and bus coaches, has grown since the open door policy in 1978 and a large sum of foreign exchange has been spent to import vehicles. Many analysts expect car sales to increase rapidly with China's entry into the World Trade Organization and imported cars will become cheaper (Agence France-Presse, 2001b). It is reported that automobile production and imports in 2001 were 2.33 million and 72,047, respectively (O'Neill, 2002). The number of mainlanders with a driver's license has more than doubled between 1995 and 2000, from 30 million to nearly 75 million (Agence France-Presse, 2001b). The growth in car ownership and driver licenses, along with the expansion and upgrading of roads throughout China, has made domestic transportation easier and has increased accessibility to many areas for holiday travel. Domestic tourism has been thriving due to this increase in mobility, which will only continue in future years.

Domestic Water Transportation

The first regular passenger shipping service in China started in 1949 between Shanghai and Guangzhou and coastal ships carrying passengers between Dalian, Tianjin, Qingdao, Shanghai, Guangzhou, Xiamen, and Xianggang have been available since 1981. Although traditionally waterways have provided a major means of communication and the main mode of trade links within China (The Economist Publications, 1986), they no longer play a prominent role today. In

1998, China had 110,300 km of navigable inland waterways, down from 144,101 km in 1957 (Guo, 1999). About a third of these waterways are navigable by steamboats. About two-thirds of the network is located in the Yangtze River basin (Shanghai) and the Xi River basin (Guangzhou). Mostly foreign visitors take water-based trips on the Grand Canal waterway system in Jiangsu and Zhejiang Provinces and through the Three Gorges of the Yangtze River between Chongqing and Wuhan. The Lijiang River cruise through the famous karst (limestone) landscape of Guilin is popular with both domestic and international visitors. Tourist boats also ply the built-up waterfronts of the Huangpu in Shanghai or the Pearl River in Guangzhou.

The inland waterways are not without problems. Flooding is an annual threat in the summer on many rivers, and most of the northern waterways are subject to silting and low water levels during the spring and winter months. Northeast China's waterways are frozen over for half of the year. Other problems relate to old vessels, outdated technology, poor management, and inadequate law enforcement, all of which hinder the development of water transport and contribute to environmental problems.

Transportation Within Cities

Tourist travel within China's cities has become much easier as the range of different modes of urban transportation has increased. Taxi operations were allowed to resume in 1979 and taxi dispatchers can be found in hotels, train and coach stations, and airports. Taxi services are available in most Chinese cities and can be hailed from the street. Services have improved with the required metering of taxis in larger cities. However, overcharging by not taking the most direct route and touting are still a source of complaints from many passengers. Drivers do not like short-distance journeys and prefer being chartered for a few days or for a long-distance trip. Electronic payment of taxi fares through the use of cash cards has been introduced in some cities, including Shanghai and Harbin ("Ride Taxi with Credit Cards," 2001). The taxi is possibly the most convenient and popular transport service for tourists visiting a new city.

Short-distance urban-rural bus transport has developed rapidly and is widely used by domestic travelers, but foreign tourists do not usually patronize it. Crowding and the rather poor conditions of the buses in some cities do not make them an attractive proposition. Minibus services are restricted to the Special Economic Zones and some major cities such as Guangzhou and Beijing. These minibuses travel specified routes and travelers get on and off of them at any point on the route.

Along with the rapid development in ground transportation has come an increase in air pollution in most Chinese cities. Some efforts have been made to address this problem. In 1999, the government banned the yellow cab minitaxis in Beijing because of the pollution that these vehicles were generating, and more recently China introduced its first hydrogen-powered minisightseeing coach on February 23, 2001 ("Shanghai Develops Hydrogen-Power Sightseeing Coaches," 2001). Mass rail transit is one of the most efficient and environmentally friendly transport modes; however, only Beijing, Shanghai, and Guangzhou have underground train networks. Guangzhou's subway with sixteen stops along the 18.5 km route is China's newest. It commenced operation in June 1998 at a cost of RMB 12.7 billion yuan ("Guangzhou-Kowloon Direct Train," 1999; "Guangzhou Underground Route," 1999). Shenzhen's underground railway will be completed in 2004 and a second line in Guangzhou is expected to be completed in April 2003 ("Shenzhen Plans Vast Rail Scheme," 2002; Pun, 2002). The Ministry of Railways also plans a new 55 km high-speed rail line link between Beijing Capital Airport and Beijing West Train Station ("Beijing to Build City High-Speed Railway," 1999).

TRANSPORTATION ISSUES IN CHINA'S FUTURE

Transportation remains one of the major barriers to tourism development in much of China but especially in rural areas, even though improvements during the last two decades have been significant. Low efficiency, poor economies of scale, poor management, and the poor safety records of air transport, railways, and road services have hindered tourism development in China. From a national perspective, unbalanced development between the coastal areas and central and western inland continues. In addition, transport networks differ considerably from one province to the next, and connections between modes of transportation within a province are poor and not coordinated, for example, in terms of scheduling. Railway and water transportation play only a minor role for international tourists, and high operating costs and poor management seem to prevail in all transport modes to a varying extent throughout the country.

China received 78 million international visitor arrivals and had about 750 million domestic tourists in 2000 ("Five Favourable Conditions," 2001). In an effort to develop a consumer economy in China, the central government has adopted a "holiday economy" policy and established the "three golden weeks" of Chinese New Year, Labor Day, and National Day when government employees are given week-long holidays ("Development of a High-Speed Transportation System," 2001). Each of these weeks exerts considerable pressure on the public transport system. During the annual forty-day Spring Festival peak transport period, which kicked off on January 9, 2001, 1.66 billion passenger round trips or more were taken by tourists, commuters, and cross-provincial workers, a 3 percent increase from the previous year ("Chinese New Year Transportation," 2001). On February 1, 2001, during the same holiday week, more than four million passengers traveled by train ("China Rail Breaks the Record," 2001). Overall, the number of nationally designated nonworking days have increased from 114 to 120 days, including weekends, public holidays, and annual vacation leave ("Five Favourable Conditions," 2001). The increasing number of nonwork days has contributed to the rising popularity of domestic tourism.

The increase in demand for domestic and outbound tourism raises the question of how to cope with it. In fact, transportation limitations have been one of the major constraints to more rapid growth in domestic tourism (Zhang, 1997). Peak demands on transport are extremely seasonal and, despite the improvements to the transport system since 1978, more transport infrastructure and efficiency improvements are needed. The situation will continue to be a challenge as more people desire to travel. By 2005 China's international inbound visitor arrivals are estimated to reach 85 million while domestic tourist numbers will soar to 1.1 billion ("Tourism Development Objectives," 2001). Even outbound tourists will top 16 million, which represents only 1 percent of the total population (this compares to 35 percent for European countries and 11 percent and 12 percent in South Korea and Japan, respectively (Chen, 2000). By 2020 China is expected to attract 170 million international visitor arrivals per year including day trips (MacLeod, 2001). In addition to expanding the country's transportation infrastructure, China will need to use technology and computerization to meet the demand that these growing numbers will put on the entire transportation system.

A Rolls Royce company report forecasts that the growth rate of air transport in China will be 9.9 percent, twice the world average, and it projects that by the year 2020, 80 million passengers in China will travel by air ("High Growth of Mainland Chinese Air Transport," 2001). However, an oversupply problem has resulted in low passenger loads ("Air Transport Increased in Capacity," 2001) and has triggered a price war. Ironically, there is a serious lack of feeder aircraft (that is, with 100 seats or fewer and a range of less than 1,000 km) to serve the remote and less-visited destinations. Potential certainly exists to have certain feeder routes developed for niche markets ("Bright Future," 2001).

Apart from air transportation, which is used extensively by foreign visitors, the problem of inadequate capacity exists in all other transportation sectors. Unfortunately, transportation improvements that are funded are sometimes poorly done and cause additional expenses in the long run.

"Bean curd" (i.e., substandard) constructions have been a continuing problem for China's roads ("Beijing-Zhuhai Expressway," 2001). New roads are less durable and have a shorter life expectancy than in more developed countries. Such roads, combined with poor maintenance, poor driving attitudes, overloaded trucks, and lack of law enforcement cause many accidents. "Negligence" and "ignorance" are often cited as major causes of traffic accidents. In January 2001, there were four coach accidents that caused 100 injuries in Guangdong Province ("Dangerous Highway," 2001). Unfortunately, these problems extend beyond the country's road network.

Guangzhou's Baiyun Airport, for example, has serious safety problems because beacon lights are blocked by debris and interference by illegally constructed cables nearby ("Vandalism of Baiyun Airport," 2001). In addition, electronic devices located in the vicinity of the airport interfere with aircraft communications and radio navigation systems, affecting communication between air traffic controllers and airplanes ("Guangzhou Civil Aviation Strengthens," 2001).

Domestic air transportation has greatly improved in terms of routes and number of flights; however, management seems to be a continuing problem. International travelers often prefer to use other airlines instead of Chinese carriers because of poor safety records (Yu and Lew, 1997). Flight departures in China are also not properly controlled and many complaints are received about delays and cancellations. Chinese airline personnel typically do not explain reasons for delays and cancellations, which further irritates passengers. Some of the delays and cancellations occur because of the need to consolidate flights due to low passenger loading (average 61 percent in China, compared to 70 percent in most other parts of the world) and the absence of sophisticated weather instruments at some airports. Furthermore, airport transportation departments lack coordination and management skills to ensure punctuality of departures. These problems extend to international flights as well. Because of their reputation for poor service, Chinese airlines have almost no first class and business class sales on international flights, causing considerable losses and the withdrawal of twenty-seven authorized flight services between China and the United States (Chang, 2001). Another reason for the low load factor is the low level of computerization in many areas, including CRS and operations management.

CAAC has proposed to restructure China's airline industry into three mega airlines, Air China, China Eastern, and China Southern, by merging them with other smaller regional airlines ("CAAC Restructuring," 2001). The intention is to reduce the number of low-efficiency, small-scale operations. This will not, however, guarantee more efficient and improved services in the new, consolidated airlines. Corporate joint ventures, greater interaction between China and other countries, more private sector competition, and greater liberalization of aviation are other tools that the government can use to improve both airlines and transportation in general in China. This would be good for tourism. Airlines, in particular, are more than transport business enterprises as they are a source of foreign exchange and trade. They also act as ambassadors and tourism promoters.

China joined the World Trade Organization (WTO) in November 2001. International business and investment opportunities are expected to increase considerably once this happens, which will result in more business visitor arrivals. Together with the development of western China, tourism will be a powerful driving force in these new developments. WTO guidelines and regulations will set new parameters for business activities in China, and will directly challenge the "socialist market economy." China will be required to open more areas for foreign investment, including air transportation for which foreign capital shareholdings will be increasing from a maximum of 35 percent to 49 percent. China's accession to the WTO will also benefit smaller tourism enterprises, leading to further modernization, and it is expected to spur improvements in the quality of service provided. With more involvement in the international arena, China's socialist policy formulation will have to change to cope with the international regulations, standards, and competition.

At the domestic level, air travel will become more popular, especially among residents in the coastal cities who have higher levels of disposable income. Low passenger load factors and the relaxation of price controls will drive airfares down and thus increase its appeal to domestic tour groups and individual travelers. Xiamen, Xi'an, and Chengdu will probably become major domestic air transport hubs. Nevertheless, most Chinese will primarily rely on rail and road transport for interprovincial and shorter travel. Long-distance coach services will proliferate with improvements of the highway system. More people in China will also use private vehicles for leisure and holiday purposes. There are no plans to develop the water transport system or build modernized cruise ports, and water transportation will remain limited in scope, primarily catering to passenger ferry and sightseeing purposes.

The development of and improvements in transportation are vital for China's tourism. A better transportation system will enable the country to operate the transport networks more efficiently and effectively, and facilitate tourism development. Intermodal transportation development and the provision of public transport interchange facilities are necessary to provide smooth connections for passengers. Given the amount of funds being invested by the central government for transportation infrastructure, it would be reasonable to expect that the country's nationwide transport system will be relatively comprehensive and modernized by 2010. The two commodities offered in transport services are goods (aircraft, trains, etc.) and services (frequency, in-flight service, etc.). Without a doubt, the supply of transportation goods in China is increasing and indications are that service quality improvements are not too far behind.

REFERENCES

Agence France-Presse (2001a). "Japan to Press on with Bid to Build Rail Link" *South China Morning Post,* January 23. <http://china.scmp.com/business/ ZZZYFCJVPGC.html>; accessed January 23, 2001.

Agence France-Presse (2001b). "Car-Licence Issues Show 150pc Surge" *South China Morning Post,* February 26. <http://china.scmp.com/economy/ZZZZUKPUPGC. html>; accessed February 26, 2001.

"Air Transport Increased in Capacity" (2001). *Takungpao Daily News,* February 5. <http://www.takungpao.com/news/20010205/big5/ke24.cht>; accessed February 5, 2001 (in Chinese).

Beijing Homeway (2000). "14 Highways to Be Built in West China" *South China Morning Post* (Hong Kong), July 24.

"Beijing Implements Radar Control on Air Transport" (2001). *Takungpao Daily News,* January 16. <http://www.takungpao.com/news/20010116/big5/ke13.cht>; accessed January 18, 2001 (in Chinese).

"Beijing to Build City High-Speed Railway" (1999). *Takungpao Daily News,* August 5. <http://www.takungpao.com/news/19990805/big5/ke12.cht>; accessed August 5, 1999 (in Chinese).

"Beijing-Zhuhai Expressway Becomes a 'Bean Curd' Project" (2001). *Oriental Daily News,* February 14. <http://www.orientaldaily.com.hk/new/new_c1/cnt.html>; accessed February 14, 2001 (in Chinese).

"Bright Future for Chinese-Made Feeder Aircraft" (2001). *Takungpao Daily News,* January 31. <http://www.takungpao.com/news/20010131/big5/ke23.cht>; accessed January 31, 2001 (in Chinese).

"CAAC Restructuring Awaiting Approval" (2001). *Takungpao Daily News,* March 14. <http://www.takungpao.com/news/20010314/big5/ke28.cht>; accessed March 14, 2001 (in Chinese).

"CAAC Will Develop Three Air Traffic Control Centers" (2001). *Takungpao Daily News,* January 12. <http://www.takungpao.com/news/20010112/big5/ke17.cht>; accessed January 13, 2001 (in Chinese).

Chang, Dan Hong (2001). "WTO and Civil Aviation Enterprise Restructuring in China" In *China Civil Aviation Magazine,* February 13. Beijing: China Civil Aviation Magazine (in Chinese).

Chen, Philip N. L. (2000). "The Development of China's Airline Industry" *Ming Pao Monthly,* December, pp. 95-98. Hong Kong: Ming Pao Enterprise (in Chinese).

Chen, Zuoer (2001). Personal communication, interview on Hong Kong Tourism, February 16, 2001 at Hong Kong and Macau Office, Beijing (in Chinese).

"China Aircraft Market Forecast" (2001). *Takungpao Daily News,* February 6. <http://www.takungpao.com/news/20010206/big5/ke17.cht>; accessed February 6, 2001 (in Chinese).

"China Changes Its Transportation Structure" (2001). *Takungpao Daily News,* January 10. <http://www.takungpao.com/news/20010110/big5/ke20.cht>; accessed January 10, 2001 (in Chinese).

"China Civil Air Passenger Volume Ranks World Number Six" (2000). *Takungpao Daily News,* December 15. <http://www.takungpao.com/news/20001215/ big5/ ke16.cht>; accessed December 18, 2000 (in Chinese).

"China Civil Air Passenger Volume Ranks World Number Six" (2001). *Takungpao Daily News,* March 5. <http://www.takungpao.com/news/20010305/big5/ ke24. cht>; accessed March 5, 2001 (in Chinese).

"China Developing a Series of High-Speed Trains" (1999). *Hong Kong Commercial Daily,* July 9. <http://www.hkcd.com.hk/data/tc1_content_c990709c106.html>; accessed July 9, 1999 (in Chinese).

China International Travel Service Hong Kong (2001). How to Go—Via Hong Kong: Sea. <http://www.cits.com.hk/english/how/main.html>; accessed April 18, 2001.

China National Tourism Administration (CNTA) (2000*). The Yearbook of China Tourism Statistics.* Beijing: China Tourism Press.

"China Rail Breaks the Record of 4 Million Passengers" (2001). *Takungpao Daily News,* February 2. <http://www.takungpao.com/news/20010202/big5/zm511.cht>; accessed February 2, 2001 (in Chinese).

"China Rail Builds Eight Information Technology Projects" (2001). *Takungpao Daily News,* February 25. <http://www.takungpao.com/news/20010225/big5/mw13.cht>; accessed February 26, 2001 (in Chinese).

China Travel Net (2002). Train Ticket Enquiry. <http:www.chinatravel1.com/ english/train/traintimetable/formothers.htm> accessed June 5, 2002.

"Chinese New Year Transportation" (2001). *Takungpao Daily News,* January 10. <http://www.takungpao.com/news/20010110/big5/zm63.cht>; accessed January 10, 2001 (in Chinese).

"Chinese-Russian Border Transportation" (2001). *Takungpao Daily News,* January 17. <http://www.takungpao.com/news/20010117/big5/ke14.cht>; accessed January 18, 2001 (in Chinese).

Civil Aviation Administration of China (CAAC) (2000). *Statistical Data on Civil Aviation of China.* Beijing: China National Aviation Publication (in Chinese).

"'Dangerous Highway' Caused 39 Injuries" (2001). *The Sun,* March 27. <http:// www.thesun.com.hk/chanels/news/200010327/20010327031457_0001.html>; accessed March 27, 2001 (in Chinese).

"The Development of a High-Speed Transportation System" (2001). *Takungpao Daily News,* January 16. <http://www.takungpao.com/news/20010116/big5/ke16.cht>; accessed January 18, 2001 (in Chinese).

"Direct Flight Between Hong Kong and Urumqi" (2001). *Takungpao Daily News,* May 11. <http://202.153.114.133/news/20010511/big5/zm74.cht>; accessed May 11, 2001 (in Chinese).

Economic Services Bureau (2001). Policy Responsibilities—Civil Aviation. <http://www.info.gov.hk/esb/respone/13.htm>; accessed April 17, 2001.

The Economist Publications Ltd. (1986). *International Tourism Reports*. No. 3, August, p. 8. London: The Economist Publications Ltd.

"Electrification of Harbin-Dalian Railway" (1999). *Takungpao Daily News*, June 2. <http://www.takungpao.com/news/19990602/big5/ke21.cht>; accessed June 2, 1999 (in Chinese).

"Eleven Pairs of Direct Trains Between Guangzhou and Kowloon" (1999). *Takungpao Daily News*, June 11. <http://www.takungpao.com/news/19990611/big5/gw56.cht>; accessed July 9, 1999 (in Chinese).

"Fastest Passenger Train Unveiled" (1999). *Takungpao Daily News*, July 9. <http://www.takungpao.com/news/19990709/big5/zm10.cht>; accessed July 9, 1999 (in Chinese).

"Five Favourable Conditions to Support China Tourism" (2001). *Chung Hwa Gong Shang Shi Bao* (Beijing), January 12, p. 2 (in Chinese).

"Goodbye to CAAC Manual Tickets" (2001). *Takungpao Daily News*, January 4. <http://www.takungpao.com/news/20010104/big5/ke11.cht>; accessed January 4, 2001 (in Chinese).

"Guangzhou Civil Aviation Strengthens Its Information Management and Communication" (2001). *Takungpao Daily News*, January 3. <http://www.takungpao.com/news/20010103/big5/ke25.cht>; accessed January 3, 2001 (in Chinese).

"Guangzhou Underground Route No. 1 Started Operation" (1999). *The Sun*, June 29. <http://www.the-sun.com.hk/channels/news/19990629/19990629015951_6267.html>; accessed June 29, 1999 (in Chinese).

"Guangzhou-Kowloon Direct Train Increased Service After the Operation of Guangzhou Underground" (1999). *Oriental Daily News*, June 29. <http://www.orientaldaily. com. hk/new/new_c10cnt.html>; accessed June 26, 1999 (in Chinese).

"Guangzhou's New Airport Will Open in 2003" (2001). *Takungpao Daily News*, March 8. <http://www.takungpao.com/news/20010308/big5/ke14.cht>; accessed March 8, 2001 (in Chinese).

"Guangzhou's New Airport Runway Design Approved" (2001). *Takungpao Daily News*, January 15. <http://www.takungpao.com/news/20010115/big5/ke25.cht>; accessed January 18, 2001 (in Chinese).

Guo, Chairen (Ed.) (1999). *People's Republic of China Yearbook*. Beijing: PRC Yearbook.

He, Guangwei (2001). Personal communication, interview on tourism development in China, February 16, 2001 at Kun Lun Hotel, Beijing (in Chinese).

"High Growth of Mainland Chinese Air Transport Market" (2001). *Takungpao Daily News*, January 4. <http://www.takungpao.com/news/20010104/big5/ke16.cht>; accessed January 4, 2001 (in Chinese).

"Investment of 800 Billion in Road Construction in the West" (2001). *Ming Pao Daily News*, March 31. <http://www.mingpaonews.com/20010331/cfd1r.htm>; accessed April 2, 2001 (in Chinese).

Kowloon-Canton Railway Corporation (2001a). East Rail Domestic and Lo Wu Services—Introduction. <http://www.kcrc.com/eng/service/erdintro.html>; accessed April 11, 2001.

Kowloon-Canton Railway Corporation (2001b). East Rail Domestic and Lo Wu Services—Train Schedules. <http://www.kcrc.com/eng/service/erdtrs.html>; accessed April 11, 2001.

Li, Raymond (2001). "China Southern Pays Compensation for Secret Deal" *South China Morning Post*, January 18. <http://china.scmp.com/business/ZZZE80JVPGC.html>; accessed January 19, 2001.

"Lintingyang Bridge Is Under Consideration" (2001). *Takungpao Daily News*, February 14. <http://www.takungpao.com/news/20010214/big5/gw44.cht>; accessed February 14, 2001 (in Chinese).

"Long-Distance Coach Services Between Beijing and Shanghai" (2001). *Takungpao Daily News*, January 16. <http://www.takungpao.com/news/20010116/big5/ke15.cht>; accessed January 18, 2001 (in Chinese).

"Lufthansa Airlines Starts Shanghai and Frankfurt Air Services" (2001). *Takungpao Daily News*, February 28. <http://www.takungpao.com/news/20010228/big5/ke26.cht>; accessed February 28, 2001 (in Chinese).

MacLeod, Calum (2001). "Mainland Opens Up to World Tourism" *South China Morning Post*, February 11. <http://china.scmp.com/lifestyle/ZZZB5VKVPGC.html>; accessed February 13, 2001.

"Magnetic Levitation Railway Between Shanghai and Hangzhou" (2001). *Takungpao Daily News*, February 8. <http://www.takungpao.com/news/20010208/big5/zm80.cht>; accessed February 9, 2001 (in Chinese).

Mak, L. M. Barry (1989). The Development of Tourism in China. Unpublished Master of Science thesis. Scottish Hotel School: University of Strathclyde.

Middleton, Victor T. C. (1988). *Marketing in Travel and Tourism*. London: Heinemann.

"New Train on the Rails Next Month" (1999). *Hong Kong Standard* (Hong Kong), September 3.

Ng, Andy. (2001). Personal communication, checking on airfare between Beijing and Shanghai, April 18, Hong Kong (in Chinese).

Ng, Eric, Barling, Russell and Lo, Joseph (2002). "CAAC Eyes Foreign Stakes." *South China Morning Post*, June 5, Hong Kong; <http://www.wisenews.net>; password protected, accessed June 6, 2002.

Ng, Eric and Reuters (2001). "Watchdog Lowers Ceiling to Rein in Airfare Rises" *South China Morning Post*, February 7. <http://china.scmp.com/business/ZZZB6HKVPGC.html>; accessed February 7, 2001.

O'Neill, Mark (2002). "Hyundai Confident of Market Potential." *South China Morning Post*, May 2, Hong Kong; <http://www.wisenews.net>; password protected, accessed June 6, 2002.

"Outstanding Performance of Shenzhen Rail Transportation" (2001). *Takungpao Daily News,* February 28. <http://www.takungpao.com/news/20010228/big5/ke14.cht>; accessed February 28, 2001 (in Chinese).

Page, Stephen J. (1999). *Transport and Tourism.* Essex: Addison Wesley Longman.

"Pan-Asian Railway in Yunnan" (2001). *Takungpao Daily News,* April 10. <http://www.takungpao.com/news/20010410/big5/ke21.cht>; accessed April 10, 2001 (in Chinese).

Pearce, P. L. (1982). *The Social Psychology of Tourist Behaviour.* Oxford: Pergamon.

Pun, Pamela (2002). "Express Opening for New Rail Line." *Hong Kong iMail,* May 4, <http://www.wisenews.net>; password protected, accessed June 6, 2002.

"Qinghai-Tibet Railway Costs 20 Billion" (2001). *Takungpao Daily News,* March 15. <http://www.takungpao.com/news/20010315/big5/mw14.cht>; accessed March 15, 2001 (in Chinese).

"Qinghai-Tibet Railway Will Not Destroy the Ecology" (2001). *Takungpao Daily News,* February 25. <http://www.takungpao.com/news/20010225/big5/mw15.cht>; accessed February 26, 2001 (in Chinese).

"Railway Development in Western China" (2001). *China Daily* (Beijing), February 8 (in Chinese).

"Regular Cruise Services Between Hainan and Vietnam" (2001). *Takungpao Daily News,* April 17. <http://www.takungpao.com/news/20010417/big5/ke13.cht>; accessed April 17, 2001 (in Chinese).

Reuters (2001). "Transrapid Seals Shanghai High-Speed Rail Contract" *South China Morning Post,* January 22. <http://china.scmp.com/business/ZZZD17OUPGC.html>; accessed January 22, 2001.

"Ride Taxi with Credit Cards" (2001). *Ming Pao Daily News,* February 23. <http://www.mingpaonews.com/20010223/ccj1r.htm>; accessed February 26, 2001 (in Chinese).

"Road Ranks Number One in China's Passenger Transportation" (1999). *Hong Kong Commercial Daily,* May 31. <http://www.hkcd.com.hk/hkce/backup1/data/tc1_ content_c990531c104.html>; accessed June 1, 1999 (in Chinese).

"Seventy-Eight Coach Companies Operate China-Hong Kong Services" (2001). *Ming Pao Daily News,* April 12. <http://www.mingpaonews.com/20010412/gnb2r.htm>; accessed April 17, 2001 (in Chinese).

"Shanghai Develops Hydrogen-Power Sightseeing Coaches" (2001). *Takungpao Daily News,* February 24. <http://www.takungpao.com/news/20010224/big5/zm68.cht>; accessed February 26, 2001 (in Chinese).

"Shenzhen Plans Vast Rail Scheme" (2002). *Hong Kong iMail,* April 29, <http://www.wisenews.net>; password protected, accessed June 6, 2002.

"Steady Growth of China's Civil Aviation" (2001). *Takungpao Daily News,* February 12. <http://www.takungpao.com/news/20010212/big5/ke20.cht>; accessed February 12, 2001 (in Chinese).

"Ten Nations' Understanding of the Trans-Asian Railway" (1999). *Ming Pao Daily News,* May 30. <http://www.mingpao.com/newspaper/archives/99-53-/taa1h.htm>; accessed June 1, 1999 (in Chinese).

"The Tenth Five-Year-Plan" (2001). *Ming Pao Daily News,* February 13. <http://www.mingpaonews.com/20010213/caa1hr.htm>; accessed February 15, 2001 (in Chinese).

"Tourism Development Objectives of the Tenth Five-Year Plan in China" (2001). *People's Daily* (Beijing), January 9, p. 3 (in Chinese).

"Vandalism of Baiyun Airport Safety Facilities" (2001). *Ming Pao Daily News,* January 26. <http://www.mingpaonews.com/20010126/ccb1hr.htm>; accessed January 30, 2001 (in Chinese).

Yu, Lawrence and Lew, Alan. A. (1997). Airline Liberalization and Development in China. *Pacific Tourism Review* 1(2):129-136.

Zhang, Qin Yang; Liu, Wen Sheng; and Wang, Bai Xue. (2001). "Market Analysis and Forecast of China Civil Aircraft" *People's Daily* (Beijing), February 9, 2001, p. 3.

Zhang, W. (1997). "China's Domestic Tourism: Impetus, Development and Trends" *Tourism Management,* 18(8): 565-572.

Zhou, Jamila (2000). "Beijing-Shanghai Expressway to Improve Traffic Flow" *South China Morning Post* (Hong Kong), December 19.

Chapter 11

An Assessment of Theme Park Development in China

John Ap

The theme park industry is relatively new in China, with some of the early parks developed only in the mid-1980s. By 1998, however, there were an estimated 2,000 to 2,500 amusement or theme park attractions (Xu, 1998; Yang cited in Xu, 1998). Some of the early large-scale parks were, in fact, amusement parks, offering rides and entertainment. Probably the first and most widely recognized theme park on the Chinese mainland was Splendid China, containing miniature replicas of major national attractions of the country, which opened in 1989 at Shenzhen. Despite the success of some parks and tremendous growth in the number of theme parks and amusement attractions in China since the mid-1980s, the industry has been fraught with problems. Many parks have not been successful from a financial and operational viewpoint, with attendance much lower than projected, and by the mid to late 1990s the industry was facing crisis. The failure of many parks and attractions has served to damage the image of the industry and tarnish its reputation. It has left many in China asking, "What happened?" Why did so many theme parks and attractions fail?

This chapter briefly traces the development of theme parks in China and examines reasons for the spectacular growth that occurred during the 1990s and issues affecting the industry today. Besides looking at the elements of success for some parks, reasons why the industry ex-

The author would like to thank Pamela Ho, King Chong, and Qi Ping Shu for their assistance in this study. The financial assistance provided by the International Association of Amusement Parks and Attractions for the evaluation study on theme park development in China is gratefully acknowledged.

perienced turmoil and why many projects failed are also examined. It is important to learn from the mistakes and to provide industry and government authorities with recommendations to ensure that future developments are successfully developed and operated.

THEME PARK DEVELOPMENT

The origins of modern theme parks are often traced to Disneyland, which opened in 1955 in Anaheim, California, but it was not for another thirty years or so that the concept took hold in China. The types of themes adopted in China included folk customs and legends (e.g., Journey to the West parks), history and culture (e.g., Splendid China and ethnic folk culture villages), animals (e.g., sea worlds and wildlife safari parks), sports and competitions, science, technology, and fantasy/amusement (e.g., Happy Valley) (Deng cited in Xu 1998; Bao, 1995). Most theme park development in China has concentrated in the major populated areas around the Pearl River (Guangzhou) and Yangtze River (Shanghai) delta areas, in the Beijing-Tianjin area and major regional cities such as Chengdu. Bao (1995) found that China's theme parks possessed the following characteristics:

1. They are a type of property run as a business enterprise with a focus on amusement and entertainment.
2. They have a specific and understandable theme with facilities, operations, and the environment of the park conforming to that theme.
3. They enable guests to escape from the routine of everyday life.
4. They are usually large and involve high levels of investment.
5. They have admission fees regarded as relatively high compared to the income level of most Chinese.

Zhang cited in Xu (1998) noted that the distinctions among different types of theme parks in China have become harder to delineate as the boundaries between theme parks, amusement parks, entertainment centers, and museums have been blurred by efforts to serve the multiple purposes of entertainment, education, and tourism. In the Chinese context, theme parks have been defined as man-made stages and properties for entertainment and recreation that feature a specific subject (Bao, 1995) and as man-made attractions that cater to tourism, recreation, and entertainment activities (Deng, 1998). Thus, the term theme park is often used interchangeably with man-made attractions.

In terms of life cycle, tourism in China, especially outbound and domestic tourism, is still at a relatively early stage and is neither as sophisticated nor as well developed as may be found in other developing countries. Thus, China has a lot of catching up to do to become more attractive and competitive in the international marketplace. In trying to catch up, one common tactic has been to copy theme parks that have been successfully developed either elsewhere in the country or internationally. Splendid China in Shenzhen is one such example.

Following a visit by Ma Zhimin, President of China Travel Service, Limited to the Miniature City Madurodam in the Netherlands, he pursued the development of a similar attraction based upon the major scenic and man-made attractions of China. Splendid China opened in 1989. It was China's first modern theme park and one of the country's most successful, receiving 3.1 million visitors in its first year of operation and recouping its capital investment within nine months. The Overseas Chinese Town Group, Ltd., which had developed Splendid China in collaboration with China Travel Service, Ltd., subsequently developed more theme parks, such as the China Folk Culture Villages (also in Shenzhen) in 1991 and Windows of the World in 1995. Both of these were successful ventures. The China Folk Culture Villages is a cultural attraction where the dwellings, customs, and arts of some fifty-five ethnic minorities from all over China are featured, and Windows of the World features miniature versions of the world's major wonders, historic sites, and scenic sights. The phenomenal success of Splendid China and China Folk Culture Villages heralded the beginning of the boom in theme park development that spread rapidly across the country. In addition, Xia (personal communication, December 6, 1999) noted that the success of a Journey to the West theme park (based on the legendary story of a monkey god and Buddhist monk) in Shijiazhuang, Hebei Province, which recouped its investment in approximately one year, led many others to jump on the theme park bandwagon. Consequently, about 260 Journey to the West parks were developed throughout the country.

Four theme parks are located in Overseas Chinese Town (OCT), a five-square-kilometer area of land in the Shenzhen Special Economic

Zone to the immediate north of Hong Kong. They are Splendid China (opened in 1989), China Folk Culture Villages (1991), Windows of the World (1995), and Happy Valley (1997). The parent company, the Overseas Chinese Town Group, Ltd., is a publicly listed company with interests in electronics, real estate, and tourism. Overseas Chinese Town was originally conceptualized as a property development project involving residential and factory development specifically targeted to overseas Chinese investors. Tourism was not part of the scheme until Ma visited the Netherlands, seized upon the theme park idea, and changed the direction of the master plan (Wang, personal communication, March 19, 2000). The initial success of the OCT theme parks was quite an achievement and they quickly became a model for theme park development throughout China. In retrospect, their initial success created false and unrealistic expectations about theme park development, which according to Wang (personal communication, March 19, 2000) and Zhong cited in Xu (1998) included the following:

- Theme parks guarantee high returns on investments.
- Simply operating a park will earn profits.
- Capital investment would be recouped within two to three years.
- Replication or copying a successful theme park will ensure success.
- Consumer demand for theme park attractions is unlimited.
- All theme parks are equally attractive.
- The larger the park, the better (without regard to project feasibility and viability).

These misconceptions were typical of the "supply-led" mentality that prevailed for much of the 1990s where the maxim was "build it and the people will come." However, China's consumer market was changing; people were becoming increasingly sophisticated and demanding value for money. Marketing and management, however, were not recognized as important factors influencing successful theme park operations. The result was widespread decline and failure throughout China's theme park industry.

Although the OCT theme parks have been quite successful, they also have their share of problems. Annual attendance has tapered from an all-time high of a combined 7.5 million at the first two parks in 1992 to a low of 4.3 million for all four parks in 1997. The experience of the OCT parks, as well as similar experiences in other parks around the country, indicates that visiting a theme park is a once-only affair for most of the Chinese market (Bao 1995; Lou, personal communication, December 6, 1999). Bao (1995) suggested that the life cycle of a theme park in China is characterized by reaching the stagnation stage within the first year or two when the peak of the cycle occurs, followed by decline in subsequent years or possibly rejuvenation if new facilities or development are provided. By contrast, it is well known in the theme park industry that repeat visitation plays a critical role in successful theme park operations.

A major reason cited for the lack of repeat visitations, and the resulting short life cycle of Chinese theme parks, is the high admission fees and other costs associated with visiting most theme parks relative to the average earnings in China. The typical entrance fee into a theme park is around RMB 100 yuan per person and the cost for a family of three, including one child, is approximately RMB 250 yuan, which is nearly half the RMB 600 yuan average monthly wage for 70 percent of China's workers (Wang, personal communication, March 19, 2000). Visiting a theme park is a luxury experience for most mainland Chinese.

Unfortunately, official statistics of the number of theme parks and related attractions in China have not been collected. No government authority has responsibility or jurisdiction over theme parks, although the Department of Planning and Development within the China National Tourism Administration (CNTA) handles many theme park matters. This situation has most probably arisen because the government's policy of promoting a market economy with socialist characteristics has resulted in less government involvement in local business ventures. Also, because many Chinese theme park developers saw little or no need to market their projects, they had little contact with tourism authorities.

Theme park development in China has been a relatively recent phenomenon that has been characterized by rapid growth following the successful experiences of the OCT parks and the Journey to the West park in Shijiazhuang. This initial success created false expectations and led to an oversupply of parks that often replicated the successful ones. A visit to a theme park would be regarded as a luxury experience for most mainland Chinese and the Chinese parks were also characterized by a short life cycle, which lacked repeat visitation. Another aspect has been an absence of the monitoring of theme park development.

ELEMENTS OF SUCCESS

The initial success of the OCT theme parks can be attributed to a number of factors (Bao, 1995, 1999; Ma, 1999; Wang, personal communication, March 19, 2000; Xia, personal communication, December 6, 1999; Zhong, personal communication, December 3, 1999). First is the management philosophy and culture of the OCT Group, which consists of the "Three Insists":

1. *Insist on quality*—it has to be high to meet tourists' needs and to provide safety, hygiene, and comfort.
2. *Have your own characteristics*—develop and maintain distinctiveness based upon a clear theme. Each OCT park has its own theme and distinctive features.
3. *Maintain your development*—ongoing enhancements in the construction and management of the attractions must be made, along with a regular program of maintenance and repairs.

The second key to success is timing. OCT's parks were the first of their type to open in China and as market leaders, they enjoyed an advantage compared to other similar attractions subsequently developed elsewhere in the country. The third factor was their location in the Shenzhen Special Economic Zone, which lies within the Pearl River Delta region comprising Hong Kong, Macao, and Guangdong Province. This is one of the richest areas in China with salaries in both Shenzhen and Guangdong among the highest in the country. In addition, Shenzhen is a "frontier town" that became nationally recognized following a visit by the former Premier Deng Xiao Ping who praised its development. Fourth, related to its regional location, the OCT theme parks have good accessibility because they are located on a main thoroughfare in Shenzhen, approximately twenty kilometers from the downtown and railway station area. Fifth, the OCT Group adopted a Hong Kong-style market-oriented management approach. Being adjacent to the Hong Kong Special Administrative Region

(SAR), the OCT Group took conscientious steps to adopt some of the best practices that market-oriented management had to offer.

The sixth factor was proper planning, careful attention to detail, and maintaining the authenticity of the cultural aspects of Splendid China and the Chinese Folk Culture Villages. In this regard, professional and expert advice was sought when planning and developing the parks. When developing Splendid China, the exhibits were replicated as authentically as possible, and craftsmen and artisans from the respective local areas were used. To maintain authenticity of the folk villages, personnel recruited to work and perform in the villages were from the respective ethnic minority groups, and materials used to construct the village were imported directly from each area of the ethnic minorities represented. The seventh, and final, factor was that the OCT Group linked up with a major tour operator, China Travel Service, Ltd., which had a share in the group, provided the necessary expertise for the development and operation of its tourism portfolio, and helped to direct tour groups to the new attractions.

Another of the more successful operations has been the Suzhou Amusement Land, which presently includes two attractions—Water World and Happiness World, opened in 1995 and 1997, respectively (Duan, personal communication, December 7, 1999). According to its Deputy General Manager, Duan Su, their successes were attributed to:

1. conducting detailed research into the needs of target customers and, in particular, developing a good understanding of the Shanghainese, their main market;
2. adopting clear-cut market and theme orientations;
3. location at the intersection of three provinces;
4. good management based upon the philosophy that "Life Lies in Activity," focusing on the importance of dynamism in theme park operations;
5. the provision of ongoing investment in facilities; and
6. adopting a vigorous marketing and promotion program.

In addition, when planning and designing the park, the park managers paid close attention to the design and facilities in order to accommodate the Chinese situation, such as adopting an entry fee structure that reflected the lower standard of living in China. As can be seen, the elements contributing to the Suzhou Amusement Land were quite similar to those of the OCT Group's theme parks. In many ways, they are models of the successful development and operation of theme park and amusement attractions (cf. Themed Entertainment Association, 1999; Goeldner, Ritchie, and McIntosh, 1999; Inskeep, 1991; Gee, Choy, and Makens, 1984). As noted, however, most Chinese theme parks have not been developed upon sound, textbook management models.

REASONS FOR FAILURE

An estimated 80 to 95 percent of the theme parks in China have been losing money ("An Empty American Dream," 1999; Wang, personal communication, March 19, 2000), including most of the over 200 Journey to the West theme parks (Qian, 1999). As a result, billions of RMB yuan in investments have either been lost or put at serious risk. Media headlines such as "China No Fun Ride for Theme Park Developers" (1999) and "What Fun: China's Theme Parks Aren't Amusing for Many Investors" (Smith, 1998) all point to an embarrassing situation. This unfortunate state of affairs has tarnished China's investment image and placed a dark cloud over the prospects of the industry. The spate of theme park failures in the 1990s has led to much soul searching by government officials, developers, industry operators, and academics in China as they try to determine why the failures occurred and how they can be prevented in the future.

To address these problems and issues, two conferences were held in 1998. One was organized by the Department of Social Development, State Development Planning Commission, and the Planning Department of the Hubei Provincial Government in May. The China National Tourism Administration (CNTA) organized a national conference on theme park development in June. I embarked upon an assessment of theme park development in late 1999. The information presented next is a synthesis of these conferences and research. In addition, a case study based on the Shanghai experience will be presented to identify and illustrate some basic and fundamental errors that have plagued theme park development in China (based on Ding, Lou, and Xia, personal communications, December 6, 1999).

Shanghai

Shanghai has a population of 13 million and is the business and financial capital of the Chinese mainland with one of the highest standards of living in China. Given these characteristics, one might expect that developing a theme park for this large and affluent community would not be difficult. With only one major amusement park in the Shanghai area (the Shanghai Amusement Park) in the early 1990s, it was not surprising that several developers were drawn to this market, and by 1996 at least seven new theme parks or attractions were under construction. At least three of these parks were foreign joint venture projects.

- The American Dream Park—with a U.S. theme (U.S. investor)
- Frobelland—a German-themed park (Taiwan investor)
- Universal Park—based on an around-the-world theme similar to Shenzhen's Window of the World
- Two Journey to the West theme parks
- Cosmos Park
- The Euro-American Amusement Park (Hong Kong investor)

The proliferation of these developments in the mid-1990s made Shanghai the center of China's theme park mania. However, within a few years (by the end of 1998) many of these attractions had run into problems. By 2000, all but one of these parks had closed and the closure of the last was imminent. The American Dream Park, which had cost US$50 million to develop, opened in 1996 and was expected to attract 30,000 visitors per day, according to the Toronto-based *Financial Post* ("An Empty American Dream," 1999). On the day that the *Financial Post* reporter visited the park in 1999, there were a total of twelve visitors. Entrance tickets were initially priced at RMB 100 yuan (about US$12.50) but had subsequently been dropped to RMB 20 yuan to attract customers.

Frobelland, which also opened in 1996, was named after the German educator who developed the kindergarten concept. Its location is a two-hour drive west of Shanghai. Smith (1998) reported that this park was projected to bring in 15,000 visitors per day, but instead was lucky to draw 150 visitors, and on some days had no visitors. In 1999, the Taiwanese investor walked away from the project leaving employees unpaid. A few days before the National Day Holiday that year, the workers went on a rampage, looting the park and taking anything of value. Armed government troops were sent in to restore order and secure the park, which was then closed down.

Universal Park, based on an around-the-world theme, opened on a trial basis, but its reception was so soft that within six months it closed down altogether. Construction of Cosmos Park commenced in 1996, but was abandoned following the poor performance of the Shanghai area's theme parks. The Euro-American Amusement Park, which was designed as a combined theme and water park project, started construction in 1996, but the principal investor died and the project floundered. Construction of the park was eventually completed; however, by 2000 it was barely surviving and the plans were to close it down. The two Journey to the West theme parks closed within a year of their opening.

Throughout China, and indeed the rest of the world, the question was asked: why have so many parks failed in such a prosperous and affluent part of the country? The answer is not simple, but can be categorized under the three headings of planning, development, and operations.

Planning

Inappropriate Location

Most of the Shanghai parks were located on the outskirts of the city where land for large-scale development was available and relatively cheap. This created a problem of accessibility as it was not easy for guests to reach these parks. Public transport was very limited and the travel time from Shanghai was at least one or two hours. According to Smith (1998):

> Amusement parks often fail because of mistaken assumptions of similarities between China and other countries. For instance, investors typically plan their ferris wheels and haunted house an hour or more outside major cities, as is customary in the West. But few people in China yet have cars. This forces parks to rely on group trips organized by companies, government offices and schools. (p. 1)

Repetition and Copying of Parks

As mentioned previously, the misconception was that all one had to do was to replicate a successful theme park and it too would make a profit. Little or no consideration was given to incorporating new or innovative facilities to give the park some individuality and distinctiveness. This led to a rampant oversupply of parks and excessive competition for attractions seeking to lure patronage from the same target market.

Inadequate Feasibility Studies

Park feasibility studies were often simplistic, unrealistic, inaccurate, and lacking in detail. In some instances, feasibility studies were not even conducted. In other instances, investors or developers did not seek the advice of the relevant experts and professionals involved in the tourism industry. Many of the inaccuracies in these studies occurred because projections were based upon the direct application of figures obtained from existing and successful parks, without considering the local situation and conditions (Bao, 1995). Some well-known foreign consultants who lacked an understanding of the particularities of the China market and had failed to customize their work accordingly also gave wrong advice. The problem of inappropriate location, cited previously, is a classic example of the failure to take into consideration the local situation.

Ineffective Evaluation of Projects

Evaluation meetings are often held to assess, endorse, or approve major development projects. Various sources *(that shall remain confidential)* have suggested that most of the failed parks did not have properly constituted evaluation meetings, and projects were not evaluated very rigorously. The meetings usually did not include economists or experienced theme park managers or operators and were typically treated as a formality with the decision already a foregone conclusion. In many instances, panel members were not provided with documentation on the project beforehand and were expected to assess the material during the meeting and return it at the end of the meeting. In addition, the information provided usually did not include detailed market and financial data and, at times, contained flawed data. However, a lack of experienced theme park professionals in China also compounded the problem in trying to find suitably qualified members to serve on the evaluation panels.

Lack of Market Knowledge and Research

Closely related to the issue of low quality development is the lack of understanding of the market. In general, the role and importance of marketing is not well recognized in China because it has been a supply-led economy (driven by government edicts) for so long. Consequently, most theme parks did not undertake a comprehensive market research study to identify customers, target segments, identify their needs and preferences, nor assess market feasibility.

Poor Design Planning

One common aspect of many failed theme parks was poor design and layout, with large distances between attractions. Without an efficient and relatively compact layout, it can be difficult to generate a lively atmosphere, especially on a slow day. This created an unnecessary inconvenience for guests who had to walk some distance from one section of the park to another. During hot or wet weather (both common in Shanghai's summer months) the inconvenience was further exacerbated.

Lack of Effective Control

A frequent comment about theme park development in China in general has been the lack of effective government control and coordination at the macro level, which has allowed the unchecked development of theme parks. Consequently, identical parks were locating in close proximity to one another and the oversupply situation was not addressed. One could argue that the failure of so many poorly planned parks demonstrated the success of liberal market economics in weeding out inefficient business activities. But in a developing country such as China, the inefficiencies of a laissez-faire approach to major infrastructure development are ill afforded.

Development

Low-Quality Development

The construction of unattractive projects that are not up to international standards created many low-quality theme parks (Yoshii, cited in Zoltak, 1998). This was often due to a low level of available investment capital relative to the size of the proposal. Lou (personal communication, December 6, 1999), for example, noted that the investment level for the Shanghai projects based on an investment/land ratio was relatively low at RMB 250,000 yuan per land unit compared to theme parks in Japan where the investment level was RMB 7 million yuan per land unit.

A related issue is the lack of maintenance and proper upkeep, which compounds the problem of an initially poor quality development. Inadequate attention to maintenance is a common problem with most development projects throughout the Chinese mainland and is not restricted to theme parks only. A third consideration is that many facilities and rides were old, even in a new park. Rides were often acquired secondhand. Smith (1998) reported, for example, that some of the rides at American Dream Park were built in the 1950s. All of these factors contributed to a low level of quality from the first day the parks opened, which detracted from the visitor experience at a time when Chinese consumers were becoming increasingly sophisticated and demanding of higher standards. In an assessment of China's theme parks, the *Financial Post* ("An Empty American Dream," 1999) pointed out:

> the quality has been so poor at so many places that several hundred have already gone out of business. Even worse, potential consumers expected to flock to the parks have gone sour to the notion of theme parks altogether. (p. C12)

Lack of Interactivity and Dynamism

With the lack of experience in theme park operations, many parks were devoid of a dynamic atmosphere and the attractions did not create a lively or fun atmosphere. Rides and displays lacked the novelty and surprise typically found in Western theme and amusement parks, which are constantly working to improve themselves and outdo their competition. Thus, the theme park visit in China ended up being a rather dull and boring experience. The quality of entertainment and shows has also been criticized as being of a low standard, which further adds to this problem.

Management/Operations

Poor Management

Poorly trained and unskilled management is a common problem in China and management staff were often unqualified or lacked experience in running a theme park business. In some cases, accusations of nepotism were made as governmental officials used their influence to have unqualified friends or relatives appointed to management positions in exchange for expediting permits and reviews.

Naiveté of Investors, Joint Venture Partners, and Local Officials

Many of the investors and developers who became involved in theme park development were also novices to the industry and, therefore, highly susceptible to believing the exaggerated claims of its potential. For foreign investors, particularly Westerners, the business mantra of "If I can sell just one item to every Chinese . . ." often attracted their involvement in a theme park project. However, without a sound and intimate knowledge of the complex and changing Chinese market, people could easily get their fingers (and money) burned, and many did. For local officials (who were often also joint investors), foreign investors were seen more as "cash cows" than as partners. When financial difficulties arose, local officials were known to demand compensation for the infrastructure support they provided and threatened the withdrawal of the generous tax breaks that were initially offered for the development.

Political Interference

Because of the blurred lines between government and business activities in China, it was relatively easy for government officials at varying levels to exert strong influence over the development process. For example, "independent experts," who were relied upon to provide objective and informed assessments upon which official opinions would be based, were often swayed by government bureaucrats to judge theme park proposals favorably. Thus, projects that were improperly conceived, had questionable feasibility, or lacked sufficient information to enable a proper evaluation were approved anyway. This occured, in part, because government officials are evaluated by the amount of foreign investment they are able to attract. Consequently, they are primarily concerned with the inputs to the system and do not really bother with the outputs (or performance) of the venture. This constant pursuit of foreign investment by government officials has a detrimental effect upon the development of theme parks because the investment itself is made paramount, at the expense of providing a viable and profitable attraction that meets the public's needs for entertainment and society's need for economic development. The signing of yet another agreement in 1999 by the Jia Ding local government authority outside of Shanghai for a new theme park project next door to the failing American Dream Park is evidence that this situation has not changed despite the lessons of the 1990s (Xia, personal communication, December 6, 1999).

The list of problems cited in relation to the Shanghai theme park development experience would certainly be applicable to most other parts of China and, in varying degrees, to some other industries. They are certainly not unique to Shanghai, although the scope and magnitude was more pronounced, allowing for a more concise understanding of the elements involved in the success and failure of this industry in China in the 1990s.

PROSPECTS FACING THE THEME PARK INDUSTRY IN THE TWENTY-FIRST CENTURY

As China's prosperity increases and its people become more affluent, domestic tourism will be further stimulated and the demand for theme park development will continue to grow and evolve. According to Ding (personal communication, December 6, 1999), the potential exists for new theme parks that are of high quality and are adapted to the unique characteristics of the China market. Government agencies, such as the powerful State Development Planning Commission and the CNTA, have been quite concerned about the state of affairs in theme park development and have taken steps to address the problem. Zhong (personal communication, December 3, 1999), an official from the CNTA who has responsibility for theme parks, has advocated that the central government should play an active role in guiding theme park development through:

1. providing planning advice and guidance;
2. collecting, compiling, and distributing theme park information for reference by developers when making investment decisions;
3. regulating the construction and operation of theme parks;
4. training managers and professional operators; and
5. publishing and disseminating relevant information that will increase the exchange of information.

This advice has been heeded and draft guidelines, which will cover theme park development under the proposed "Standard Rating System for Quality Tourist Attractions," have been developed by the China National Tourism Administration (CNTA, 1999). This is a first step on the road to recovery. If the government is able to assume and facilitate the roles mentioned, it will certainly help the industry become stronger and more profitable in the future. Examples of successful and bad practices have been documented, and the bad practices identified certainly provide a basis for recommendations on what needs to be done to develop a successful theme park or attraction. These recommendations include the following.

Planning

- Prepare and establish guidelines for theme park and attractions development.
- Coordinate theme park and attraction development (by the central government) to avoid duplication and to monitor oversupply.
- Establish a national theme park and attraction database, which inventories existing parks, those under construction, and proposed projects.
- Locate parks and attractions in areas that are in close proximity to the major domestic markets, which are easily accessible or can be readily serviced by public transport.

- Develop clear and distinctive themes for each project in order to minimize duplication.
- Conduct detailed and properly prepared market research and feasibility studies to develop a good understanding of consumers and to identify appropriate target markets.
- Prepare market forecasts that are realistic and based upon local conditions rather than using the forecasts of successfully operating theme parks elsewhere in the country.
- Conduct detailed and properly prepared financial feasibility studies, which incorporate not only the capital inputs of a project but also its outputs and performance from a financial perspective. Measures used to assess performance include the preparation of profit and loss statements over a five to ten year period, cash flow statements over a five to ten year period, and calculation of the return on investment.
- Use independent professional and expert advice. Avoid using plans and feasibility studies that have been prepared in-house for major decisions and/or the final decision concerning the project.
- Seek the advice and input of an experienced theme park operator when preparing the plans and designing the project.
- Appoint independent and appropriately qualified evaluation panel members to assess and evaluate the project plans and feasibility studies.
- Adopt a compact design to create dynamism and atmosphere within the park, and to ensure that distance between attractions is not too great.

Development

- Develop parks and attractions to a high standard and, wherever possible, to international standards. Guests are now more sophisticated and expect to receive value for money.
- Develop a regular maintenance program and set aside funds for such purposes.
- Avoid the use of dated secondhand rides that lack novelty and are not attractive to guests; be creative and innovative.

Operations

- Appoint appropriately qualified and experienced management staff who understand business principles and the market system.
- Identify and adopt a mission statement and a corporate philosophy.
- Adopt an effective management structure to achieve the aims of the mission statement and its application in operating the park.
- Establish effective orientation and training programs. Ongoing training programs should be developed and provided for all levels of staff.
- Examine the feasibility of establishing a theme park executive development program to provide training for theme park professionals and managers.
- Prepare and implement an effective marketing program to promote the theme park. This also includes target marketing, adoption of various pricing policies, and the establishment of a good network of distributors for the product.
- Develop partnerships and strategic alliances between parks, attractions, travel and tourism businesses and organizations, and sponsorship partners.
- Examine means to identify and develop the repeat market. The "once only" phenomenon of theme park visitation in China needs to be investigated and consideration of a range of measures should be examined to develop the repeat market, including special events, pricing schemes, and product renewals and innovations.

Despite the challenges and problems experienced, some parks have been successful. Mistakes have been made and, hopefully, lessons have been learned. Because of the unique social and economic environment in which China's theme parks were developed in the 1990s, clear-cut recommendations can be developed that have implications for similar operation well beyond China's borders. Existing and prospective theme park operators in China, as well as other key players in the industry, need to reflect upon the mistakes made. Any major new parks developed in the future will need to model the successful business practices that continue to benefit the more successful parks. Gone are the days of the rampant replication and copying of parks in inappropriate locations. Future parks will be larger, more attractive, of higher quality, and developed to international standards. There will be fewer parks but they shall be strategically located. This will become the norm as the unprofitable parks gradually close and the industry becomes more efficient. The creation of a positive environment that facilitates properly planned and feasible theme parks is necessary before the industry gets back on its feet. Intervention by the central government at the macro level will be needed. In conclusion, the boom and bust of the Chinese theme park industry in the 1990s has certainly been a roller coaster ride. As the industry picks itself up from the bust, the ride to the top again will be a slow but cautious one. The theme park industry is the business of fun and it is time for the fun to begin once again.

REFERENCES

An Empty American Dream: Once Misty-Eyed Over the Potential Demand for Theme Parks in China, Foreign Investors Are Getting a Reality Check (1999). *The Financial Post* (Toronto), August 5, p. C12.

Bao, Jigang (1995). Theme Park Development—An Example of Shenzhen. Unpublished PhD Dissertation. Department of Geography, Zhongshan University (in Chinese).

Bao, Jigang (1999). Personal communication, interview, December 10, 1999.

China No Fun Ride for Theme Park Developers (1999). *The Sydney Morning Herald,* August 4, p. 22.

CNTA (1999). *Standard Rating System for Quality Tourist Attractions.* Beijing: CNTA Press (in Chinese).

Deng, Zongde (1998). The Present Situation and Perspectives on Chinese Amusement Parks. *China Tourism News,* March 31, p. 3 (in Chinese).

Gee, Chuck, Choy, Dexter, and Makens, James (1984). *The Travel Industry.* Westport, CT: AVI Publishing.

Goeldner, C., Ritchie, B., and McIntosh, W. (1999). *Tourism: Principles, Practices and Philosophies,* Eighth Edition. New York: John Wiley and Sons Inc.

Inskeep, Edward (1991). *Tourism Planning: An Integrated and Sustainable Development Approach.* New York: Van Nostrand Reinhold.

Ma Zhimin (1999). Views on the Development of Chinese Theme Parks. *China Tourism News,* May 25, p. 3 (in Chinese).

Qian, Wei (1999). China Tourism 2010—New Role for a New Millennium. In Heung, V., Ap, J., and Wong, K. (eds.), *Proceedings of the Asia Pacific Tourism Association Fifth Annual Conference—Tourism 2000: Asia Pacific's Role in the*

New Millennium (Volume 1), August 23-25, Hong Kong: The Hong Kong Polytechnic University, pp. 17-30.

Smith, Craig S. (1998). What Fun: China's Theme Parks Aren't Amusing for Many Investors. *The Asian Wall Street Journal,* July 20, p. 1.

Themed Entertainment Association (1999). *Project Development Guidelines: For the Themed Entertainment Industry,* Second Edition. Burbank, CA: Themed Entertainment Association.

Xu, Ju Feng (1998). Summary of a Symposium on Theme Parks and Cultural Recreation Performance in China. *Tourism Tribune,* Vol. 13, No. 5, pp. 18-22 (in Chinese).

Zoltak, James (1998). China: Theme Park Market for New Millennium. *Amusement Business,* September 14, p. 2.

SECTION IV:
TOURISM MARKETS

Chapter 12

Tourism Marketing in the People's Republic of China

Suosheng Wang
John Ap

The People's Republic of China has long been regarded as an exotic tourist destination, especially following the lifting of the "Bamboo Curtain" when, after three decades of isolation from the rest of the world, foreign pleasure tourists were allowed to visit the country. The introduction of the open door policy in 1978 marked the beginning of modern tourism in China. Initially, many of the visits were made by overseas and compatriot Chinese returning to visit family, relatives, and friends. At the time, facilities to accommodate visitors were basic and limited. However, as more facilities were provided to accommodate the needs of foreign tourists and, as further areas were opened up for tourists to visit, tourism boomed. In 1979, one year after the open door policy was introduced, there were 362,000 foreign tourist arrivals. Twenty years later, foreign tourist arrivals (excluding compatriots from Taiwan, Hong Kong, and Macao) totaled 7.3 million, a twenty-fold increase, and tourism income amounted to US$14.1 billion compared to US$44.3 million in 1979 (CNTA 2000). Based on World Tourism Organization (WTO) statistics, China now ranks fifth and seventh in the world, in terms of tourist arrivals and foreign exchange earnings, respectively (WTO 2000).

Due to the lure and fascination of China as an exotic destination, early demand often outstripped supply, and problems arose in trying to accommodate the needs of foreign tourists. There was constant growth in tourist arrivals and marketing China was not really an issue. Promotional efforts made by CNTA in the early 1980s routinely included participation in international travel trade shows and the invitation of foreign travel journalists to visit China. The purpose of these promotional activities was mainly to propagate the achievements made since reform and the introduction of the open door policy. It was not until 1989, when the events of the Tiananmen Square incident led to a 22 percent drop in tourist arrivals, that Chinese tourism officials began to address the role, need, and importance of marketing.

In order to develop a better and more complete understanding of inbound tourism in China, an overview and assessment of tourism marketing at the national level is presented to provide some insights into the current tourism marketing situation in China. We begin with an examination of the inbound market profile and a short description of the organization responsible for national-level tourism marketing and its structure. The nature and state of funding for tourism marketing and the promotional activities undertaken by the China National Tourism Administration (CNTA) are also examined. Finally, an assessment of these activities and identification of tourism marketing issues currently facing China are presented and discussed.

CURRENT MARKET SITUATION

There are five major inbound markets to China—Japan, South Korea, the United States, the ASEAN countries, and Europe (Yang 1997) (Table 12.1). Based on statistics from CNTA (2000), the three biggest markets in Asia are Taiwan, Japan, and South Korea. Taiwanese tourists are usually listed in the category of "compatriots" together with Hong Kong and Macao visitors (Lew 1995). In 1999, tourists from Taiwan exceeded a landmark number of 2.5 million, making Taiwan the largest international tourist-generating market.

The compatriot markets of Hong Kong and Macao largely reflect the domestic and day trip market due to considerable cross-border activity. In 1999, this market represented 61.7 million visitors. Family visits that occurred during various festivals throughout the year make up the bulk of this market, especially to neighboring Guangdong Province. Since the Asian economic downturn that began in mid-1997, the level of cross-border activity actually increased: by 13 percent in 1998 and 14 percent in 1999. This increase was largely attributed to Hong Kong and Macao residents crossing the border for shopping in the special economic zones of Shenzhen and Zhuhai, respectively.

TABLE 12.1. Foreign Visitor and Compatriot Arrivals from the Major Tourist-Generating Countries

Country	1998	1999	Growth (%)
Japan	1,572,100	1,855,200	18.0
Korea	632,800	992,000	56.8
Russia	692,000	833,000	20.4
United States	677,300	736,400	8.7
Malaysia	300,100	372,900	24.2
Mongolia	364,800	354,500	−2.8
Singapore	316,400	352,500	11.4
Philippines	256,500	298,300	16.3
United Kingdom	242,900	258,900	6.6
Germany	191,900	217,600	13.4
Canada	196,000	213,700	9.1
Thailand	144,300	206,400	43.0
Australia	186,400	203,500	9.2
Indonesia	104,600	182,900	74.9
France	138,000	155,600	12.7
Compatriot Markets			
Hong Kong/Macao	54,075,000	61,671,000	14.0
Taiwan	2,174,600	2,584,600	18.9

Source: CNTA (2000).

The Japanese account for approximately one-third of China's foreign arrivals (excluding compatriot visitors). In 1999, arrivals from Japan reached 1.86 million, an increase of 18 percent over the previous year. South Korea has emerged as a key inbound market since 1994 and has recorded the highest percentage of increase in arrivals. Since 1995, the rate of increase has slowed a little, but in 1999 South Korea surged again, with nearly 992,000 Koreans visiting China. It is currently China's second biggest foreign tourist-generating market.

The ASEAN countries of Malaysia, Singapore, Philippines, Thailand, and Indonesia have long been important tourist-generating markets for China, in part due to their large number of overseas ethnic

Chinese residents (Lew 1995). Visitors from these countries were important in helping China adjust to the decline in North American and European visitors following the 1989 Tiananmen Square incident. In 1995, the total number of visitors from these five ASEAN countries surpassed one million for the first time (1.04 million). By 1999, the total number of arrivals reached 1.41 million, reflecting growing leisure and business ties between China and Southeast Asia.

The primary inbound markets include the United Kingdom, Germany, France, and Russia. In 1999, arrivals from these four countries reached 1.47 million, with the Russians representing 57 percent of the European market. A large percentage of Russian visitors are cross-border (owing to the extremely long border that the two countries share) and budget-conscious tourists (Xu 1997). Over recent years, arrivals from these markets have increased at a relatively slow and steady rate. The United States ranked fourth among foreign visitor arrivals to China in 1999. From 1979 to 1987, the United States had consistently been China's second largest foreign tourist market (Yu 1992). The size of this market has remained steady and growth has been slow compared to Asia, including Russia. In 1999, there were 736,000 tourists from the United States, an increase of 9 percent over the previous year.

The foreign inbound market to China is now dominated by the Asia region. This no doubt reflects the growing affluence and economic prosperity of the region, and further growth is expected to continue as the economic crisis gradually subsides and disposable incomes increase. The long-haul Western markets of the United States and Europe have generally been steady although growth compared to the Asian market has been slow. Except for Russia, the Western markets are generally regarded as offering higher yields (higher expenditures per visitor) and their slow and steady growth suggests that these markets have probably reached a stage of maturity. Rejuvenation of these markets will be needed if China is to maintain and increase the lucrative profits they offer.

TOURISM MARKETING AT THE NATIONAL LEVEL

In China, tourism marketing activities at the national level are organized and conducted through the Department of Marketing & International Liaison of CNTA. The department comprises six divisions with a team of approximately thirty members, excluding personnel working in the overseas tourist offices (see Figure 12.1). The functions of the department include: market research, promotional campaigns both at home and abroad, producing and distributing promotional materials, and international communication and liaison.

Marketing research work was emphasized by CNTA when China's inbound tourism business shifted from "seller's market" to "buyer's market" at the end of the 1980s. Instead of contracting research work to consulting firms, CNTA conducted most of its research work in-house. However, due to limited budgets set aside for research and a lack of professional researchers, CNTA's marketing research work

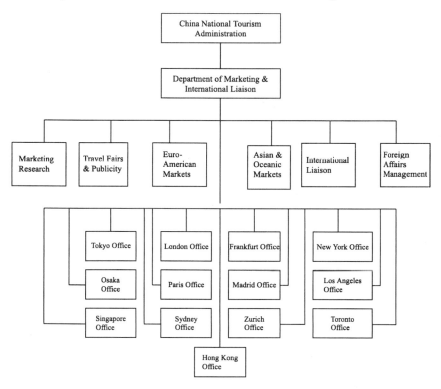

FIGURE 12.1. Organizational Chart of China National Tourism Administration's Department of Marketing International Liaison and Overseas National Tourist Offices.

was largely dependent on the travel information collected by its overseas offices. Besides, cooperation with international tourism organizations such as the World Tourism Organization and the Pacific and Asia Travel Association has recently become an important channel for China's tourism marketers to understand the newest features and trends of tourism development in the world.

The department launches overseas promotional and marketing campaigns mainly through its thirteen overseas offices. Currently, there are five overseas offices in the Asia Pacific area (Tokyo, Osaka, Singapore, Hong Kong, and Sydney); three in North America (New York, Los Angeles, and Toronto); and five in Western Europe (London, Frankfurt, Paris, Madrid, and Zurich). The main task of these offices is to implement the marketing strategies formulated by the department for each of the respective market areas. Zhang, Yu, and Lew (1995) noted that direct contact with the international market has generally been through these overseas offices, which have primarily acted as liaison offices. Thus, CNTA's marketing efforts are, in fact, quite limited.

Domestic tourism marketing and promotional activities, on the other hand, are largely dependent on the provincial tourism bureaus. All provincial governments have a tourism bureau with responsibilities for tourism planning, management, and promotion. There is also a third tier of tourism administration at the municipal and county levels. Given that the provincial and local tourism bureaus are not directly affiliated with CNTA, their influence on the provinces in terms of tourism marketing is quite limited. A decade ago, Bailey (1990) commented upon the state of tourism and said CNTA was

> handicapped by lack of expertise, lack of funds and an inability to implement the policies and regulations that it formulates. Particularly hard to monitor are price controls. Quality control—especially of tour guides, tourist restaurants, shops and hotels—is difficult to follow through. Effective promotion has been another problem area. (p. 44)

While quality control issues have been addressed over the past years and the expertise of tourism professionals has improved through various training programs and formal overseas education, marketing and promotion still remain a challenge. In contrast with the tourism marketing organizations of some nearby places, including Singapore,

Malaysia, and the Hong Kong Special Administrative Region, which have established independent and influential tourism boards specializing in tourism marketing and promotion, China lags behind. The functions and activities of CNTA's marketing and international liaison department are quite limited and can hardly be compared with the activities of its neighbors. An examination of the promotional budget helps to illustrate this point.

Information about the promotional budget for tourism is limited and is not always publicly available on an annual basis. However, some statistics were released from 1991 to 1993. Although this information is dated, it is presented to provide some insights into the nature and limited amount of funds available, and the constraints that China's tourism bureaus operate under. In 1992, when China launched its first Visit China Year, CNTA's promotional budget received a remarkable tenfold increase amounting to 30 million yuan (approximately US$3.6 million) (Xu 1996a). However, in comparison to Korea, Hong Kong, Singapore, and Malaysia, CNTA's promotional budget was very small. It was approximately one-tenth of some of its nearby competitors in the early 1990s (Table 12.2), and is not likely to change in future years.

TABLE 12.2. Selected Tourism Marketing Budgets in the Asia Pacific Region

Country/Region	1991 (Thousand U.S. dollars)	1992 (Thousand U.S. dollars)	1993 (Thousand U.S. dollars)
Australia	–	61,772,000	75,909,000
China	360,000	3,600,000	3,600,000
Hong Kong	20,164,000	22,406,000	24,187,000
Indonesia	12,291,000	14,724,000	21,357,000
Japan	21,149,000	24,919,000	29,835,000
Korea	71,491,000	76,750,000	88,997,000
Malaysia	32,364,000	39,026,000	–
New Zealand	18,238,000	19,945,000	–
Philippines	10,250,000	17,899,000	21,691,000
Singapore	43,616,000	–	–

Source: CNTA, 1995.

According to Xu (1996a), the promotional funds allocated annually to the overseas offices were approximately US$100,000 each, which was hardly comparable to the resources enjoyed by other major tourist destination offices. For example, the Singapore Tourist Promotion Board's overseas tourist office in London had an annual promotional budget of US$1.12 million, more than ten times CNTA's London office budget. The lack of funding, no doubt, restricted the ability of China to promote and market its tourism products. The low budget was due to several reasons. For one, marketing has traditionally played a low priority role in socialist countries, which are more supply driven. This, combined with the fact that little tourism marketing activity was needed to promote China to foreign tourists prior to 1989, make it understandable why resources of the same magnitude as those of China's neighbors were not provided, nor probably even necessary.

As provincial and local tourism bureaus are financially independent from CNTA, these bureaus can independently conduct their own marketing activities. The size of promotion funds of the provincial tourism bureaus varies considerably (Table 12.3). The province with the largest fund was Zhejiang with more than 4 million yuan (about US$500,000), and the smallest was Ningxia with only 50,000 yuan (about US$6,000). The provinces of Ningxia and Qinghai, which had the smallest marketing budgets, really did not have the resources to conduct tourism marketing and promotional activities on their own. These provinces relied on financial support from CNTA and participated in nationwide promotional campaigns. Although the funding situation at the provincial level and in some of the major cities varied considerably, those with larger amounts of funding could exercise a higher degree of autonomy, which can dilute efforts at the national level to project a clearly defined and consistent theme in the marketplace.

TOURISM MARKETING AND PROMOTION

To boost international tourism, CNTA has developed various marketing strategies for its major market segments. For example, in 1996 the strategies adopted by CNTA for various markets were outlined by He (1996) as follows:

Taiwan—promote indirectly through Hong Kong and Macao.

Japan—continue to attach importance to the Japanese market and focus attention on various geographic market segments and the elderly market.

South Korea—strengthen marketing research to ensure its future and stress China's integrative image when launching promotional campaigns.

ASEAN countries—develop and introduce new tourist products to meet the different demands of potential tourists.

Euro-American markets—increase the distribution channels for China's tourist products by strengthening cooperation with outbound tour operators and the airlines.

Hong Kong—strengthen contacts and cooperation with Hong Kong's tourism industry, develop mutually complementary products and attractions, and improve China's quality standards to those of Hong Kong.

These strategies indicate that CNTA has been aware of the importance of developing specific strategies for each major market, with a particular focus on the short-haul Asian markets. According to Beria (1996), different marketing strategies were used and greater attention was paid to the Japanese market as CNTA developed special study tours, as well as tailor-made tours for middle-aged and elderly Japanese visitors. As for the Western markets of Europe and North America, the main tour operators doing Chinese travel business have been the small- to medium-sized travel companies dominated by overseas Chinese (Xu 1996b). CNTA has made efforts over an extended period of time to encourage large foreign tour operators to enter the China market; however, its efforts have not been too fruitful. Reasons for this may include

- a reluctance on the part of large foreign tour operators to engage in business with China;
- the quality of China's tourist product has not met the expectations and requirements of large operators; and
- communication and language barriers.

In 1998, CNTA issued "Provisional Measures on Setting up Joint-Venture Travel Agencies," which would allow joint venture (JV) travel agencies to be established in China. Since these "provisional

TABLE 12.3. Marketing and Promotion Budgets for Provincial and Selected City Tourism Bureaus

Province/City	1992 (RMB yuan)	1993 (RMB yuan)	1994 (RMB yuan)
Zhejiang	2,012,000	2,636,000	4,760,000
Hainan	1,250,000	3,720,000	3,650,000
Beijing City	2,280,000	2,820,000	3,210,000
Fujian	1,500,000	2,200,000	2,500,000
Shanghai City	2,250,000	1,540,000	2,500,000
Shanxi	1,260,000	1,300,000	1,950,000
Jiangsu	1,000,000	1,200,000	1,400,000
Tianjin	600,000	900,000	1,200,000
Henan	300,000	600,000	1,200,000
Anhui	680,000	750,000	950,000
Liaoning	700,000	650,000	900,000
Guangdong	400,000	600,000	720,000
Shandong	538,000	620,000	700,000
Shaanxi	800,000	600,000	600,000
Jilin	500,000	600,000	500,000
Sichuan	300,000	400,000	500,000
Hubei	300,000	300,000	500,000
Hunan	350,000	410,000	480,000
Hebei	500,000	450,000	400,000
Guizhou	300,000	350,000	400,000
Guangxi	286,000	308,000	360,000
Heilongjiang	80,000	120,000	200,000
Jiangxi	120,000	220,000	150,000
Gansu	400,000	100,000	120,000
Xinjiang	120,000	240,000	120,000
Qinghai	120,000	50,000	80,000
Ningxia	50,000	40,000	50,000
Total	19.84 million (U.S. $2.32 million)	24.33 million (U.S. $2.85 million)	30.9 million (U.S. $3.62 million)

Source: CNTA, 1995.

measures" were issued, several JV agencies have been set up and the most significant JV to date has been the one established between Japan's big tour operator JTB (Japan Transport Bureau) and China's CITIC Travel Corporation in Beijing. Among the international tour operators that have set up a JV travel company in China, most are involved in the inbound travel business. CNTA also hopes that, with the entry of big international tour operators such as Japan's JTB, distribution channels will expand widely.

To improve the situation for the inbound travel market, CNTA should not only further strengthen its contacts with large operators, but seek to substantially improve its product quality as well. Zhang, Yu, and Lew (1995) pointed out that more aggressive marketing, including regional and international cooperative campaigns, should be undertaken. However, China must understand international market demands and develop appropriate travel products and services.

Since 1992, CNTA has introduced a campaign of annual tourism promotional themes. The purpose behind the designation of a theme for each year has been to present a sampler of images and focus on different aspects of China's rich culture, history, and nature, as well as her fast-expanding holiday resorts (Beria 1996). In addition, the themed campaign provides an opportunity to shape China's tourism image over time. Through these annual themed promotional campaigns, China has been able to periodically demonstrate its abundant tourism resources and present its diverse and rich products to various markets to satisfy differing demands. Themes adopted have included Visit China '92, China Landscape '93, China Heritage '94, China Folklore '95, and China Holiday Resorts '96. In 1997, a second Visit China Year was launched, followed by China City & Country Tour '98, China Eco-tour '99, and the New Millennium Tour 2000. The annual theme campaign provides a focus for all of CNTA's major promotional activities. Local tourism marketing departments throughout China, as well as leading Chinese tour companies and hotels, are also advised by CNTA to promote these designated themes.

Some problems were encountered with the adoption of the yearly themes, especially in the early years. The challenge for Chinese marketers was to project a unified image, but media coverage and promotion in the overseas markets was limited due to a lack of resources. With themes changing annually, there was inadequate time to effectively promote the themes, which may have created confusion in the marketplace. Thus, efforts to raise the awareness of potential international tourists may not have been as effective as desired.

The promotion of a destination image is far from an easy task. China's image, especially in the West, is dominated and influenced by the media. This, unfortunately, is something that has been beyond the control of the tourism officials and it must be recognized that overseas media influence far exceeds any of CNTA's promotional efforts. Zhang, Yu, and Lew (1995) observed that

> [t]he reputation of China's tourist industry is less than desirable and leaves much room for improvement. In fact, a clear and positive tourist image of China has yet to be truly established. . . . The tight control that China's central government exerts over political dissent is discussed in the Western media almost as much as is the country's economic miracle. This is an important issue for some potential travelers, particularly from the US and Europe. No matter how many "Visit China" campaigns the CNTA plans, they may have less impact on the major international markets than images presented in foreign outlets of a Chinese government that suppresses individual political freedoms. (p. 240)

Besides the larger image problem of China in the international arena, China's tourist image has also been seriously affected by some problems of its own. Tourist safety in China has become a serious concern for the international travel industry (Zhang, Yu, and Lew 1995; Yu and Lew 1997). The abduction of a tour boat and subsequent murders of a Taiwanese tour group and the boat's crew on Qiandao Lake in 1997 sent shock waves throughout the industry and resulted in a three-month self-imposed ban of inbound tour groups from Taiwan. Although the situation has improved since that time, the future success of international tourism to China will require continued vigilance to safeguard the personal safety of international tourists by both the government and private sector. More recently, a series of bus accidents have resulted in the death of Hong Kong tourists in Guangdong Province and this is posing a threat to bus transportation safety ("Dangerous Highway" 2001) and raising the concerns of the traveling public. This problem has been an ongoing concern of organizations such as the Travel Industry Council of Hong Kong, which oversees outbound travel matters.

Another area of concern has been the lack of quality in service provision. It has been suggested that China should make greater efforts to provide better quality service. Visitor discontent and complaints often due to poor staff attitudes and service will continue to further tarnish China's image unless concerted efforts are made to address this problem.

In order to truly improve and establish China's destination image, more attention needs to be paid to the existing problems in China's tourism industry and to establish more positive and effective tourism images by genuinely addressing these problems. Such problems pose as substantial obstacles for prospective tourists as they decide whether to visit China. Moreover, prior to any actual promotional campaigns being launched, more research should be undertaken to identify and assess tourist demand and preferences, as well as their perceptions of China.

ISSUES AFFECTING THE DEVELOPMENT OF CHINA'S TOURIST MARKETS

In order to maintain a steady and high rate of tourism growth, China should pay attention to and address a number of issues concerning its marketing and promotional activities. First, China's international tourist products tend to be old-fashioned and highly structured. They have been largely designed for culture-oriented sightseeing tour groups. The itineraries have included fixed tour routes, tour contents, activities, meals, shopping, and shows, with little innovation. These kinds of products can no longer suit the demands of contemporary international tourists who are seeking more independence and greater flexibility and choice in developing their itineraries. Examples of new products that may be appealing to international tourists include holiday resort products such as Hainan Island, which is now becoming popular among German tourists, and an adventure tour along the famous Silk Road in China's Xinjiang Uygur Autonomous Region. Realizing that a large FIT (fully independent tourist) market exists, travel agencies such as China International Travel Service are currently promoting and offering a new type of tour product (the "seat-in" or "join-in" tour) where FITs, upon arrival in the country, may sign up and join a tour.

A second problem is that the distribution channels for marketing tourism to China have narrowed and become more congested. As mentioned previously, few global and large tour operators have been including China in their distribution brochures because long-haul markets have been dominated by small- to medium-sized travel companies largely owned by overseas Chinese. As a result, China finds it hard to enter into other distribution channels oriented toward niche markets and specialty tours. Many cultural exchange organizations, religious organizations, large private companies, and various kinds of clubs are organizing international and incentive tours, which are becoming a huge market. However, China does not have distribution channels to tap such markets.

A third issue that hinders China's marketing efforts has been the limited resources that CNTA has for marketing and promotion. As indicated previously, China's main competitors have promotional budgets up to ten times greater. Unlike other countries, which may have a stable source of marketing funds from tourism taxes or commissions, CNTA's marketing funds mainly come from the central government's annual financial allocation, which are specific and limited. Due to budget restrictions, CNTA finds it hard to compete with other Asian countries. Provincial and local tourism bureaus have tended to reduce resources for tourism promotion.

Fourth, with the rapid development of today's Internet and e-commerce travel business, thousands of destinations—regions, countries, states and provinces, cities, and park systems—are using and taking advantage of Web sites to market their destinations and travel products. While e-commerce is an effective tool in tourism promotion and purchase of tour products and services, the development of e-commerce especially for inbound business in China has only been recent. Most Web sites of mainland Chinese travel companies are primarily used as a communication tool for product orientation and promotion of corporate image. Some issues exist for China's tourism authorities and travel companies in fully applying e-commerce in travel business operations, such as the need to adapt the use of e-commerce to existing travel-related regulations and restructure traditional Chinese ways of operating a business.

Fifth, the central government's tourism marketing strategies and those of private enterprises generally have not complemented one another. When CNTA launched a series of theme-year activities in

1992, it designed and prepared a series of corresponding tour products (such as package tours and itineraries). However, domestic travel companies took little or no interest in selling these "products" because they did not see them as being attractive to consumers. Such tensions and problems between government national tourist organizations and the industry are common and have been previously experienced elsewhere, such as in Singapore and Australia.

Sixth, there are some issues to be addressed with respect to the Chinese compatriot market. This category makes up the largest number of "international" tourists. However, most of the cross-border visits by Hong Kong and Macao residents involve commuting to the adjacent special economic zones of Shenzhen and Zhuhai, and making family visits to Guangdong Province. In 1999, the value of tourist receipts from the huge 61.7 million Hong Kong and Macao compatriot markets represented 42.1 percent of China's total tourism receipts, slightly more than the 41.6 percent of revenue contributed by the 8.4 million foreign tourist market. Although the receipts provided by the Hong Kong and Macao compatriot markets were sizable, this segment of the market tends to spend, on average, one-seventh as much as their foreign counterparts. This, no doubt, has implications for the host communities especially in Guangdong Province, in terms of crowding and the straining of resources. Given this situation, targeting the higher yielding foreign visitor market is more desirable.

Difficulties are faced by mainland China in accessing the important Taiwanese market. Kinship, nostalgia, diverse attractions, and business opportunities have been the main reasons for Taiwanese visiting the mainland (Yu 1992). However, little can be done by mainland Chinese tourism marketers to boost this market. Xu (1997) identified a number of difficulties in developing the Taiwan market. The first problem is the nonavailability and nonexchange of tourism information. It is difficult for mainland marketers to obtain information about Taiwan's outbound tourism market, and potential Taiwanese tourists do not know where to find tourist information about the mainland. This situation leads to a greater mismatch between market demand and supply, which eventually reduces the mainland's competitiveness. Despite the difficulty in obtaining information directly on the Taiwan outbound market, it can be obtained indirectly through the Taiwanese tourism offices in North America or from organizations such as the Pacific Asia Travel Association.

The second problem is that the Taiwan tourism industry can easily enter and engage in business with the mainland. However, the mainland Chinese cannot easily enter Taiwan to launch direct promotions as they can in other markets. As a result, destination marketers know little about the actual demand of this major market. A third problem is that mainland promotional materials are not allowed in Taiwan, thus hindering the dissemination of market information.

Finally, there is the matter of marketing cooperation between the mainland, Hong Kong, and Macao. Tourism in the Pearl River Delta (PRD) region, which encompasses Hong Kong, Macao, and Guangzhou in Guangdong Province, has become more interdependent in recent years. Annually, more than two million international tourists visit both China and Hong Kong on the same trip (Lai 1996). In order to jointly promote the PRD area, the Hong Kong Tourist Board (HKTB), which was formerly known as the Hong Kong Tourist Association (HKTA), Macao Government Tourist Office (MGTO), and China's Guangdong Provincial Tourism Bureau (GPTB) formed a working group in 1993 called the Pearl River Delta Tourism Marketing Organization, through which they promote the PRD area (HKTA 1993). Given that Guangdong's marketing resources (both budgetary and human resources) are well below those of Hong Kong and Macao, it may be hard to achieve substantial effects from this cooperative effort without the support from CNTA. Also, when compared with China's other famous attractions such as Beijing, Xi'an, and Guilin, Guangdong is not one of the long-haul tourist's top choices when deciding to visit China. As mentioned in the *Travel Business Analyst* ("Final Report of Market Profile on Pearl River Delta" 1993), "Although Guangzhou, the capitol of Guangdong, is a famous city in China, its historical sites are not as attractive as those in Beijing, Xi'an and Kaifeng; and its scenic spots and facilities are not as good as those of Guilin, Hangzhou and Suzhou" (pp. 102-103). It would probably be more effective for the tourism authorities in Hong Kong and Macao to expand marketing cooperation to all of China rather than confining their cooperation to the PRD. The historic change of sovereignty of both Hong Kong and Macao to China in 1997 and 1999, respectively, has provided a golden opportunity for CNTA to establish and develop closer cooperation with the HKTB and MGTO.

SUMMARY

Although China's tourism industry has boomed in terms of international tourist arrivals, it has potential for greater achievements in the future. In order to compete effectively in the international marketplace, in terms of its tourism marketing and promotion activities, China still has much room for improvement. Specifically, there is need to strengthen marketing research and identify tourists' needs in order to allocate and utilize the very limited resources available effectively. The Asian markets of Taiwan, Japan, South Korea, and the ASEAN countries are China's major inbound markets, and China needs to reexamine and strengthen efforts in these markets. Although China is focusing on its theme-year campaign activities, an assessment and evaluation should be conducted to examine the extent to which the campaign is achieving the objectives that have been set. Perhaps a single theme lasting for several years, such as is used in Singapore and Hong Kong, would be a more effective use of limited resources. China should further improve its marketing environment through

- a review of its existing product offerings so that it can develop new products to satisfy changing market needs;
- the expansion of the distribution channels for its products;
- the full utilization of e-commerce for purchases and business transactions to be made; and
- the development of professional marketing and promotion skills.

There is also need to establish a clearer and more positive destination image for China in the global marketplace. Taiwan is China's biggest offshore market, and effective means to access this market need to be identified in the current tense and awkward political climate. With the return of sovereignty of Hong Kong and Macao, CNTA should strengthen its linkage with the HKTA and MGTO, and make the most use of this opportunity for tourism cooperation and joint marketing activities to link the resources of these two special administrative regions beyond the Pearl River Delta.

In conclusion, this overview and assessment has provided a glimpse into the nature and characteristics of tourism marketing in China. In a sense, the awakening of the Chinese Dragon from a tourism perspective has yet to occur. There is room for improvement and with the World Tourism Organization projecting that China will become the leading player for both inbound and outbound travel by 2020 (WTO 1998), many opportunities exist for industry professionals both within and outside of the country to identify and pursue. Tapping China, both as a destination as well as a major source of tourists, will provide rewards for astute tourism professionals and businesspeople.

REFERENCES

Bailey, M. (1990). China. *EIU International Tourism Reports,* No. 3, 22-48.

Beria, B. (1996). China Beyond 1997. *Asia Travel Trade,* June, 26-28.

China National Tourism Administration (CNTA) (2000). *The Yearbook of China Tourism Statistics.* Beijing: National Tourism Administration of the PRC.

" 'Dangerous Highway' Caused 39 Injuries." (2001). *The Sun* March 27. <http://www.the-sun.com.hk/channels/news/200010327/20010327031457_0001.html>; accessed March 27, 2001 (in Chinese).

He, G. (1996). Work Report of China National Tourism Industry. *Travel Industry* (in Chinese) May, 6-7. National Tourism Administration of the PRC.

Hong Kong Tourist Association (HKTA) (1993). Press Release about the Pearl River Delta. Hong Kong: Hong Kong Tourist Association.

Lai, L. K. (1996). All for One & One for All. *Asia Travel Trade,* June, 30-34.

Lew, A. A. (1995). Overseas Chinese and Compatriots in China's Tourism Development. In A.A. Lew and L. Yu, eds., *Tourism in China: Geographical, Political, and Economic Perspectives.* Boulder, CO: Westview Press, pp. 155-175.

Travel Business Analyst (1993). Final Report of Market Profile on Pearl River Delta for Hong Kong Tourist Association. 102-103.

World Tourism Organization (WTO) (1998). *Tourism Highlights 2020.* Madrid: WTO.

World Tourism Organization (WTO) (2000). *Tourism Highlights 2000,* Second Edition. Madrid: WTO.

Xu, F. (1996a). Retrospect of China's Tourism Marketing for Ten Years. *Tourism Marketing* (in Chinese), 1 (January), 1-55.

Xu, F. (1996b). Minutes of the National Tourism Marketing Seminar. *Tourism Marketing* (in Chinese), 6 (December), 1-9.

Xu, F. (1997). Situations of China's Inbound Tourism Markets in 1996. *Tourism Marketing* (in Chinese), 1 (February), 1-7.

Yang, W. Z. (1997). Improve the Marketing Mechanism of International Tourism. *Tourism Marketing* (in Chinese), 4 (August), 1-10.

Yu, L. (1992). Emerging Markets for China's Tourism Industry. *Journal of Travel Research,* 31 (1): 10-13.

Yu, L. and A. Lew (1997). Airline Liberalization and Development in China. *Pacific Tourism Review,* 1(2):129-136.

Zhang, G., L. Yu, and A. Lew (1995). China's Tourism: Opportunities, Challenges, and Strategies. In A. A. Lew and L. Yu, eds., *Tourism in China, Geographic, Political, and Economic Perspectives.* Boulder, CO: Westview Press, pp. 237-244.

Chapter 13

Short- and Long-Haul International Tourists to China

Xiaoping Shen

China's rich tourism resources are due to its vast and diverse territory, its civilization of over 5,000 years, and its ethnic diversity with fifty-six nationalities. These combine to total over 4,600 identified scenic spots and places of historical interest, with many more that have not been cataloged (Yang, 1989; Jeffrey and Xie, 1995). The interest that China holds for international tourists and the potential of China's international tourism are tremendous. In 2000, China received 83.48 million international visitors compared to 57.59 million in 1997 (Han, 2001; CNTA, 1998; note that these numbers include day excursionists). The majority of international visitors (about 78 percent) are compatriots from Hong Kong, Macao, Taiwan, and overseas Chinese (who reside in a foreign country but hold Chinese passports). Foreign visitors (who entered China with foreign passports) exceeded 10 million for the first time in history in 2000 and showed an impressive increase of 2.6 million or 35 percent from 1997 (Han, 2001). For the purposes of this chapter, short-haul foreign visitors are those from either an Asian country or a country that shares a border with China such as Russia, while long-haul foreign visitors are from all other areas in the world: Europe, America, Oceania, and Africa. Although smallest in number of visitors (3 million in 1997), long-haul visitors tend to spend more time and money in China than the short-haul visitors, are the group that has the greatest potential to grow, and are a major marketing segment for China's National Tourism Administration (CNTA).

Most previous research on China's international tourism studied overall international tourists (Gerstlacher, Krieg, and Sternfeld, 1991; Gormsen, 1995), comparison between compatriots and foreigners

(Gerstlacher, Krieg, and Sternfeld, 1991), overseas Chinese as tourists to China (Lew, 1995), or individual foreign sources such as America (Zhang, 1989), England (Jeffrey and Xie, 1995), and Germany (Gormsen, 1990). Some studies focus on specific regions, such as Guilin, Suzhou, and Beidaihe (Xu, 1999), Huang Shan and Dali (Gormsen, 1990), and Guizhou (Oakes, 1998). In addition, most prior works studied international tourism development in the period of the 1980s (Gerstlacher, Krieg, and Sternfeld, 1991; Gormsen, 1990; Zhang, 1989; He, 1989) or up to the beginning of the 1990s (Gormsen, 1995, Wen and Tisdell, 1996). Few, if any, have done in-depth analysis on long-haul tourists in China particularly in the 1990s after the effects of the Tiananmen Square incident in 1989. This chapter focuses on long-haul visitors, with an emphasis on major tourist sources in Europe, North America, and Oceania for which data are available, and analyzes the growth of these long-haul markets in comparison with short-haul markets, the characteristics and motivations of long-haul visitors, the spatial variation of their visitations, and the changes during the past decade.

FOREIGN VISITORS IN CHINA

Although foreigners have visited China for a variety of reasons tracing back at least 2,000 years, most scholars and travel agents agree that China's commercial tourism industry started only after 1978. More specifically, the First All China Tourism Conference held in January 1978 in Beijing has been considered by many as the starting point of modern commercial tourism in China (He, 1989; Gerstlacher, Krieg, and Sternfeld, 1991). As one of the major policies of the economic reforms announced in 1978, China used tourism as a key component in gradually opening its doors to foreign goods, visitors, and investments in the 1980s. According to the World Tourism Organization (WTO), China ranked fifth in the world as an international tourism destination, behind France, the United States, Spain, and Italy since 1996 (World Tourism Organization, 2000). The WTO has predicted that China will be the number one global destination for international tourists by 2020.

According to *The Yearbook of China Tourism Statistics,* published by the China National Tourism Administration (CNTA, 1995, 1998), foreign visitors increased from 230,000 in 1978 to 7.4 million in

1997 (Figure 13.1). (Unless otherwise indicated, the statistical data cited in the research are from various annual issues of *The Yearbook of China Tourism Statistics* published by the China National Tourism Administration.) In other words, it soared more than thirty times in twenty years, despite a significant drop (20-30 percent) in 1989 and 1990 due to the Tiananmen Square incident. Although foreign visitors accounted for only 13 percent (1997) of the total international visitors (which included Hong Kong, Macao, and Taiwan compatriots), they generated 41.7 percent of the total revenue from international tourism in 1997 (Figure 13.2). Thus, the average foreign visitor spent 4.8 times as much in China as did the typical compatriot visitor.

Within the foreign visitor population, long-haul visitors spent the most on their trip, usually staying in China for a few more days than Asian short-haul visitors, which included some border-crossing day excursionists. More important, only a very small percentage of residents of long-haul origin countries have ever visited China, meaning that this market segment has a greater potential for growth than does the compatriot and short-haul (Asian) foreign market, if the friction of distance can be ameliorated.

The term *foreign visitors* is used instead of *foreign tourists* in part because China does not directly collect and publish purposes of trip information for international visitors, but also because most foreigners visit China for multiple purposes. Indirectly, it might be possible to separate foreign tourists from visitors because nontourists technically need an invitation from a Chinese unit, e.g., government agency, organization, academic institution, tourism agency, or company to visit China. However, this is complicated because not all foreign visitor follow this rule and ethnic Chinese who hold foreign passports are allowed to visit their families without any special invitations. Information for group tours could be used to identify vacationing tourists, but the growing number of individual tourists and those combining business and sightseeing, such as most conference attendees, would be excluded. In fact, no matter what the primary purpose of the visit is, most foreigners in China spend some time as tourists, including long-term students, employees of overseas companies, and foreign experts consulting with government agencies, all of whom are not included in the foreign visitor counts of CNTA. Due to these problems, this chapter focuses on the broader category of foreign visitors, rather

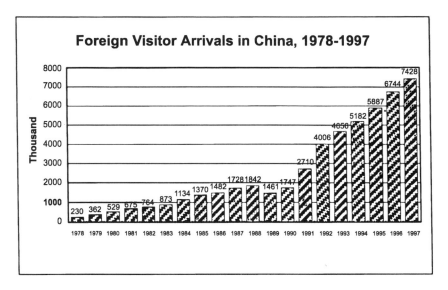

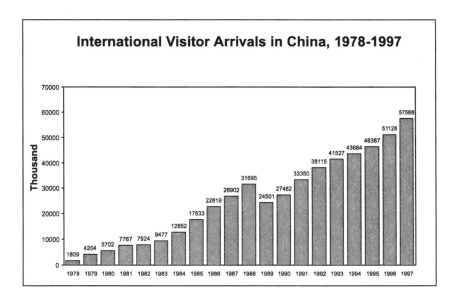

FIGURE 13.1. Foreign Visitors in China, 1978-1997. (*Source:* CNTA, 1990-1998.)

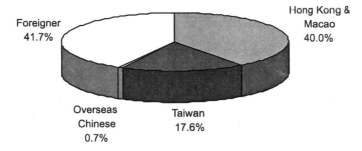

FIGURE 13.2. International Tourism Revenues, 1997. (*Source:* CNTA, 1998.)

than trying to tease out a subcategory of tourists from the officially published numbers.

GROWTH OF LONG-HAUL FOREIGN VISITORS

Despite the time-space convergence that has created an ever smaller global village, travel distance remains a major barrier to human interaction. The farther apart the two places, the more difficult it is to overcome the distance barrier, and the fewer face-to-face interactions occur. In tourism, long-haul foreign visitors not only have to overcome distance, but also cultural and language barriers and higher financial costs. Therefore, they are generally smaller in numbers and relatively slower in growth than short-haul visitors.

Similar to the situation in the 1980s (Gormsen, 1995; Gerstlacher, Krieg, and Sternfeld 1991), a handful of countries in Asia continue to generate the majority of foreign visitors to China. The proportion of Asian visitors among all foreign visitors to China even increased in the 1990s. In 1997, China's 4.4 million Asian visitors accounted for almost 60 percent of all foreigners, an increase of 7 percentage points in seven years (from 52.4 percent in 1990, cf. Table 13.1). Among them, Japan alone generated more than one-fifth of all foreign visitors in 1997, although its percentage share was reduced from 33 percent in 1981 (Gormsen, 1995). East and Southeast Asian countries, such as Japan, South Korea, Mongolia, Malaysia, Philippines, and Singapore have been the main sources of foreign visitors since the beginning of commercial tourism in China. This has been due to the proximity to

TABLE 13.1. Foreign Visitor Arrivals by Nationality and Region, Select Years 1990-1997

Nationality	1990	%[a]	1992	1995	1997	%[a]	% of Visitors to Total Country Population, 1997
Total	1,747,315	100	4,006,427	5,886,716	7,428,006	100	0.13[b]
Japan	463,265	26.5	791,523	1,305,190	1,581,747	21.3	1.25
South Korea	–	–	–	529,467	781,119	10.5	1.70
Mongolia	–	–	–	261,940	342,881	4.6	14.29
Malaysia	–	–	–	251,758	361,308	4.9	1.72
Philippines	78,872	4.5	137,944	219,722	276,656	3.7	0.38
Thailand	67,906	3.9	147,219	173,342	168,508	2.3	0.28
Singapore	71,658	4.1	152,830	261,467	316,825	4.3	9.05
Others	233,471	13.4	618,502	416,269	582,048	7.9	0.03
Asia	915,172	52.4	1,848,018	515,469	4,411,092	59.4	0.19[b]
United Kingdom	78,934	4.5	129,839	184,912	227,907	3.1	0.39
France	50,735	2.9	116,165	118,494	131,286	1.8	0.22
Germany	56,178	3.2	121,257	166,528	184,712	2.5	0.23
Italy	26,262	1.5	56,983	63,721	65,139	0.9	0.11
Netherlands	13,783	0.8	20,777	34,948	52,257	0.7	0.33
Russia[c]	109,805	6.3	895,243	489,329	813,681	11.0	0.55
Others	110,563	6.3	179,626	396,962	413,891	5.6	0.13
Europe	446,260	25.5	1,519,890	1,454,894	1,888,873	25.4	0.26
United States	233,193	13.3	346,303	514,850	616,438	8.3	0.23
Canada	47,573	2.7	93,140	128,762	174,092	2.3	0.58
Others	22,776	1.3	55,961	53,643	76,636	1.0	0.02
America	303,542	17.4	495,404	697,255	867,166	11.7	0.12
Australia	50,175	2.9	75,610	129,368	156,840	2.1	0.85
New Zealand	10,027	0.6	16,162	22,883	28,296	0.4	0.79
Others	3,295	0.2	13,748	6,283	8,305	0.1	0.12
Oceania	63,497	3.6	105,520	158,534	193,441	2.6	0.67
Africa	12,582	0.7	26,740	40,805	49,134	0.7	0.01
Others	6,262	0.4	10,855	16,873	18,300	0.2	0.05

Source: CNTA (1995, 1998); Getis, Getis, and Fellmann (1998).
[a] Percentage share of foreign visitors in the year
[b] Excluding China
[c] "Former Soviet Union" from 1990 to 1992, and "Russia" from 1993

China, common roots in history and culture, a large number of ethnic Chinese in some of these countries, and laws that allow their citizens to freely travel to China.

The number of long-haul visitors from Europe (except Russia), America, and other non-Asian countries have also grown almost every year. From 1978 to 1986, American and European visitors increased by a two-digit annual growth rate, but changed to one-digit in 1987, followed by a 4.6 percent decrease for American visitors in 1988 and then big drops for all visitors in 1989 and 1990 (Gerstlacher, Krieg, and Sternfeld 1991). The growth rate of international visitors bounced back in 1991 when all foreign visitors, including Americans and Europeans, increased about 40 percent from the previous year. However, the growth rate for long-haul visitors has been slower than that of Asian visitors in the 1990s, resulting in declining proportions in the foreign visitor totals (cf. the 1997 column in Table 13.1). The proportion of Americans declined from 17.4 percent in 1990 to 11.7 percent in 1997, although the number of American visitors more than doubled to 867,166 in 1997. Long-haul European visitors were in the same situation. Excluding Russian visitors who were mostly border-crossing day-trippers, other European visitor totals dropped from 19.2 percent in 1990 to 14.4 percent in 1997.

The percentage of a country's total population visiting China provides another perspective of the difference between long-haul and short-haul travelers (cf. the last column in Table 13.1). Among major Asian source countries, the highest ratio of visitors to population in 1997 reached an amazing 14.29 percent in Mongolia. This was probably due to the shared language and culture in Mongolia and China's Inner Mongolia. Other Asian countries, such as Japan, South Korea, Singapore, and Malaysia had over 1 percent of their population visiting China in 1997 (assuming no repeat visits in that year). By contrast, all European countries except Russia had visitation rates lower than 0.5 percent.

In North America, Canada generated fewer total visitors, but they represented 0.58 percent of its population, which was 2.5 times that of the United States. This is not surprising due to the longer and friendlier relationship between Canada and China. Canada established diplomatic relations with the People's Republic of China in 1970 whereas the United States did so in 1979 (Encyclopaedia Britannica Online 2000a,b). Chinese people consider Canadians as friends from Dr. Bethune's home country, a household name in China as an example of selflessness. Dr. Bethune was a Canadian volunteer surgeon who helped the Chinese Army during WWII and gave his life in China. To Canadians, the Chinese are their friends too. For example, Canada's current Prime Minister Jean Chrétien has visited China four times since he was elected to the office in 1994, and led the largest delegation (with more than 600 people) in Canadian history to China in February 2001 (Yang, 2001). The relationship between China and the United States has greatly improved during the past two decades; however, it is still not as close as that of China and Canada.

Australia and New Zealand both had relatively high percentages of visitors relative to their population probably due to their relative nearness to China. As European and North American countries are the largest international tourist sources in the world (World Tourism Organization, 2000), their smaller numbers and proportions going to China are a clear indication of the impact of the combined friction of distance, language, cultural, and financial barriers on tourist behavior.

In addition, "views of China as a poor, desolate, isolated country with a suppressed people tyrannized by a ruthless government" (Lambrianidis, 2000, p. 9) are common among peoples in West Europe and North America, which further discourages tourists from those regions from visiting China. Very often Americans returning from their first trip to China comment on how surprised they were by what they saw (Bessette, 1999; Lambrianidis, 2000) and how the visit could "change any stereotypical ideas and preconceived notions I have been carrying in my mind about what the Chinese people are all about" (Bessette, 1999, p. B1). However, as the barriers to international travel decline and the number of repeat visitors to China increases, and as tourist services in China improve and China continues to open its society, these stereotypical views will gradually fade even in the more distant corners of the world.

CHARACTERISTICS OF LONG-HAUL VISITORS

The age, sex, and occupation of foreign visitors are reported by CNTA annually at the continental and national levels for selected countries. These data are used to compare the characteristics of short-haul and long-haul visitors and how they have changed between 1992 and 1997 (i.e., the period after the Tiananmen Square incident disruption).

Sex Ratio

The ratio of males to females among foreign visitors to China was about 6:4 in the 1980s, although organized group tours reported slightly more women than men (Gerstlacher, Krieg, and Sternfeld, 1991). In the 1990s, the sex ratio was even higher for males at about 2:1. The ratio even reached 7:3 in 1993 and 1994. This reflects a growth in business travel, which was seen as becoming increasingly important even in the late 1980s (Roehl, 1995). Variation in sex ratios was significant among major source countries, as well, with a clear division between short-haul and long-haul visitors observed (Table 13.2).

Generally speaking, short-haul visitors tended to be more balanced in gender than long-haul visitors. The most balanced ratios in 1997 were for countries bordering China, including Russia (1:1), Mongolia (55:45), and nearby Thailand (53:47). At the same time, however, the most unbalanced sex ratios were also among the short-haul countries. Several Asian countries, including Japan, South Korea, and the Philippines had ratios at the level of 3:1 in 1997. Long-haul visitors were also very unbalanced in gender, but the ratios were similar for the major source countries at the level of about 2:1.

The changes in sex ratios from 1992 to 1997 were in opposite directions for long-haul and short-haul visitors. All of the short-haul countries, except Japan, saw an increase in the proportion of female visitors to China, ranging from 0.3 percent for Singapore to 12 percent for Russia. This probably reflected greater access to China as a leisure destination for many Asian countries. Long-haul visitors, on the other hand, saw a decline in the percentage of female visitors to China, ranging from a 3 percent decrease for Australia to an 11 percent drop for Italy. This decline was likely the result of business travel increasing at a faster rate than leisure travel from long-haul origin countries (Roehl, 1995).

The male:female ratio from different countries can point to variations in the general composition of the visitor groups. When men and women travel together they are more likely to be on a vacation, whereas

TABLE 13.2. Percentage of Foreign Visitor Arrivals by Age and Sex, 1992-1997

Regions	1992 % (N = 4 million)						1997 % (N = 7.4 million)					
	Under 17	17-30	31-50	Over 50	Male	Female	Under 17	17-30	31-50	Over 50	Male	Female
Total	**3.9**	**26.2**	**44.1**	**25.8**	**66.3**	**33.7**	**3.4**	**20.9**	**44.5**	**31.2**	**67.5**	**32.5**
Asia	3.5	23.8	43.2	29.5	70.5	29.5	3.0	21.0	43.5	32.5	70.2	29.8
Europe	3.3	31.2	45.3	20.3	62.3	37.7	2.8	24.6	49.5	23.1	61.2	38.8
Europe (Excl. Russia*)	4.1	21.7	44.5	29.6	62.8	37.2	3.1	19.5	45.4	32.0	69.7	30.3
America	6.6	20.8	43.3	29.4	62.7	37.3	6.0	13.5	39.9	40.6	67.2	32.8
Oceania	6.2	23.9	46.8	23.2	64.1	35.9	6.8	15.1	41.8	36.3	67.1	32.9
Africa	5.6	25.2	44.5	24.7	71.0	29.0	2.7	23.6	32.7	41.1	77.5	22.5
Short Haul												
Japan	3.3	20.0	39.1	37.7	69.9	30.1	2.9	17.3	38.4	41.3	75.4	24.6
Philippines	3.0	32.7	48.9	15.3	82.7	17.3	1.3	32.5	45.8	20.4	75.5	24.5
South Korea	-	-	-	-	-	-	3.2	17.8	50.1	28.9	74.9	25.1
Singapore	5.5	20.2	43.3	31.0	61.5	38.5	5.8	15.9	43.1	35.2	61.2	38.8
Thailand	4.1	20.2	40.6	35.1	54.5	45.5	4.3	21.3	39.9	34.5	52.9	47.1
Mongolia	-	-	-	-	-	-	1.2	39.9	47.5	11.4	54.6	45.4
Russia*	2.6	37.7	45.8	13.9	61.9	38.1	2.3	31.4	54.9	11.4	50.0	50.0
Long Haul												
U.K.	5.6	22.4	43.3	28.7	62.6	37.4	3.6	17.2	41.9	37.2	71.3	28.7
France	4.9	19.8	44.6	30.6	58.5	41.5	4.5	18.4	41.6	35.6	66.4	33.6
Germany	3.1	19.8	42.4	34.7	62.8	37.2	2.8	16.4	43.2	37.6	70.5	29.5
Italy	4.1	21.7	44.9	29.4	62.5	37.5	2.0	17.7	47.6	32.7	73.4	26.6
U.S.A.	6.9	19.8	42.5	30.9	62.0	38.0	5.9	13.2	40.0	40.8	66.7	33.3
Canada	6.5	22.5	45.3	25.8	63.8	36.2	6.8	13.0	40.2	40.0	68.5	31.5
Australia	6.8	24.2	45.3	23.7	63.8	36.2	7.2	14.3	42.1	36.4	66.7	33.3

Source: CNTA (1993, 1998).
*"Former Soviet Union" in 1992 and "Russia" in 1997.
Note: See Table 13.1 for country totals.

single male travelers are more likely to be on business trips (although this may be combined with leisure activities, as well). More balanced sex ratios may indicate a higher degree of leisure vacationers relative to business travelers. The relative decline in female visitors from long-haul origin countries was probably related to a significant drop in the percentage of foreign visitors taking group inclusive tours (GIT) through Chinese travel agencies (from 31 percent of foreign visitors in 1992 to 27 percent in 1997).

Distance also seems to be a factor, as family-oriented vacations are seldom long-haul in nature due to the financial, psychological, and physical stresses of travel. This further reduces the proportion of women from long-haul origin countries, even though quite a few long-haul source countries are the wealthiest nations in the world. Finally, the status of women in the source country may be reflected in the sex ratio of visitors to China. In Japan and South Korea, for example, women traditionally play a more restrained role in public and economic life, which may account for their lower percentages among visitors from those countries.

Age

Age distribution is the principal demographic variable available on visitors to China. The age group of thirty-one to fifty years comprised the largest number of visitors and accounted for about 40 percent of total foreign visitors to China in the 1980s (Gerstlacher, Krieg, and Sternfeld, 1991). This group has since increased to about 44 percent in the 1990s (Table 13.2). The percentage of the thirty-one to fifty-year-old age group from major source countries, whether long-haul or short-haul, has been mostly around 40 to 45 percent. This was generally so for both 1992 and 1997. Among short-haul source countries, Japan had the smallest number of visitors from the thirty-one to fifty-year-old group (38 percent) and Russia had the largest (54 percent) in 1997. They both also represented the bottom and top, respectively, among China's major source countries.

Compared to the steady percentages of the middle adult group, the shift from youths to older adults was rather significant in the 1990s. From 1992 to 1997, almost all of the decline in the percentage shares occurred among the youth age group (seventeen to thirty), with a corresponding growth in the older adult group (over age fifty). The over-

all percentage of foreign visitors over fifty years old reached 31 percent in 1997, the highest during any year in the prior two decades
(CNTA, various years). For some source countries (e.g., Japan and
the United States), this older group was the largest age group to visit
China in 1997. However, in terms of total numbers, all of the age
groups were much larger in 1997 than in 1992. A decline in percentage share here (Table 13.2) represents only the slower growth of one
age group relative to the others and the overall changing demographic
structure of foreign visitors to China. The shares of older adult visitors from long-haul source countries is overall higher and more uni-
form, ranging from 32 to 40 percent, in comparison to short-haul origin countries, which ranged from 11 to 41 percent. The percentage
(and number) of older adult visitors grew tremendously from several
long-haul source countries in the 1990s, including Canada (reaching
15 percent in 1997), the United States (10 percent in 1997), Netherlands (10 percent), and Australia (13 percent). The aging trend in
some long-haul countries probably plays some role in the changes.

Occupations

Data on the occupation of foreign visitors are collected from the
customs entrance form and reported by CNTA annually (CNTA,
1990). Although visitor occupations have been reported by CNTA
since the 1980s, a major change in the classification system occurred
in 1991, making comparison between 1980s and 1990s impossible
for most categories. For example, in the 1980s, the largest visitor occupation group was that of worker/farmer, which accounted for over
21 percent of all visitors, followed by business and business management occupations (at about 15 percent and 18 percent, respectively)
(Gerstlacher, Krieg, and Sternfeld, 1991). "Official" was a small category in the 1980s, and only accounted for 2 to 3 percent of foreign
visitors. After the classification change in 1991, the "official" occupation jumped to 9.7 percent and reached a peak of 11.9 percent in
1992. The significant increase in visitors in this group was probably
caused by two factors: (1) a change in the Chinese definition of official, and (2) the impact of the Tiananmen Square incident. The old
and new English statistical reports both use the term official, but the
Chinese version was changed from *guanyuan* (meaning "government
official") to *xingzhen guanli renyuan* (meaning "administrator"),

which is a category in both English and Chinese on the customs entrance forms. In China, there is no significant difference between government official and administrator. Outside of China, however, administrator has a broader connotation than government official, which can cause confusion in the ultimate interpretation of occupation statistics.

The year 1992 was when sanctions against China by many Western countries for the Tiananmen Square incident were either cancelled or significantly reduced. Many foreign government visits that had been cancelled in 1989 were being rescheduled, thereby resulting in the increased number of visits by "officials."

Even though comparisons with the 1980s are not possible, differences can be compared between 1992 and 1997 (Table 13.3). In 1992, long-haul visitors were much more concentrated than short-haul visitors in two occupation categories: officials and businesspeople (totaling about 40 to 50 percent in those major source countries). Although a visitor's occupation is not directly related to the purpose of a trip, it is reasonable to expect a higher proportion of business and government trips to China at a time when global media encouraged vacationers to stay away. For long-haul visitors there was a universal decline in percentage of officials, clerks, and businesspeople. As discussed previously, it is important to keep in mind that the number of visitors in 1997 was higher than that in 1992 in almost every occupation category, except a major drop for farmer and a slight decrease for the officials and worker categories. The category that registered the highest gain was "others," which more than doubled for almost every country from 1992 to 1997.

The occupational structures of long-haul and short-haul visitors to China differ in many ways. First, the percentage of visitors from the "official" occupation category dove into the single digits (around 5 percent) for short-haul visitors in 1997, about half that of long-haul visitors. Second, while the proportion of businesspeople traveling to China generally declined from 1992 to 1997, this was greater for long-haul visitors than among short-haul visitors. Russia even showed a 19 percent increase in the businesspeople category from 1992 to 1997. Third, the major long-haul source countries (except Australia) had large percentage increases in the category of "nonemployed" from 1992 to 1997, while short-haul countries did not change either way during this period.

TABLE 13.3. Percentage of Foreign Visitor Arrivals by Occupation and Nationality, 1992-1997

Regions	1992								1997							
	Technician	Official	Clerk	Business	Server	Worker	Others	Non-employed	Technician	Official	Clerk	Business	Server	Worker	Others	Non-employed
Total	**10.2**	**11.9**	**11.0**	**22.5**	**5.7**	**13.8**	**17.6**	**7.3**	**8.1**	**6.1**	**6.8**	**17.7**	**6.7**	**6.5**	**31.3**	**16.8**
Asia	9.1	9.6	10.2	22.1	6.5	15.8	16.9	9.9	6.8	4.8	7.8	15.9	7.0	7.7	34.3	15.7
Europe	9.5	13.3	11.8	20.4	4.9	15.0	21.4	3.6	7.9	6.5	4.6	22.9	6.5	6.2	26.0	19.3
Europe (Excl. Russia*)	13.3	24.8	18.4	20.8	5.3	5.2	8.3	3.9	12.5	10.4	6.6	10.9	5.3	4.6	19.5	30.2
America	16.0	15.3	11.4	27.4	5.3	5.0	10.6	8.9	13.7	11.0	6.9	15.5	6.0	1.6	27.9	17.4
Oceania	13.2	12.5	10.2	35.7	4.9	5.3	10.9	7.4	13.7	8.4	6.8	17.7	5.8	1.6	34.0	11.9
Africa	15.6	15.6	12.8	32.9	6.1	6.9	7.3	2.9	5.7	6.0	11.1	19.6	5.2	4.9	24.6	22.8
Short Haul																
Japan	9.4	11.6	13.8	19.6	8.8	11.1	14.1	11.5	6.1	5.6	10.8	16.7	5.1	1.5	39.0	15.3
Philippines	7.6	3.2	4.0	15.5	3.1	54.0	9.4	3.2	6.3	1.7	2.3	5.4	20.3	38.1	23.5	2.4
Korea	-	-	-	-	-	-	-	-	5.6	3.3	6.2	17.4	4.3	7.4	39.4	16.4
Singapore	10.9	10.1	8.2	31.3	5.8	4.0	15.7	14.0	11.1	7.7	6.4	16.5	7.5	0.8	35.1	14.9
Thailand	7.5	7.8	8.2	40.8	4.9	3.1	11.3	16.4	8.1	3.5	7.2	16.5	9.9	2.6	35.4	16.6
Mongolia	-	-	-	-	-	-	-	-	6.3	5.7	7.1	22.1	7.1	3.6	13.7	34.3
Russia*	6.8	5.4	7.2	20.1	4.6	21.8	30.5	3.5	1.8	1.4	1.9	38.8	8.2	8.4	34.6	5.0
Long Haul																
United Kingdom	16.6	19.4	13.9	25.2	5.6	4.7	9.4	5.3	16.0	12.3	7.4	13.7	5.9	1.4	23.1	20.2
France	14.9	24.0	16.0	21.9	4.6	3.6	10.0	4.9	12.3	10.5	7.5	12.5	5.1	0.9	21.5	29.7
Germany	11.1	31.2	22.4	15.9	4.7	3.3	8.1	3.3	13.9	11.3	6.9	11.3	4.4	2.2	18.7	31.3
Italy	12.3	27.5	23.0	22.1	4.9	2.1	5.4	2.8	11.8	13.5	7.1	13.1	4.0	1.3	15.6	33.7
United States	16.9	15.9	11.3	24.3	5.7	4.7	11.3	9.9	15.0	11.8	6.3	14.0	6.4	1.4	27.0	18.1
Canada	14.1	13.8	11.1	31.8	4.9	4.9	10.8	8.6	11.8	10.7	8.6	17.5	5.2	1.2	29.0	16.0
Australia	13.7	12.7	11.1	29.9	5.8	5.8	12.5	8.6	14.3	8.8	7.0	16.6	6.2	1.4	33.6	12.1

Source: CNTA (1993, 1998).
* "Former Soviet Union" in 1992 and "Russia" in 1997.
Note: Nonemployed describes those visitors who have no defined occupation.

Nonemployed refers to visitors who have no occupation, such as housewives, students, and retired people. The age distribution showed us that visitors under thirty years old were on the decline; therefore, the increase in the nonemployed category would be mainly from retirees and housewives. Table 13.3 shows that Western European countries all had very high percentages in the nonemployed category (about 30 percent), followed by North American countries (16 to 18 percent). However, the two extremes in the nonemployed category were both from the short-haul group of countries: Mongolia (34 percent), Russia (5 percent), and the Philippines (2.4 percent). Given the economic constraints of people in the Philippines and Russia, the low percentage of unemployed travelers can be understood. The story for Mongolia is a bit different. The large number of nonemployed from Mongolia are herders who cross the land border into China. They consider themselves as "nonemployed" when filling out the customs forms because they have no paid occupation.

In summary, the demographic characteristics of various long-haul visitors tend to be similar, both in their occupational distributions and in the changes experienced from 1992 to 1997, whereas short-haul visitors vary much more in both of these patterns. From 1992 to 1997, more men than women visited China, and visitors over fifty years old were on the rise. Official and businesspeople occupied a declining share of the visitor totals, indicating that China attracted broader interest among its foreign visitors at the turn of the millennium. The increase of percentage share in both the older adult group and the nonemployed category indicates a growing number of retirees among China's long-haul visitors.

SPATIAL CONCENTRATION AND CHANGES

Although China is a vast country with a huge list of spectacular natural, cultural, and historical attractions, foreign visitors actually tend to be concentrated in only a few dozen places due to the limits of time, money, and accessibility. CNTA annually reports the number of foreign visitors received in about fifty major cities by nationality (Table 13.4). Eleven major source countries were identified in the statistics for both 1992 and 1997, including five short-haul countries, Ja-

TABLE 13.4. Percentage Change of Foreign Visitors by Nationality in Selected Cities, 1992-1997

City	Total %G[a]	Japan %92[b]	Japan %C[c]	Philippines %92	Philippines %C	Singapore %92	Singapore %C	Thailand %92	Thailand %C	Russia %92	Russia %C	UK&Fr&Ge[d] %92	UK&Fr&Ge %C	US&CA[e] %92	US&CA %C	Australia %92	Australia %C
Beijing	55	31	-8	1	0	3	1	2	0	4	-1	17	-4	12	2	2	1
Changsha	732	35	-20	1	0	6	-1	2	-1	2	4	15	-7	19	0	2	6
Chengdu	57	25	26	1	0	6	3	3	0	0	0	20	-2	18	9	2	0
Chongqing	232	16	1	1	0	5	2	2	4	0	0	31	-24	24	-14	2	0
Dalian	132	72	-27	0	0	1	0	1	0	4	-2	2	0	4	-1	0	0
Fuzhou	11	24	5	3	-1	20	-5	1	0	1	-1	3	2	12	2	1	1
Guangzhou	23	15	-2	1	0	9	-5	4	-2	0	0	12	-4	15	-6	3	0
Guilin	11	25	-3	0	0	5	-3	2	-1	0	0	18	0	13	1	3	-1
Haikou	67	19	3	1	0	26	-6	9	-4	0	0	7	-2	9	-2	2	-1
Hangzhou	57	25	-2	1	0	8	4	2	1	0	0	10	-2	13	-3	2	1
Harbin	30	18	7	0	1	2	1	0	2	65	-38	2	4	3	5	0	1
Huangshan	295	41	-21	4	-3	12	13	3	1	0	0	7	-4	14	-3	1	1
Kunming	204	19	-7	0	1	9	6	18	-3	0	0	11	-1	10	0	2	0
Nanjing	49	22	6	1	0	8	0	4	-3	0	0	14	-3	12	-1	2	0
Nantong	741	67	-2	1	0	1	1	1	0	0	0	3	2	8	9	1	0
Ningbo	169	42	-10	19	-9	5	2	2	0	0	0	12	-4	9	3	2	1
Qingdao	229	40	-12	1	4	2	3	1	-1	1	1	10	-5	13	-7	2	-1
Qinhuangdao	838	27	-17	3	0	8	0	3	2	12	0	11	-2	11	-4	3	-1
Quanzhou	137	13	9	21	-4	38	-1	1	0	0	0	1	3	2	3	0	0
Sanya	476	24	15	0	0	14	-7	2	-1	1	0	18	-14	11	-6	2	-1

Shanghai	66	48	-2	2	0	3	1	1	0	1	-1	11	-2	12	-1	1	1
Shantou	-41	4	4	0	0	15	1	61	-20	0	0	2	2	4	3	1	1
Shenyang	207	27	-11	0	0	3	-1	1	-1	27	-9	4	0	7	-3	1	0
Shenzhen	133	23	-3	1	0	1	3	0	1	0	0	3	2	3	7	0	1
Shijiazhuang	643	44	-24	2	-1	3	1	1	0	3	1	10	-5	14	-1	2	4
Suzhou	31	42	-7	0	0	4	1	1	0	0	0	18	-6	11	-1	2	-1
Tianjin	318	41	-26	1	-1	3	-1	1	-1	2	-2	8	-4	10	-5	2	-1
Urumqi	21	26	-12	0	0	1	0	1	-1	46	6	8	-4	5	0	1	0
Wuhan	401	23	9	1	0	4	-1	2	-1	0	0	21	-12	28	-15	3	-2
Wuxi	58	41	3	0	0	7	3	1	0	0	0	16	-8	13	-6	1	0
Xiamen	121	12	3	1	-11	29	-6	3	-3	0	0	3	1	5	4	1	2
Xi'an	20	26	9		0	4	-3	1	-1	0	0	25	-6	16	-1	2	0
Yanbian	403	9	-7		0	0	0	0	0	5	-4	1	0	4	-3	0	0
Zhengzhou	460	30	-7	1	1	6	-1	4	-2	1	4	8	2	12	-3	2	0

Source: CNTA (1993, 1998).

a Percentage growth from 1992 to 1997. Calculated as: (visitors in 1997 – visitors in 1992) / visitors in 1992.

b Percentage share of visitors in 1992.

c Percentage change of visitors between 1997 and 1992. Calculated as: percentage share in 1997 – percentage share in 1992.

d United Kingdom, France, and Germany.

e United States and Canada.

pan, the Philippines, Singapore, Thailand, and Russia; and six long-haul countries, United Kingdom, France, Germany, the United States, Canada, and Australia.

The statistics provide interesting information on "who visited where," and make spatial analysis possible. However, since the data were collected by hotels that are officially designated to receive foreign guests, they are not comparable with the more accurate statistics collected at customs, which include day excursionists and people staying in other types of accommodations. For example, about 800,000 Russian visitors entered China in 1997, but only about 200,000 hotel stays were reported. At the regional level, duplicate counting of visitors who stayed overnight in several different places within the region of study is a problem. Visitors who are on multidestination itineraries, therefore, are more represented in the data than those who are not. Thus, the total number of foreign visitor stays reported by the fifty-nine major cities was 20 percent greater than the total foreign visitors who entered China in 1997.

There was an interesting division among the reported countries. The number of regional visitors from the six long-haul countries all exceeded their customs numbers at China's ports of entry. It is easy to understand that long-haul visitors stayed longer and visited several places in one trip since their cost and effort to get China are much greater than that of short-haul visitors.

On the other hand, the five short-haul countries varied greatly in this in 1997. Japan and Singapore were very much overcounted at the regional level (similar to long-haul travelers). Thailand is almost the same, but regional accounts for Russian and Filipino visitors were fewer than half of their port of entry counts. Although this may cause some confusion, it in fact reveals the different visitors' behavior patterns in China. Russian visitors, for example, were mostly border-crossing day excursionists, looking for business or trading opportunities; even if they stayed overnight, they seldom stayed in star-rated hotels designated for foreigners due to their financial constraints. Unlike Russians, most Japanese visitors stayed in the official foreign guest hotels and visited several different places during their trip. Once again, long-haul visitors showed greater similarity among themselves than did short-haul visitors.

Regional Variations and Changes

Unlike compatriots from Hong Kong, Macao, and Taiwan, who have ethnic and ancestral roots in China and may visit places in small towns or rural areas for family reasons, the majority of foreign visitors have no such ties to places in China. Therefore, they primarily go to the most popular tourist destinations and end up being highly concentrated in only a handful of cities in China, especially Beijing, Shanghai, and Guangzhou (Figures 13.3 and 13.4). In addition to these, the top seven most visited cities included Xi'an, Guilin, Shenzhen, and Hangzhou, which together attracted 70 percent of total foreign visitors in 1992 and 58 percent in 1997 (keeping in mind the biases in this data as indicated previously).

Although the regional concentration of foreign visitors was still very strong in 1997, there was also an emerging trend toward greater dispersion. This trend was evidenced not only by the decline in the share of visitors in the top seven cities, but also by corresponding increases in foreign visitors in medium-sized and interior cities (Table 13.4). None of the cities that reported the fastest growth from 1992 to 1997 were primary destinations: Qinhuangdao (838 percent), Nantong (741 percent), Changsha (732 percent), and Shijiazhuang (643 percent). In fact, rates of growth in arrivals of the top seven cities were all lower than 70 percent over the five-year period, compared to most other cities, which saw their foreign arrivals double, triple, or even grow eight times by 1997.

The spatial diffusion of foreign visitors reflects a natural instinct of humans to avoid repetition and to explore new places. Along with the opening up of China after economic reforms in 1978, services in interior places have gradually been improved and more foreigners are now repeat visitors to China. The spatial diffusion of foreign visitors is an inevitable trend that will continue to grow well into the next century. However, the primary positions of Beijing, Shanghai, and Guangzhou will not be challenged because of their economic, political, and cultural importance, as well as their positions as the principal gateways and transportation hubs for the country.

As important as the main destinations were, there were still differences in the way short-haul and long-haul visitors toured China. Short-haul visitors tended to have their favored places in China that they visited more often than others. For example, Korean visitors

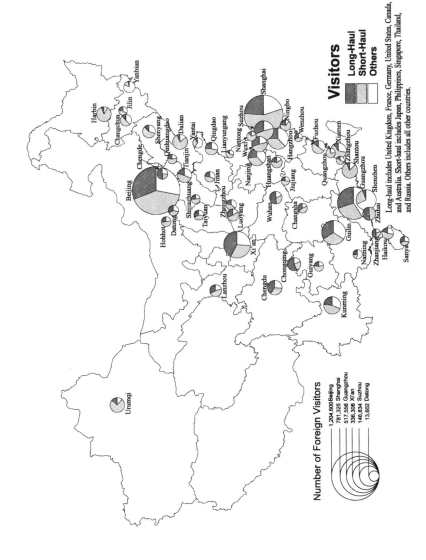

Visitors

- **■** Long-Haul
- **▥** Short-Haul
- **□** Others

Long-haul includes United Kingdom, France, Germany, United States, Canada, and Australia. Short-haul includes Japan, Philippines, Singapore, Thailand, and Russia. Others includes all other countries.

Number of Foreign Visitors

| 1,204,600 Beijing |
| 781,325 Shanghai |
| 517,556 Guangzhou |
| 336,308 Xi'an |
| 146,834 Suzhou |
| 13,602 Datong |

FIGURE 13.3. Foreign Visitor Arrivals in Selected Cities, 1992. (*Source:* CNTA, 1993, 1998.)

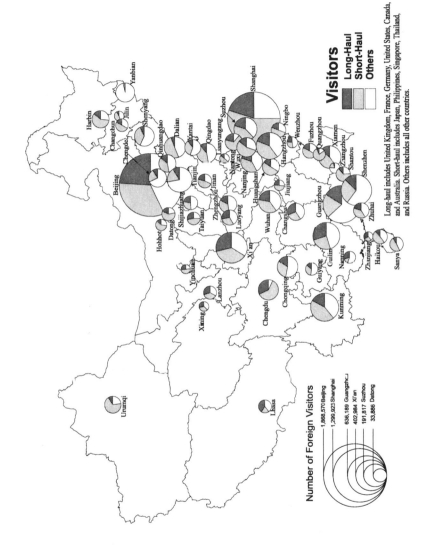

Long-haul includes United Kingdom, France, Germany, United States, Canada, and Australia. Short-haul includes Japan, Philippines, Singapore, Thailand, and Russia. Others includes all other countries.

Visitors
- Long-Haul
- Short-Haul
- Others

Number of Foreign Visitors
- 1,868,570 Beijing
- 1,299,923 Shanghai
- 636,189 Guangzhou
- 402,984 Xi'an
- 191,817 Suzhou
- 33,886 Datong

FIGURE 13.4. Foreign Visitor Arrivals in Selected Cities, 1997. (*Source:* CNTA, 1993, 1998.)

257

were highly concentrated in Yanbian, which is an ethnic Korean autonomous city, and in northeast China and the Bo Hai Bay region, which is close to the Korean peninsula. Thai visitors favored Shantou, the hometown of a large number of Chinese descendants in Thailand, and Kunming with its close proximity to Thailand and great ethnic and scenic diversity. In addition, short-haul visitors tended to visit their favorite places repeatedly while they were exploring other places.

Long-haul visitors, on the other hand, have less knowledge about China, and also less freedom due to the language and culture barriers. Their first trip to China typically consists of visits to the most important tourist attractions, including Beijing, Shanghai, Xi'an, and Guilin. However, since even long-haul visitors have a desire to explore new places, they tend to visit more diverse destinations on subsequent trips. It is actually quite easy to tell if a foreign tour group is composed of first-time visitors or repeat visitors simply by examining the itinerary.

In examining changes in the spatial distribution of foreign visitors in China by nationality from 1992 to 1997, two trends become evident (Table 13.4). First, there has been a rapid increase of foreign visitors to medium-size and interior cities. Second, the intensity of visitation by certain short-haul nationalities in particular cities has declined over the years. Major concentrations of this type included Thai visitors in Shantou, Japanese visitors in Dalian, Singapore visitors in Fujian Province, and Russian visitors in Harbin. Both of these trends reflect the tendency of people to start from something familiar and then to try something new.

Motivation for nonbusiness travelers can be summarized in the following categories:

1. Visiting family, relatives, and friends
2. Visiting a hometown or origin place of ancestors
3. Visiting the place they themselves or their parents have lived in the past
4. Visiting a place where they can speak the same language
5. Visiting places with similar culture, religion, or geographic proximity
6. Visiting places with famous attractions
7. Exploring new places

The interest and propensity of visitors to take a particular trip declines from motivation 1 to 7. Interest in making multiple visits to the same place is reduced even faster down this list. Many short-haul visitors to China are motivated by the first five categories while long-haul visitors are mainly motivated by the last two categories and have, therefore, been growing at a slower rate. To the long-haul visitor, China is the destination and experience to be had. Kunming may be significantly different from Dalian for short-haul visitors, but it is just another Chinese city in the eyes of long-haul visitors. This is simply because their motivational frame of reference is shaped by the many barriers that long-haul visitors must overcome in making a China trip—barriers that are far less substantial for short-haul visitors.

CONCLUSION

In the year 2000, twenty-two years after commercial tourism started, foreign visitor arrivals in China exceeded 10 million (Han, 2001). Tremendous increases in foreign visitors came from every major source country in the world. However, due to the barriers of distance, culture, cost, and knowledge, long-haul visitor numbers grew slower and showed different demographic and spatial touring patterns in comparison to short-haul visitors from other Asian countries.

The analysis in this chapter revealed many common characteristics among long-haul visitors no matter what part of the world they came from. These included sex ratio and the trend of increasing male visitors, a uniformly higher percentage of middle-age and older adult visitors that has been growing, a higher percentage of visitors in the occupation category "official," and distinct patterns of spatial distribution and diffusion.

Short-haul visitors, on the other hand, were found to have much greater diversity in these characteristics, often showing extreme highs and lows, making them more difficult to generalize. This is due to the significant differences in economic conditions, purposes of visits, border-crossing opportunities, and relationships to China that exist for short-haul countries. Distance tends to even out these differences for long-haul countries and will continue to be the biggest challenge that China faces in growing its long-haul visitor market.

REFERENCES

Bessette, Claire (1999). China Visit Changes Tallman's Perceptions. *The Day* (October 18):B1.

CNTA (1990-1998). *The Yearbook of China Tourism Statistics.* Beijing: China Tourism Publishing House.

Encyclopaedia Britannica Online (2002a). History: Canada since 1920: Canada between the wars. <www.eb.com:180/bol/topic?eu=119752>, accessed June 6, 2002.

Encyclopaedia Britannica Online (2002b). International Relations, American Uncertainty. <www.eb.com:180/bol/topic?eu=10837>, accessed June 6, 2002.

Gerstlacher, Anna, Krieg, Renate, and Sternfeld, Eva (1991). *Tourism in the People's Republic of China.* Bangkok: Ecumenical Coalition on Third World Tourism.

Gormsen, Erdmann (1990). The Impact of Tourism on Regional Change in China. *GeoJournal* 21(1/2): 127-135.

Gormsen, Erdmann (1995). International Tourism in China: Its Organization and Socio-economic Impact. In Lew, Alan A. and Yu, Lawrence (Eds.), *Tourism in China* (pp. 63-88). Boulder, CO: Westview Press.

Han, Zhuping (2001). Woguo qunian jiedai waiguo luyouzhe tupo qianwan renci daguan (China Received Over 10 Million Foreign Visitors Last Year). *Renmin Ribao (People's Daily)* (January 11):1.

He, Guoping (1989). An Analysis of Tourism Development in the People's Republic of China: Government Policy from 1978 to 1989. Master thesis, The George Washington University.

Jeffrey, Douglas and Xie, Yanjun (1995). The UK Market for Tourism in China. *Annals of Tourism Research* 22(4):857-876.

Lambrianidis, William (2000). An American View of China. *The Recorder* (September 13):9,10.

Lew, Alan A. (1995). Overseas Chinese and Compatriots in China's Tourism Development. In Lew, Alan A. and Yu, Lawrence (Eds.), *Tourism in China: Geographic, Political, and Economic Perspectives* (pp. 155-178). Boulder, CO: Westview Press.

Oakes, Tim (1998). *Tourism and Modernity in China.* London: Routledge.

Roehl, Wesley S. (1995). The June 4, 1989, Tiananmen Square Incident and Chinese Tourism. In Lew, Alan A. and Yu, Lawrence (Eds.), *Tourism in China: Geographic, Political, and Economic Perspectives* (pp. 41-62). Boulder, CO: Westview Press.

Wen, Jie and Tisdell, Clem (1996). Spatial Distribution of Tourism in China: Economic and Other Influences. *Tourism Economics* 2(3):235-250.

World Tourism Organization (2000). *Tourism highlights.* Madrid: World Tourism Organization.

Xu, Gang (1999). *Tourism and Local Economic Development in China, Case Studies of Guilin, Suzhou and Beidaihe.* Richmond, UK: Curzon Press.

Yang, Guoqiang (2001). Jiang Zeming huijian Janada zongli Chrétien. (Jiang Zeming Met Canadian Prime Minister Chrétien.) Renming *Ribao (People's Daily, Overseas Edition),* (February 14):1.

Yang, Z. (1989). Exploit Tourist Resources and Develop Tourism Industry in China. *Problemy Tourystyki* 12:13-15.

Zhang, Yongwei (1989). American Tourists to China: A Marketing Perspective of Perceived Tourism Quality in China. PhD dissertation. Southern Illinois University.

Chapter 14

Leisure in China

Honggen Xiao

Much research has been conducted into the nature and significance of leisure. Although leisure is popularly thought of as the opposite of work, it is generally defined in terms of "freedom from constraint," "time left over after work," or "free time after obligatory social duties have been met" (Torkildsen, 1992:25). However, according to Parry, leisure as a social phenomenon involves social constraint and social obligation and can best be thought of as being embodied in a whole way of life. Such an idea of leisure even invokes the concept of culture (Parry and Parry, 1977). The complexity and diversity of leisure are also illustrated by Kaplan, who, from a sociological point of view, argued that "nothing is definable as leisure per se and almost anything is definable as leisure, given a synthesis of elements" (Kaplan, 1975:19).

Contrary to the understanding of leisure as a commodity of time and a state of mind, Goodale and Godbey described leisure as a way of living when they expressed the view that "leisure is living in relative freedom from external compulsive forces on one's culture and physical environment so as to be able to act from internally compelling ways which are personally pleasing, intuitively worthwhile, and provide a basis of faith" (Goodale and Godbey, 1988:28). Generally, researchers to date have attempted to approach the conceptualization of leisure as "free time," "activity," "a state of being," "an all-embracing and holistic concept," and even as "a way of living" (Torkildsen, 1992:25-33). According to Dumazedier (1967), for example, the three primary functions of leisure are relaxation, entertainment, and personal development. Within these three activities, people find, respectively, recovery from fatigue, deliverance from boredom, and liberation from daily automatism. It is based on this understanding and conceptual interpretation that this discussion of leisure in contemporary Chinese society is developed.

CHARACTERISTICS OF LEISURE IN CHINA

Leisure in China had a very different pattern prior to China's economic expansion in the late 1980s and 1990s. In the first place, the income of Chinese families was very low. Discretionary income was limited and rarely allocated to leisure activities, recreation, and leisure travel. After meeting their daily expenses, most Chinese families devoted their discretionary income to building or purchasing homes, to their children's education, to the expenses involved in the marriage of sons and daughters, and to the purchase of durable goods.

The fashion in the purchase of durable goods by Chinese families, for example, had been changing with the times from the purchase of the "three major durable goods" of watch, bicycle, and sewing machine in the late 1970s and early 1980s to those of television, refrigerator, and motorcycle in the late 1980s. This is especially true during the later periods of Mao's era and the first ten years of the post-Mao era (1976-1986). According to a survey of urban residents conducted by *Economic Daily* ("Family Vacation Survey," 1982), participation in leisure and leisure-based travel on a yearly basis was uncommon, accounting for 23 percent of the surveyed families in large cities, 15 percent in medium-sized cities, and 8 percent in small cities and towns. Most of the travel taken by residents of smaller cities involved shopping trips to nearby larger cities.

A second characteristic of leisure in China prior to the recent economic expansion was that leisure activities were limited in scope and poor in quality. Participation rates were even low for the occasional leisure activities in which people did participate. Not only did the majority of the Chinese have difficulties affording leisure and recreation activities, but the poor state of leisure facilities further worsened the situation. In the *Economic Daily* study cited previously, urban residents participated in (in order of frequency) visiting parks and zoos, suburb outings, and weekend sports.

A third feature of earlier leisure in China was the striking difference between urban and rural residents in the provision of leisure facilities and, consequently, in their participation in such activities. Although leisure facilities such as cinemas and theaters, gardens and parks, and museums and libraries were popular for urban residents, rural people could hardly find anywhere to go or anything to do in their leisure time. Common mass leisure and recreation facilities such as nightclubs, karaoke TV, theme parks and other man-made attractions, and cafeterias and bars, have been only a recent phenomenon in China, even for residents in larger cities.

Finally, considerable irregularity existed in the leisure behavior patterns of people in China (Xiao, 1997; Huang and Xiao, 2000). For one, leisure and recreation were not pursued solely for their own sake. Business or visiting friends and relatives played an important role in the leisure behavior of the Chinese. For another, irregular and intensive periods of leisure took place during traditional holidays, festivals, and events. These far outnumbered regular leisure activities during weekends and after work. This partly accounted for a high seasonality in leisure activities at the time. Overall, leisure behavior in China prior to the 1990s was deeply embedded in the Chinese mentality and social structure that was formed following the establishment of the People's Republic of China in 1949. From the standpoint of the Chinese in the 1970s and 1980s, outgoing leisure behavior was easily and readily associated with "idleness" and "hedonism" and was, therefore, strongly discouraged by government officials. For most families, the inherited Confucian ideology of "working for the next generation" still strongly prevailed, although the Chinese Communist Party tried to expand this to incorporate the good of the broader society, as well.

Ever since the Chinese government formulated and carried out the economic reform and open door policy, which was initiated in late 1978, contemporary Chinese society has seen rapid changes in its economy. In the 1990s, due to improved international relations, advances in information technology, partial privatization of the Chinese economy, and the increasing globalization of China's trade, the distance between China and the rest of the world has become remarkably shortened. Major transformations in China's social policies have also taken place, with increasing free time and consumer choice, which has had a direct effect on leisure provision and management.

On one hand, China's economic success has contributed to a remarkable increase in people's disposable income, by means of pay raises and more diversified sources of incomes. For example, the nationwide pay raise, under the State Council Pay Raise Act for public sectors and state-owned enterprises, enacted in October 1993, has provided the salary-earning class with higher incomes and, consequently, has increased the likelihood of leisure expenditures (Liu, 1995).

On the other hand, the new system of labor and employment has intensified the rhythm of work in daily life and, as a result, has increased competition and work pressure in a hitherto relatively easy, although simple, life for most Chinese. Intense competition and the strains of work have brought about a greater awareness of the need for leisure and recreation. A study of the leisure market in Shanghai found that 92 percent of the surveyed respondents expressed a need and expectation to participate in leisure and recreation activities, including taking short vacations during the newly implemented two-day nonwork weekends (Su, Ding, and Zhou, 1996). The five-day work week, introduced in China in May 1995, lengthened the available leisure time in a week and, as a result, many public and private leisure facilities, recreation centers, and tourist attractions have experienced a boom in participation rates. There has also been a steady growth of vacation trips on weekends.

The increasing awareness of leisure needs has, interestingly, been reflected in the growing membership in labor unions in the 1990s (Zhou, 1993). Unions have now achieved a wider scope of acceptance in China than they had in the past. Most medium-size private enterprises have their own unions. In government and other public sector bodies, a labor union hierarchy has been established, which operates down to the smallest work unit. Through such unions, the rights of members can be better protected, and their public welfare (including group social activities, weekend excursions, and other leisure activities) has been extended to a wide cross section of the society. Furthermore, union activity funds, which are supported by public money, member fees, and income from union business activities have become substantial sources for organizing leisure activities for union members.

LEISURE PRODUCTS IN CHINA

In China, leisure participation occurs through a wide range of resources, services, facilities, and management. Although leisure facilities and services have not been as well developed in China as in more developed nations, there has recently been a marked emphasis on leisure and recreation product design in urban and, to a lesser degree, rural planning policies (Du, 1999). To meet the diverse needs of the leisure market, a range of facilities is needed, both indoor and outdoor, in urban and rural areas, and on both land and water. Because of government land use policies and finance regulations, the provision and management of leisure and recreation in China (with no distinction of urban and rural differences for the ease of presentation) can be mainly classified into two categories: the public sector and the private or commercial sector.

The Public Sector

Leisure products and provision of the public sector are primarily planned and constructed by various governmental organizations, such as the planning and land use departments of central, provincial, municipal, and local governments. Their goals are to enhance the living standards of residents by ensuring the availability of leisure and green space in urban and rural settings. Although the management and operation of public leisure facilities take various forms and may, sometimes, serve overlapping purposes in terms of product functions and categorization, the provision of this sector is generally for nonprofit purposes. Leisure products and provisions in the public sector mainly include:

- *Entertainment-related products:* cinemas, theaters, Chinese opera houses, music (concert) halls, unions clubs, dance halls, open air museums (such as model villages and model towns, which have been especially established to show visitors traditional ways of life that have already disappeared), staged performances of traditional dances or rituals, exhibition halls and fairs, cultural parades, and "cultural centers" (a general term for open public space for entertainment and gathering)
- *Education-related products:* public libraries, readers' clubs, adult education centers, convention, exhibition, and meeting halls, museums, zoological parks (zoos), and education bases of patriotism and socialism (specified by China's central government, including mausoleums, cemeteries and tombs of revolutionary martyrs, monuments, and some historical sites and relics)

- *Culture and art-related products:* museums, art centers, and galleries, Chinese opera houses, historic preservation sites, cultural palaces, and cultural districts
- *Indoor and outdoor sports-related products:* playgrounds, sports stadiums, gymnasiums, swimming pools, tennis courts, golf courses (although some tennis courts and most golf courses are commercial provisions), taiji and wushu (martial arts) centers, roller skating courts, soccer fields, baseball fields, basketball courts, badminton courts, volleyball courts, ice skating rinks, and ski slopes
- *Recreation-related products:* urban parks and gardens, play spaces, lakes, beach and river access, pavilions, chess and card houses, children's play parks, theme parks, and other man-made attractions

The Private or Commercial Sector

A greater diversity exists in the provisions of leisure products and facilities by the private or commercial sector. These are generalized into the categories of (1) state-designated tourism resorts, (2) theme parks and man-made attractions, (3) community-based leisure activities, and (4) commercial sports facilities.

State-Designated Tourism Resorts

State-designated tourism resorts are extensive resort complexes with a comprehensive product and service mix intended to satisfy the needs of diverse leisure and tourist markets. On October 4, 1992, the State Council of the People's Republic of China approved the establishment of state tourism resorts, and in the next few years twelve resort complexes were planned to be created ("State Designated Tourism Resort Complex Series," 1993). The government secured the land, provided conceptual planning and development regulations, and leased development sites to private commercial ventures. The resorts provide a wide range of private leisure products and services, from resort hotels and villas to recreation and entertainment facilities, from land games to water sports, and from spas and hot springs to casino gambling and horse racing. Seaside and beach resorts are the most popular forms, comprising six of the twelve state tourism resorts, including Silver Beach Resort in Beihai (Guangxi Autonomous

Region), Yalong Bay Resort in Sanya (Hainan Province), Meizhou Island Resort in Putian (Fujian Province), Golden Stone Beach Resort in Dalian (Liaoning Province), Stone Old Man Resort in Qingdao (Shandong Province), and Heng Sha Island Resort in Shanghai. Five of the resorts are located in river and lake settings, including Dianchi Lake Resort in Kunming (Yunnan Province), Hangzhou River Resort in Hangzhou (Zhejiang Province), South Lake Resort in Guangzhou (Guangdong Province), Suzhou Taihu Resort in Suzhou (Jiangsu Province), and Wuxi Taihu Resort in Wuxi (Jiangsu Province). Wuyi Mountain Resort in Fujian Province is the only mountain resort among the twelve state-designated tourism resorts.

Theme Parks and Man-Made Attractions

The 1990s witnessed a boom in the construction of theme parks, amusement parks, and other man-made attractions in China. In September 1989, the Splendid China theme park (with an investment of RMB 100 million yuan, approximately US$12 million at the exchange rate of one U.S. dollar equaling RMB yuan 8.8 at that time) in Shenzhen became an immediate success and marked the beginning of this massively popular investment trend (Yu, Y. S., 1998). Over 180 theme parks had been constructed or were under construction by the end of 1995 (Chen, 1998).

Yu Xuecai (1998) and Yu Yingshi (1998) have identified several distinct characteristics of theme parks and man-made attractions in China. China's man-made attractions are highly concentrated geographically. Most are found in China's more economically open and developed regions of the Pearl River Delta (in South China), the Yangtze River Delta (in East China), and the region surrounding the Bo Hai Sea (in North China). Found here are the best known of China's man-made attractions: Splendid China, China Folk Culture Village, Windows of the World, Valley of Happiness, Miracle of the World, Towns of Three Kingdoms, Towns of the Song Dynasty, Towns of the Tang Dynasty, Parks of the World, the Wu Culture Park, and the Suzhou Entertainment Park. In striking contrast to natural and historical attractions, these man-made attractions have very clear themes and are more entertainment and participation oriented, even when they are miniaturized copies of real places.

To create these experiences, huge and extensive investments have been made in the planning, construction, and promotion of theme parks. For example, the initial investment of each of the theme parks and man-made attractions just listed exceeds RMB 100 million yuan (approximately US$12 million), with some as high as RMB 1,180 million yuan (approximately US$143 million).

Theme parks and man-made attractions have become major forms of entertainment and recreation for the domestic leisure and tourist market in China. Chen (1998) reported that China's theme parks and man-made attractions catered to 210 million domestic visitors annually. Although the continuing growth in the construction of such attractions has been criticized as resulting in an oversupply and waste of resources, marketing authorities believe that theme parks, entertainment parks, and man-made attractions will continue to be an important form of leisure and recreation into the new century, especially for urban residents (Meng, 1998).

Community-Based Leisure Facilities

Community-based leisure facilities are the third form of private, commercial leisure provision in China. This includes dance halls, karaoke and other nightclubs, teahouses, cafeterias, restaurants (including fast food) and bars, saunas and parlors, bowling alleys, multifunctional centers found in urban hotels, and other commercial places that offer nonwork leisure, recreation, and entertainment. These facilities are places of social gathering and provide leisure primarily for local residents. They became increasingly popular in the 1990s and represent an important indicator of social and cultural change in the modernization of China's socialism (Fei, 1998).

Commercial Sports Facilities

Commercial sports facilities in China are provided both indoors and outdoors, including tennis courts, golf courses, bowling rinks, shooting ranges, archery ranges, body exercise facilities, skating and skiing, swimming pools, fishing, surfing, scuba diving, horse racing, and even bungee jumping. Although many sports facilities for the general public are provided by the institutions and communities for non-profit purposes, commercial sports are generally regarded as a luxury way of leisure, catering to vacationers, hotel guests, first-time learners, excitement and thrill seekers, special interest groups, and some professional players. These facilities are often found in deluxe hotels, resort hotels, comprehensive resort complexes (such as the state-designated tourism resorts), commercial sports centers, and professional clubs.

Leisure and Domestic Tourism in China

In the late 1990s, domestic tourism emerged as a very significant segment in China's leisure economy (Table 14.1). Data from the China National Tourism Administration (CNTA) showed that in 1999 more than half of the Chinese population participated in some kind of domestic tourism, and their expenditures accounted for 71 percent of China's total tourism receipts (CNTA, 2000; He, 2000).

As a form of leisure activity, domestic tourism displays a number of distinct motivational and behavioral characteristics. Based on studies in South China (Xiao, 1997), northeast China (Huang and Xiao, 2000), and Shanghai (Su, Ding, and Zhou, 1996), the motivational and behavioral characteristics of general leisure and domestic tourism can be summarized as follows.

First, in terms of the needs and motivations of domestic tourists, leisure and recreation-related expectations were dominant. The studies cited here found that domestic tourists went on vacation primarily for the purposes of gaining physical and mental recovery, seeking pleasure and entertainment, getting away from work pressure, and having a change of environment. This was in direct opposition to the motivation of adventure, novelty seeking, or knowledge seeking that

TABLE 14.1. Major Statistics of Domestic Tourism in China, 1999

	Urban Residents	Rural Residents	Total
Domestic Trips (million)	284.00	435.00	719.00
% of Total Population	94.80	47.00	57.60
Domestic Tourism Expenditure (million RMB yuan)	174,823	108,369	283,192
Average Expenditure per Person (RMB yuan)	614.80	249.50	394.00

Source: China National Tourism Administration (2000), p. 559.
Note: RMB yuan 1 million = US$120,000.

has been more commonly expressed by long-haul travelers of longer duration. CNTA's comprehensive survey report on China's 1999 domestic tourist market (CNTA, 2000:419) indicated that "while the number of long haul travelers (those who travel with a duration of four days or more and visit at least three cities) has increased by 3.5 percent compared to the previous year, short distance travelers (those traveling for less than three days and visiting one or two cities) are still dominant in the domestic tourist market, accounting for 94.5 percent." The survey also reported that "vacation for leisure and relaxation is a very important motivation for short excursion trips, accounting for 62 percent of the respondents, while 43 percent of long haul travelers go on sightseeing trips" (CNTA, 2000:20-21). This partly supports the findings of the three previous studies cited earlier.

Second, with regard to vacation patterns and behavior, there was a strong distance-decay factor in destination choice. The longer the distance between origin and destination, the lower the number of visitor arrivals. The northeast China case study, for example, found that most domestic trips were within a 350-kilometer (217 miles) radius of the origin, while residents in Shanghai preferred an even shorter distance of 200 kilometers (124 miles) for their leisure and holiday activities. Age, gender, occupation, and income were other factors exerting influences on travel patterns and preferences. The three studies found that Chinese residents between twenty-one and fifty years of age had greater aspirations for leisure and recreation than other age groups, that men had a stronger desire for vacation trips than women, and that residents with higher incomes and better education (such as government officials, cadres, technical personnel, large company employees, and private businesspeople) had a correspondingly higher level of leisure participation and a wider range of leisure activities, including more leisure travel.

Third, although Chinese residents demonstrated regional diversity and variety in their holiday and activity preferences, consistency could still be observed to a considerable extent. In the study of leisure preference in south China, for example, residents in Fujian put a priority on entertainment and recreation-related activities, including parks and gardens, public recreation centers, theatergoing and attending performances. Natural scenery, karaoke and nightclubs, weekend shopping, and religious sites and activities were secondary in importance to them. This was consistent with the results of the northeast

China study in which puppet stages, movie studios, and cinema palaces were selected as the most preferred sites for leisure by the respondents. Moreover, as was revealed in the Shanghai study, sports and recreational activities, vacations at beaches and spas (hot springs), and natural scenery or landscape within a short and accessible radius were popular leisure activities, especially for family or group vacationers.

Fourth, unlike international tourism and other forms of domestic travel, the domestic tourist market in China shows little seasonality in vacation behavior. Data for 1999 (CNTA, 2000) showed that 26.9 percent of trips were taken in the winter (January-March), 20.7 percent in the spring (April-June), 24.3 percent in the summer (July-September), and 23 percent in the fall (October-December). This pattern was also seen in the three case studies. The high winter percentage was a result of the Chinese New Year, the most important holiday period on the Chinese calendar, when many people throughout China travel home to celebrate with family members. China recently introduced several other weeklong holidays to encourage increased consumer spending. These, along with the maturing of China's domestic travel industry, could change the seasonal travel patterns in the future, possibly increasing the summer proportions and making the overall pattern more similar to those found in other parts of the world (with a summer peak).

Last, there was a strong two-way flow of holiday trips between cities and rural areas in China. Urban residents demonstrated a trend of going to the rural areas for leisure and vacation, the rural population finds it equally attractive to spend their holidays and vacations in nearby cities.

CONCLUSION: TOWARD THE EMERGENCE OF A LEISURE INDUSTRY

With the further development of the Chinese economy and people's increasing awareness of, and need for, leisure and recreation, leisure and domestic tourism in China have an enormous potential for growth. In response to the growing need for mass leisure, the China National Tourism Administration ran a nationwide promotional campaign in 1996, defining that year as "the Year of Leisure and Vacation." This event created a boom in leisure activities and a growing range of leisure products and provisions in the late 1990s. Nevertheless, problems and drawbacks still exist. Despite the current scope of development and potential for further growth, leisure and domestic tourism in China are still in their infancy. Management, planning, and marketing issues, such as traffic congestion, visitor congestion, inadequate upkeep of facilities, and poor visitor behavior are leading to the degradation of destinations and infrastructure systems. These will need to be better addressed for China's leisure industry to properly mature.

Moreover, local and regional economic development will continue to play a vital role in the integration of tourism and leisure into the everyday lives of the Chinese people, and the evolution of a leisure-oriented society in China. Many domestic tourist activities and facilities today have been targeted for international tourists and are far beyond the consumption capabilities of the local residents. For a developing country such as China, an increase in per capita GNP and personal incomes is still a prerequisite before a broad range of both simple and sophisticated tourism and leisure pursuits can be available to all. To adequately prepare for the emergence of China's leisure industry, and the subsequent coming of a leisure-oriented society, leisure-related education and research should be emphasized, resulting in better-qualified personnel who can manage the development of this promising future. To date, there has been a lack of such educational programs, both in the curriculums of comprehensive universities and at more specialized tourism and tourism-related institutions. The addition of such offerings could at least prepare future leaders with the "How-To's" and the "Should-Do's" to facilitate the evolution of a leisure industry and of a leisure-oriented society in China.

REFERENCES

Chen, G. Z. (1998). Thoughts on the Current Development of Man-Made Attractions in China. In Wenchan Shun (Ed.), *Regional Tourism Planning and Development* (pp. 79-84). Beijing: Geological Publishing House (in Chinese).

China National Tourism Administration (2000). *The Yearbook of China Tourism.* Beijing: China Tourism Publishing House (in Chinese).

Du, S. C. (1999). Towards the Sustainable Development of Tourism Through Scientific Planning and Enhanced Quality. *Tourism Research,* No.7: 6-7 (in Chinese).

Dumazedier, J. (1967). *Toward a Society of Leisure*. New York: W.W. Norton.

Family Vacation Survey of Chinese Residents in Cities and Towns (1982). *Economic Daily* in Public and Opinion Section (August 14) (in Chinese).

Fei, X. T. (1998). "On Modernization and Chinese Tradition: An Invited Speech." China Central Television: Education Channel (November 28) (in Chinese).

Goodale, T. and Godbey, G. (1988). *The Evolution of Leisure*. State College, PA: Venture Publishing.

He, G. W. (2000). Carry Forward the Cause, Forge Ahead into the Future, and Strive for the Construction of China As a Powerful Country of Tourism: Work Report Delivered at the 2000 National Tourism Conference (Beijing, China, January 17). *Tourism Management* No. 2: 2-13 (in Chinese).

Huang, A. M. and Xiao, H. G. (2000). Leisure-Based Tourist Behavior: A Case Study of Changchun. *International Journal of Contemporary Hospitality Management* 12(3): 210-214.

Kaplan, M. (1975). *Leisure Theory and Policy*. New York: Wiley.

Liu, D. Q. (1995). Summary of Speeches Delivered at the Symposium on Tourism Development and Planning. *Tourism Tribune* 10(2): 5-13 (in Chinese).

Meng, H. (1998). A Discussion on Man-Made Tourist Attractions. In Wenchan Shun (Ed.), *Regional Tourism Planning and Development* (pp. 76-78). Beijing: Geological Publishing House (in Chinese).

Parry, N. and Parry, J. (1977). Theory of Culture and Leisure. In *Proceedings of Leisure Studies Association Conference,* University of Manchester, September (pp. 37-46).

State Designated Tourism Resort Complex Series *China Tourism News* (1993). In Planning and Development Section (19 October-20 November) (in Chinese).

Su, W. C., Ding, F., and Zhou, Z. N. (1996). On the Present State of the Weekend Holiday-Making of Shanghai Citizens and a Survey of Its Trend. *Tourism Tribune* 11(2): 23-25 (in Chinese).

Torklldsen, G. (1992). *Leisure and Recreation Management*. London. Chapman and Hall.

Xiao, H. G. (1997). Tourism and Leisure in China: A Tale of Two Cities. *Annals of Tourism Research* 24(2): 357-370.

Yu, Y. S. (1998). The Phenomenon of "Man-Made Attractions": A Theoretical Investigation. In Wenchan Shun (Ed.), *Regional Tourism Planning and Development* (pp. 66-70). Beijing: Geological Publishing House (in Chinese).

Zhou, L. H. (1993). On the Importance of Social Survey in Labor Union Work. *Journal of China Labor Union* (August): 35-37 (in Chinese).

Chapter 15

Mainland Chinese Outbound Travel to Hong Kong and Its Implications

Zhang Qiu Hanqin
Carson L. Jenkins
Hailin Qu

China's population of approximately 1.2 billion, its fifty-six distinct nationalities, its recorded history of over 5,000 years, and its territory of 9.6 million square kilometers all contribute to a cultural and natural resource base that provides the country with enormous potential for tourism development. At the same time, tourism in China is distinct in that it was not recognized nor encouraged by the Chinese central government prior to 1978. Like many of the former socialist countries of Eastern Europe, China had travel restrictions both within and outside of the country, for fear of Western ideological contamination. At the Chinese Communist Party's Third Plenary Session of its eleventh Congress in 1978, the party leadership decided to shift its emphasis from political struggle to economic reconstruction. The Four Modernizations of industry, agriculture, science and technology, and national defense were the guiding principles of President Deng Xiao Ping's new era. These principles were reflected in a more open stance to the outside world and the open door policy was to have dramatic impact on the development of China's tourism sector. Although much has now been written on the development of tourism in China (Zhang and Qu, 1996; Zhang, Pine, and Zhang, 2000), less attention has been given to China's rapidly developing domestic tour-

This chapter is one of the outputs from a major research project on Mainland Chinese Travel Demand Patterns for Hong Kong. The authors wish to acknowledge the funding provided by the Hong Kong Polytechnic University for this study (GT075).

ism market and to China's newly emerging outbound market. The latter is the focus of this chapter, particularly in relation to the Hong Kong Special Administrative Region (SAR), which was returned to Chinese sovereignty in 1997.

CHINA'S OUTBOUND TRAVEL

China had one of the highest economic growth rates in the Asia Pacific region in the 1990s. From 1993 to 1999, China's annual real gross domestic product (GDP) growth was, on average, the highest among the major countries in the region, ranging from 7 to 13 percent, even though the annual inflation rate was also the highest in the region in those years. China clearly experienced rapid economic growth, but also varying degrees of political stability. Since the June 4, 1989, Tiananmen Square incident, the Chinese leadership has shown a considerable capacity to regulate the pace of reform, thereby easing social strains and building consensus among different groups within society.

In 1991, the Chinese government renewed its pledge to accelerate the economic transformation of Chinese society by introducing further initiatives to advance the liberalization of the national economy. As a result, the annual GDP at both national and individual levels increased considerably. Over the twenty-year period from 1978 to 1999, China's national GDP increased 13.7 times and per capita GDP grew from RMB 379 yuan to RMB 6,705 yuan (RMB 10 yuan = US$1.21), nearly an eighteen-fold increase (China State Statistical Bureau of PRC, 1999).

Along with this growth, the average living standard of the Chinese population has steadily improved, especially for the residents of the major coastal provinces, cities, and special economic zones of Shenzhen and Zhuhai, Guangdong Province, Shanghai, Beijing, and Tianjin. Residents of these areas have higher disposable incomes and represent the bulk of the current market for outbound travel. Although the majority of Chinese remain predominantly rural, the total size of this urban market is impressive and the proportion of the population traveling overseas is growing precipitously. Over the past two decades the percentage of Chinese population traveling internationally grew from 0.3 percent in 1984 to 2.4 percent in 1999 (China State Statistical Bureau of PRC, 1999). China's large population base gives it the numerical potential to become a huge international outbound source country. In fact, the World Tourism Organization predicts that China will be the fourth largest outbound tourist-generating country in the world by 2020 (WTO, 1997). Within the Asia Pacific region, China is the largest tourism market for Hong Kong.

The ability to travel outside of China depends on two essentials: adequate income to afford international travel and official permission to do so. As more Chinese have the financial ability to travel internationally, the determining factor has become if, when, and where they are allowed to do so. Hong Kong and Macao became the first international destinations that Chinese tourists could visit in the mid-1980s, when travel to these "territories" of China were opened up on an "experimental" basis for business travel (Lew, 2000).

A major change in the central government's policy on international travel occurred in 1990 when Chinese nationals were officially allowed to join leisure tours organized by the China Travel Service (CTS) to Hong Kong, Macao, and several Asian countries, including Malaysia, Singapore, and Thailand (Yatsko and Tasker, 1998). These were the first officially designated "tourism liberalizing countries." To meet the high and growing demand for outbound travel, the Philippines was added to this list in 1992, followed by Australia in 1997, and South Korea and New Zealand in 1998 (Lew, 2000). Although the China National Tourism Administration (CNTA) has officially approved overseas holiday tours to only these few Asia Pacific countries, travel agents in China have indicated that there is, in practice, no restriction on the destinations that can be offered as long as a visa can be obtained. In recent years, travel agencies have introduced tours to nontourism liberalizing countries including Japan, the United States, and Europe. However, obtaining a visa to travel to these other destinations is a long and costly process.

The development of China's outbound tourist market follows the classic "ripple effect." Just as a pebble dropped into a pond generates ever-widening ripples, so the growth of outbound travel over time becomes more geographically distant. The first ripple was the growth in domestic tourism within China. The second ripple was travel to Hong Kong, starting in 1983, a proximate destination and the focus of this chapter. The third ripple effect comprises the intra-Asia travel starting in 1990. The addition of New Zealand and Australia marks the beginning of the fourth ripple, in which the high demand in China for travel beyond Asia, which is still very limited for leisure purposes, will gradually expand to encompass the entire globe.

Although easier than in the past, international travel for Chinese nationals in China is still not a simple proposition. Chinese nationals use either passports or travel permits for visits to the Hong Kong and Macao Special Administrative Regions. For foreign travel they use one of four types of passports: private, official, ordinary (sometimes called "official ordinary"), and diplomatic. The official and ordinary passports are essentially the same, except that the traveler with higher status within China, such as a Communist Party cadre, would be issued the official type. Private passports are valid ranging from only one foreign trip to an unlimited number of trips over a five-year period. Ordinary passports range from one trip up to two years, and official passports from one trip to five years. Most private passports are used for only one trip and a traveler needs to go through the same procedures each time he or she travels internationally. Passports for official or business travel are mainly for people who work for the government, including local administration and state-owned enterprises. The cost of travel when using an official or diplomatic passport is fully paid for in some way by the government. Unlike a private passport, which is issued by the local Public Security Bureau, the Foreign Affairs Office issues the official or business passport at the provincial level.

DESTINATION HONG KONG

Since the formation of the People's Republic of China in 1949, outbound travel statistics have not been well collected nor maintained. While there has always been some business and official travel, private travel was not officially allowed until 1983. Starting from that point, Chinese nationals were allowed to join organized tours to visit their relatives in Hong Kong, and starting a year later to Macao. Thus, the first international tours from China, known as "visiting relatives" tours, were to Hong Kong. These were mainly bus tours in which travelers stayed with their relatives for a short period of the time, which gradually expanded to eight day-seven night packages. The Hong Kong government set a quota on these tours, which began in

1983 with just one or two buses or groups a day. This has increased steadily to 1,500 a day in 1998 ("HKTA Attempts 'Re-entry'," 1998).

Demand for tours to Hong Kong was strong from the beginning. After a slowdown in 1989 and 1990 due to the June 4 Tiananmen Square incident, Chinese arrivals to Hong Kong subsequently surged in response to a relaxation in the foreign exchange regulation in China. Hong Kong was also interested in attracting more mainland visitors, especially as more and more were passing through Hong Kong to the first international destinations opened for leisure travel. To take advantage of its position as a transportation hub, the Hong Kong government launched a seven-day free (no-charge) visa policy in 1993 for Chinese nationals who transited in Hong Kong and held a return airline ticket to another country. This reduced the cost of a visit to Hong Kong and made such a stopover, if only for shopping purposes, more attractive.

There was a brief period of stagnation between late 1993 and 1994 due to economic austerity measures implemented in China, but subsequent growth in mainland arrivals was strong throughout the latter part of the 1990s. This was fostered by the introduction of the shorter workweek, the further opening of China's foreign exchange market, and the addition of new international destinations to the tourism liberalizing country list. For example, starting in May 1995, China implemented a five-day workweek for government employees. The resulting increase in leisure time, along with additional holidays, has allowed more people from neighboring Guangdong Province to visit Hong Kong on short trips, either for business or to visit friends and relatives.

As a result of these policy and social changes, the number of mainland Chinese traveling to Hong Kong increased from 214,854 in 1984 to 3,083,859 in 1999 (an annual growth rate of 23 percent) (Table 15.1). By 1999, the China market comprised more than 29 percent of the total international visitor arrivals to Hong Kong, making it by far the Special Administrative Region's major source of visitors. In one year, tourist receipts from mainland Chinese visitors were up by 33 percent, from HK$8 million in 1993 to HK$10.6 million in 1994 (HK$10 = approximately US$1.28). These receipts ranked third among Hong Kong's visitor markets, and at HK$14.25 million in 1998 they made up 27 percent of Hong Kong's total tourist receipts (HKTA, 1998). (HKTA, previously named Hong Kong Tourist Association, was renamed the Hong Kong Tourism Board on April 1, 2001.)

TABLE 15.1. Visitors to Hong Kong from China and All Countries, 1984-1999

Year	Visitor Arrivals from Mainland China	Growth (%)	Visitor Arrivals from All Countries	Growth (%)	Share of Hong Kong (%)
1984	214,854	—	3,303,719	—	7.0
1985	308,978	43.8	3,656,717	10.0	8.0
1986	363,479	17.6	4,052,641	10.0	9.0
1987	484,592	33.3	4,917,044	17.5	10.0
1988	683,604	41.1	6,167,221	25.4	11.0
1989	730,408	6.8	5,984,501	−3.0	12.0
1990	754,376	3.3	6,580,850	10.0	11.0
1991	875,062	16.0	6,795,413	3.3	13.0
1992	1,149,002	31.3	8,010,524	17.9	14.0
1993	1,732,978	50.8	8,937,500	11.6	19.0
1994	1,943,678	12.2	9,331,156	4.4	21.0
1995	2,243,245	15.4	10,199,994	9.3	22.0
1996	2,311,184	3.0	11,702,735	14.7	20.0
1997	2,297,128	0.6	10,406,261	−11.1	22.0
1998	2,597,442	12.9	9,574,711	−8.0	27.0
1999	3,083,859	18.7	10,678,460	11.5	29.0

Source: HKTA/HKTB, 1993-1999.
"—" means data not available

Tourist receipts from mainland Chinese were first reported by the Hong Kong Tourist Association in 1993, when the liberalization of currency restrictions made it possible for mainland Chinese visitors to contribute economically to the Hong Kong SAR's tourism industry because the amount of money that mainland Chinese travelers could spend in Hong Kong was limited before 1993. Mainland Chinese tourists spent HK$8.0 billion in that year, which was 13 percent of total tourist receipts of HK$60 billion. Due to the Asian economic crisis, Hong Kong's total tourism receipts dropped 15 percent in one year to HK$9.26 billion in 1997. However, total spending from China in that year gained a moderate 2.4 percent, reaching HK$15.6 billion.

The gain was the result of a 3.1 percent increase in per person expenditure for visitors from the mainland (Table 15.2). China was one of Hong Kong's few visitor markets that experienced an increase in per capita spending throughout the 1990s. Especially in 1997, expenditures continued to increase when all other Asian visitor markets declined. The per capita spending of mainland Chinese visitors in that year was the third highest group after the Taiwanese and North Americans, and the mainland market overtook Japan to become the biggest contributor of total tourist spending in Hong Kong. Mainland Chinese visitors contributed 22 percent of Hong Kong's total visitor receipts in 1997 (HKTA, 1998). There was a decline in expenditure from HK$6,782 per capita trip in 1997 to HK$5,487 in 1998. The lower per capita spending could be the result of shorter stays made by visitors, which fell from 5.0 to 3.9 days between 1997 and 1998 (HKTA, 1999).

Mainland Chinese travelers used three modes of transport to come to Hong Kong: land (30 percent), air (57 percent), and sea (13 percent) (HKTA, 1999). More than 60 percent of mainland visitors had household incomes over RMB 20,000 yuan per year, which places them in China's upper-middle class. Once in Hong Kong, visitors from mainland China spent most of their money on shopping, with the amount increasing annually from 1993 to 1997 (Table 15.3).

TABLE 15.2. Per Capita Visitor Expenditures of Mainland Chinese in Hong Kong, 1993-1999

Year	Growth (%)	Per Capita Trip Expenditures (HK$)	Growth (%)	Per Capita Daily Expenditures (HK$)	Growth (%)
1993	–	5,270	–	921	–
1994	32.8	5,469	3.8	904	−1.8
1995	29.3	6,128	12.0	1,048	15.9
1996	10.6	6,581	7.4	1,203	14.8
1997	2.4	6,782	3.1	1,363	13.3
1998	−8.5	5,487	−19.1	1,411	3.5
1999	−5.4	4,370	−20.4	1,118	−20.8

Source: HKTA/HKTB,1993-1999.

TABLE 15.3. Expenditure Categories of Mainland China Visitors in Hong Kong, 1993-1999

Major Items	1993 (%)	1994 (%)	1995 (%)	1996 (%)	1997 (%)	1998 (%)	1999 (%)
Shopping	56	56.5	61.0	63.5	65.1	64.6	63.8
Hotel Bills	18	20.6	18.7	16.7	14.9	15.5	14.0
Meals*	14	14.0	13.0	11.2	11.8	9.8	12.2
Tours	6	3.4	2.5	4.5	3.8	5.6	4.2
Other	4	5.5	4.8	3.0	3.2	3.1	4.3
Entertainment	2	–	–	1.1	1.2	1.4	1.5

Source: HKTA/HKTB,1993-1999.
*Meals outside hotels

Many mainland visitors are attracted to Hong Kong as a "shopping paradise" where they can find products that are often scarce in China. Hotel expenses comprised the second largest expenditure item, although this category has steadily declined in relative importance in the 1990s, as has the category of meals taken outside of hotels, which was the third largest expenditure item.

As noted previously, wealth and income are not evenly distributed in China; residents living in the coastal cities and provinces have much higher incomes than those living in rural areas. In particular, three areas are the sources of two-thirds of Hong Kong mainland visitors. These are Guangdong Province, which is adjacent to Hong Kong and shares similar culture, language, and traditions; Shanghai and its adjacent provinces of Zhejiang and Jiangsu; and Beijing and its coastal neighbor of Tianjin (Table 15.4). Guangdong Province, with its major city of Guangzhou, has steadily declined in overall importance from 76 percent in 1994 to 46 percent in 1999. At the same time outbound travelers from the other major source regions have been increasing. Visitors from Shanghai and Beijing reached peak proportions in 1998, while all of the other regions shown in Table 15.4 continued to increase in percentage into 1999. This suggests that the wave of outbound travel has expanded from the country's three major cities (Beijing, Shanghai, and Guangzhou) to their hinterlands. In the future, this trend is likely to continue to expand and also include more visitors from remote areas of China.

TABLE 15.4. Location of Residence of Mainland China Visitors to Hong Kong, 1994-1999

Cities/Provinces	1994 (%)	1995 (%)	1996 (%)	1997 (%)	1998 (%)	1999 (%)
Guangdong Province	76.0	69.5	62.0	57.9	47.7	45.6
Shanghai	2.3	3.5	5.0	4.2	5.0	3.6
Beijing	2.1	2.9	3.0	3.8	5.4	4.9
Jiangsu Province	2.2	2.1	3.0	2.2	3.4	3.5
Zhejiang Province	1.6	1.6	3.2	5.1	4.6	5.8
Tianjin	0.2	0.3	0.4	0.4	0.3	1.7
Subtotal	84.4	79.9	76.6	73.6	66.4	65.1
Other	15.6	20.1	23.4	26.4	33.6	34.9

Source: HKTA/HKTB, 1993-1999.

For most of the 1990s, Hong Kong was a single destination for the majority of mainland visitors, many of whom were using it as their first trip outside of China proper (Table 15.5). This changed dramatically in 1998 following further government relaxation in offering exit visas from China. From 1997 to 1998, the proportion of multidestination travelers doubled, from about one-third to two-thirds of mainland visitors to Hong Kong. The average number of destinations visited (including Hong Kong) also doubled from 1.3 in 1993 to 2.5 in 1999. This growth continued into 1999, which may reflect a saturation in mainland visitor levels to Hong Kong, as well as indicating the pent-up demand for international travel in China.

Thailand has been the most popular destination visited in addition to Hong Kong, followed by Singapore and Malaysia. All three of these countries have large numbers of ethnic Chinese and a moderate level of economic development. During the Asian economic crisis, which started in Thailand in July 1997, the currencies of Thailand, Singapore, and Malaysia depreciated significantly. As a result, it has been more affordable for Chinese residents to travel to Singapore, Thailand, and Malaysia since the renminbi currency of mainland China was relatively stable.

TABLE 15.5. Trip Type and Other Destinations Visited by Vacation Travelers on Their Hong Kong Trip

Trip Type	1993 (%)	1994 (%)	1995 (%)	1996 (%)	1997 (%)	1998 (%)	1999 (%)
Single-destination trip	82	79	78	76	65	34	29
Multidestination trip	18	21	22	24	35	66	71
Overnight destinations visited[a]							
Thailand	13	16	16	19	26	53	59
Singapore	10	9	6	11	16	28	28
Malaysia	4	5	5	9	16	26	27
Philippines	*[b]	1	1	*	*	1	1
France	*	*	1	1	2	*	*
Germany	*	*	1	1	2	*	*
Netherlands	*	*	*	*	1	*	*
United States	1	*	1	1	1	*	*
Australia	*	*	*	1	1	1	*
Japan	*	*	*	1	1	*	*
Taiwan	1	*	*	*	1	*	*
Italy	*	*	1	*	*	*	*
South Korea	*	*	*	*	*	2	3
Average number of destinations visited (including HK)	1.31	1.34	1.35	1.56	1.83	2.48	2.53

Source: Hong Kong Tourism Board, 1993-1999.
[a] "Overnight Destinations Visited" percentages are greater than the total "Multi-destination Trips" for each year due to more than one country being visited by some travelers.
[b] * means figure is less than 0.5%

MAINLAND TOURISTS

Although the demographic characteristics of all international visitors to Hong Kong remained stable through the 1990s, these same characteristics for mainland Chinese visitors changed from 1993 to 1999 (Table 15.6). In 1993, almost twice as many males traveled from China to Hong Kong than females, a slightly higher rate than for all international travelers. By the end of the decade, however, many more women travelers were visiting Hong Kong from China, at a rate far higher than for international visitors overall. This interesting phenomenon reflects three aspects of Chinese travel to Hong Kong: the ease of such travel, the large family and friends component of such

TABLE 15.6. Demographic Profile of China and All Countries' Visitors to Hong Kong, 1993-1999.

Demographic Characteristics	All Countries		China	
	1993	1999	1993	1999
Gender (%)				
Male	62	64	65	59
Female	38	36	35	41
Age (%)				
0-15 years	5	5	2	4
16-25	11	10	10	10
26-35	26	28	27	33
36-45	27	27	28	27
46-55	18	18	19	15
56-65	10	8	11	8
66+	5	4	3	3
Mean age (# years)	39.1	38.3	39.6	37.6
Marital status (%)				
Married	73	71	86	80
Other	27	29	14	20
Occupation (%)				
Senior white collar	57	58	43	47
Junior white collar	20	19	29	28
Blue collar	5	3	12	5
Housewife	6	6	4	6
Other	12	13	12	14

Source: HKTA,1993-1999, *A Statistical Review of Tourism.*

travel, and the importance of shopping as a major activity during a Hong Kong visit.

In terms of age distribution, mainland Chinese visitors were more likely to be in the twenty-six to thirty-five age group, and less likely to be in the oldest and youngest age groups than was the case for international visitors overall. The small proportion of the youngest and oldest segments was even more pronounced earlier in the 1990s than it was by 1999. Mainland visitors were more likely to be married than their foreign counterparts, although this had changed by 1999 and is likely to further decline as divorce laws become more liberalized in China. Senior white-collar occupations predominated among all visitors to Hong Kong, reflecting the importance of business travel, although the percentage of senior managers from China was lower than those from other countries. Instead, the proportion of junior white-collar workers was much higher among mainland Chinese visitors. This may be attributed to the recruitment of junior level management from China to work for Hong Kong-based multinational companies (Zhang and Qu, 1996). These workers frequently travel between China and Hong Kong for both business and family reasons.

Early in the 1990s, China visitors tended to stay much longer (close to a week) in Hong Kong compared to the overall international market (Table 15.7). The newness of the Hong Kong destination, limitations on travel to other destinations, and the seven-day free visa policy for Chinese transit travelers to Hong Kong all contributed to the longer stay of Chinese travelers. By the end of the decade, this number was closer to international travelers overall (3.5 to 4 nights). At the same time, however, the proportion of mainland visitors who were in Hong Kong for the first time was almost the same in 1999 as in 1993, which was much higher than for international visitors overall. This proportion went as high as 60 percent in 1997, which reflects the continued expansion of China's outbound tourism, for which many first-time travelers are making Hong Kong an important part of their overseas trip experience. Many of those who have been to Hong Kong before are bypassing the city for their second or third international trip. This is becoming easier as increasing numbers of Chinese cities develop direct international flights (Yu and Lew, 1997).

About two-thirds of the Chinese travelers stayed in commercial accommodations (although this was as low as 52 percent in 1996), compared to three-quarters of the overall international visitor market. Al-

TABLE 15.7. Trip Characteristics of Mainland China Tourists Visiting Hong Kong and All Countries Visiting Hong Kong, 1993-1999

Visitor Characteristics	All Countries		China	
	1993	1999	1993	1999
Length of stay (nights)	3.8	3.4	6.7	3.9
Number of visits to HK (%)				
First time	46	40	53	51
More than once	54	60	47	49
Accommodation type (%)				
Commercial	84	75	65	65
Others	16	25	35	35
Purpose of visit (%)				
Vacation	58	49	34	53
Visiting friends/relatives	5	12	12	19
Business/meetings	29	30	36	18
En route	6	7	17	10
Others	2	2	2	1
Travel arrangement (%)				
All-inclusive package	30	27	24	37
Air + hotel package	16	25	8	35
Nonpackage	54	48	68	28

Source: HKTA/HKTB, 1993-1999.

ternative accommodations include family and friends, which is not surprising given that the percentage of visiting friends and relatives is higher for mainland visitors.

Business travel showed an interesting decline in importance for mainland Chinese travelers from 1993 to 1999, while vacation travel increased. At the start of the decade business travel was far more important for Chinese travelers in comparison to others, while the opposite was true by the end of the decade. Much of this business in the early 1990s was government funded and some exploitation of this benefit occurred. A government crackdown on such abuses occurred in the mid-1990s, reducing the proportion of quasibusiness travel from China. Due to the geographic proximity between mainland China and Hong Kong, en route travelers from mainland China are about double those of international travelers overall.

POLICY IMPLICATIONS FOR HONG KONG

The number of visitors to Hong Kong from mainland China does not fully reflect actual demand because they continue to be controlled and shaped by government policies. Hong Kong has limited control over these policies, although the introduction of the seven-day free visa program in 1993 seems to have spurred an increase in visitation at that time. Chinese government's policies have had a much more direct impact on Hong Kong visitation, from the initial opening of China in the 1980s to the introduction of the five-day work week in 1995 and the subsequent relaxation on international outbound travel in the late 1990s. The HKTB has lobbied for positive policies for the China outbound travel market and its top agenda item has been to make exit visas easier for Chinese tour groups. Further relaxation of rules governing the issuance of travel document by the Chinese government will undoubtedly boost outbound leisure travel considerably from China.

The Hong Kong tourism industry has also been lobbying China to increase daily quotas of mainland visitors to Hong Kong. China has done this, in part to help Hong Kong's hotel industry during the Asian financial crisis. In 1998, for example, CNTA increased the number of daily Chinese leisure visitors to Hong Kong by 358, placing the daily quota at 1,500 ("HKTA Attempts 'Re-entry'," 1998). This was increased by 500 more in the year 2000. The 2,000 daily visitors from China were expected to bring HK$2.2 million worth of business to Hong Kong every day.

Under the current political atmosphere and economic conditions in China, outbound vacation travel should continue to expand. Hong Kong will continue to be the first to benefit from this trend. The growing importance of the China market has significant implications for tourism-related businesses in Hong Kong, including retailing, catering, and hotels, which must strive to ensure that they provide a high level of visitor experience and satisfaction. Recently many complaints were filed against inbound tour agents in Hong Kong due to a lack of or poor service quality. In a story reported in the *South China Morning Post* ("Protecting Tourists," 1999), 200 mainland tourists were left stranded in the SAR in the small hours of the Lunar New Year Holidays, without a guide to meet them, nor any idea of where they were to stay. This was one in a series of incidents that damaged Hong Kong's reputation as a major tourist destination.

Mainland Chinese are now providing about 30 percent of Hong Kong's tourism receipts, with an average daily expenditure of HK$5,487 per head. If those numbers are to increase, the Hong Kong SAR must offer a fairer and more reliable service than it is giving at the moment. This may mean recruiting staff with Mandarin speaking ability and providing service training particularly geared to the mainland Chinese clientele. Word-of-mouth advice from friends, relatives, or business associates is ranked very highly by mainland Chinese travelers as a source of information (Zhang, 1999). Therefore, it is extremely important to ensure their satisfaction so as to sustain and increase current travel volumes to Hong Kong.

The HKTB also needs to shift greater emphasis to the China market and design appropriate marketing strategies for it. Hong Kong has seen erosion of its regional competitiveness due to the Asian financial crisis and resulting currency depreciation, which have made Thailand, Singapore, and Malaysia less expensive destinations to visit. The mainland market has certainly helped the Hong Kong tourism industry through the difficult times experienced by the Asian financial crisis. Therefore, the HKTB needs to work with the Hong Kong tourism industry to develop more competitive packages and attractive tourism products geared toward mainland Chinese visitors.

It is still relatively difficult for mainland Chinese to obtain the necessary travel documents required to leave the country. Obtaining passports and visas are the main problems. Travel agencies and tour operators in Hong Kong could work with their China counterparts to assist travelers in obtaining these documents. Currently, travelers are required to obtain a sponsor in order for Beijing to issue them a visa to travel to Hong Kong. The HKTB has been lobbying the central government to change this policy and allow visa-free access for mainland Chinese tour groups, but this has not yet been approved.

Mainland Chinese spend more than 60 percent of their money on shopping when visiting Hong Kong. Some of them come mainly for shopping, not only for themselves, but also for their friends and relatives. Information and itineraries that focus on both discount shopping venues and brand label shopping at discounted prices would be highly attractive to this market. Incentives such as membership discount cards and special discounts for repeat visitors could encourage them to spend more in Hong Kong.

Providing more information to mainland Chinese about travel to Hong Kong is essential. The HKTB found a lack of information about Hong Kong travel opportunities available in China. Currently, the HKTB has two branch offices in China, one in Beijing and the other in Shanghai. In addition to the advertising that the HKTB provides, tour companies in Hong Kong and China should disseminate promotional material through joint efforts with airlines and ground transportation companies. They also need to open more branch offices in major cities in China to promote Hong Kong to the China market.

The HKTB needs to systematically monitor and track developments and changes in the travel patterns and needs of mainland Chinese visitors through periodic research. Since 1993 the HKTB has been conducting a "Research Review" of the mainland Chinese market. The International Market Research Study (IMRS) is also undertaken annually to supply attitudinal information concerning Hong Kong as a tourist destination in the eyes of consumers in key source markets. Just as important, travel service decision makers in China and Hong Kong should be surveyed on a regular basis for strategic planning input, including the possibility of forming joint promotional alliances and business partnerships.

CONCLUSION

Although the initial reforms associated with China's 1978 open door policy have had dramatic impacts on the development of inbound tourism to China, the longer-term impacts of the reforms are bringing about even greater change in China's domestic and outbound travel markets. As has been the historical experience in other countries, the travel and leisure industry has been a beneficiary of the rapid growth of China's per capita income. The expanding middle class in China has begun to participate in intraregional Asian travel. China has done better than most other Asian economies in weathering the region's recent economic crisis, and as a result it has become an important tourist source for some of these countries.

The outbound travel market will likely continue to grow, provided that economic growth in China continues to raise people's incomes, particularly those of the middle class. A second proviso is that the Chinese government does not continue to artificially limit outbound travel. If these two conditions are met, and they are certainly not guaranteed over the short term, there is no reason why China's outbound travelers would not become a major regional and global force, shaping the travel industry market in the next decade and beyond.

REFERENCES

China State Statistical Bureau of PRC (1999). *China Statistical Yearbook.* Beijing: China Statistics Press.

HKTA Attempts "Re-entry" (1998). *Travel News Asia.* May 29.

Hong Kong Tourist Association/Board (HKTA/HKTB) (1993-1999). *A Statistical Review of Tourism.* Hong Kong: Hong Kong Tourist Association.

Hong Kong Tourist Association (HKTA) (1998). *A Research Review of Mainland China.* Hong Kong: Hong Kong Tourist Association.

Lew, A.A. (2000). "China: A Growth Engine for Asian Tourism." In C. Michael Hall and Stephen Page (Eds.), *Tourism in South and South East Asia: Issues and Cases* (pp. 268-285). Oxford: Butterworth-Heinemann.

Protecting Tourists (1999). *South China Morning Post,* February 23, 14.

World Tourism Organization (1997). *World Tourism Organization Report: Budgets of National Tourism Administrations.* Madrid: World Tourism Organization.

Yatsko, Pamela and Tasker, Rodney (1998). Outward Bound: Just in Time, Ordinary Chinese Catch the Travel Bug. *Far Eastern Economic Review* (March 26) 66-67.

Yu, Lawrence and Lew, Alan A. (1997). Airline Liberalization and Development in China. *Pacific Tourism Review* 1(2): 129-136.

Zhang, Guangrui, Pine, Ray, and Zhang, Qiu Hanqin (2000). China's International Tourism Development: The Present and Future. *International Journal of Contemporary Hospitality Management* 12(5): 282-290.

Zhang, Q.H. (1999). The Underlying Factors Affecting International Tourist Arrivals to Hong Kong. Unpublished PhD thesis. Glasgow: University of Strathclyde.

Zhang, Q.H. and Qu, H. (1996). The Trends of China Outbound Travel to Hong Kong and Its Implications. *Journal of Vacation Marketing* 2(4): 373-381.

SECTION V:
CONCLUSION

Chapter 16

World Trade and China's Tourism: Opportunities, Challenges, and Strategies

Lawrence Yu
John Ap
Zhang Guangrui
Alan A. Lew

As demonstrated in the chapters collected in this volume, China's tourism has experienced great changes in the last two decades. China's tourism industry has been transformed from a virtually non-economic activity before the mid-1970s to a major economic force in the national economy today. Two decades of development have yielded both positive experiences and hard lessons. As the Chinese economy continues to grow at a rapid pace, China's tourism industry faces great opportunities and challenges for future development. This concluding chapter identifies and discusses the pressing issues confronting China's tourism industry in the new millennium, with particular emphasis given to the impacts of the market opening measures that China will be required to adopt since its recent accession to the World Trade Organization.

OPPORTUNITIES

The World Tourism Organization has projected that China will be the top tourism destination in the world by 2020 (WTO 1997). China's political environment, travel infrastructure, diversity of attractions, and improving services have all come together to make tourism to China increasingly accessible for international visitors. The China National Tourism Administration (CNTA) is determined to turn China into a leading world tourism destination by 2020, when more than 135 to 145 million international visitors are forecasted to arrive annually, about doubling that of 1999 ("Air China and Foreign Airlines" 2000; "China's Tourism Industry" 2000; He 2000). Total tourist income is estimated to exceed RMB 3.3 trillion yuan and account for 8 percent of the gross domestic product by 2020.

Such an aggressive development goal provides China's tourism industry tremendous opportunities for growth. Opportunities for tourism development in China are widespread, and much of it is self-evident in rich and diverse tourism resources. An incredible diversity of landscapes and cultures stretch across the vastness of China, bringing great potential for specialized tourism that focuses on cultural and ethnic heritage and sustainable ecotourism. These forms of tourism have been growing steadily. Ecotourism and adventure travel has been aggressively packaged and promoted in many parts of China as tourism developers have realized the importance of protecting the resources that tourists come to enjoy in the first place. For instance, Anhui Province introduced nine eco/adventure tour packages for both international and domestic tourists in 2000 ("Anhui's Ecotour Products" 2000). These include a wild animal safari; a mountain bike tour in the Huangshan Mountains; southern Anhui hiking; Xin'an and Tianxian rivers and Caihong Valley drifting; Lake Taiping underwater swimming; and a grotto and geological surveying tours.

A major catalyst for future tourism growth in China is its entry into the World Trade Organization. The widely recognized benefit of joining the World Trade Organization for China's tourism industry is that it will force greater efficiency in the microenvironment of business management and operations, including financial management, service competitiveness, and tourism information management. The streamlining of tourism payments, the development of e-commerce in the tourism sector, and international service standards have been identified as key areas in the modernization of China's tourism industry. In addition, tariff cuts on imported vehicles will end the chronic affliction of a shortage of tourism vehicles with modern amenities, although traffic congestions could also rise.

China has gradually improved its transportation infrastructure over the past decade. Efforts have been made by the Chinese government at various administrative levels to develop an efficient transportation network linking tourism destinations. In 2000 alone, US$12 billion were invested in China in new airport construction, airport facility upgrading, and new aircraft (Sinclair 2000). A modern and efficient highway system has been built to connect major Chinese tourist cities and link them to secondary cities. The development of the national and regional highway system has provided new opportunities for automobile travel and motel development.

The explosive growth of domestic tourism and outbound tourism stimulated by China's striking economic growth, the relaxing of overseas travel procedures, and the three newly instituted weeklong national holidays (May Day, National Day, and the Spring Festival) has offered opportunities for further tourism development for both Chinese and international travel companies. The need for mid-scale and budget hotels for the increasing numbers of domestic tourists has drawn great interest from international hotel firms. The transportation of Chinese outbound tourists to overseas destinations is now facilitated by international airlines, which have formed strategic alliances with the Chinese airlines. These growth opportunities will continue to attract international travel, transportation, and hospitality firms to develop and standardize China's tourism operations.

The success of China's economic growth has drawn attention worldwide, from politicians to businesses and the general public. Given the opportunity, the Chinese people are demonstrating the entrepreneurial skills and integrity that have made expatriate Chinese so economically successful the world over (Lew 1995). China is making every effort to achieve the goal of being the leading tourism destination in the world in twenty years.

CHALLENGES

Along with the numerous opportunities identified previously (as well as in Chapter 1), China will continue to encounter strong challenges in the areas of international competition, domestic industry consolidation, transportation infrastructure, and environmental enhancement. Global competition will increase and intensify as multinational travel firms enter the Chinese market now that China has entered the World Trade Organization. These capital-rich and experienced firms will attract the best local managers and professionals by offering better compensation and benefits. Domestic Chinese travel companies could be directly affected by the brain drain of experienced managerial and professional personnel to the international firms. International travel firms can also develop a loyalty marketing strategy by working with other international airlines, hotel chains, restaurant chains, and shopping centers in China to the exclusion of some domestic businesses, thus forcing consolidation and increasing economic leakage in the Chinese economy. The arrival of the international travel firms will definitely erode the market share of inbound tourism held by the domestic travel companies, and some domestic travel companies might be forced out of business or compelled to merge with other companies ("Opportunities and Challenges" 2000).

Although China has many advantages in its diversity of tourist resources, these may not be brought into full play due to inflexible business operations, ineffective promotion, and undesirable level of services. Other Asian countries and areas, especially the ASEAN countries, Hong Kong, and Taiwan, are more competitive than China in this region owing to their successful economies, well-developed tourism infrastructure, quick access to information, flexible business operations, wide international connections, and effective promotion with the help of powerful regional tourist associations. The reputation of China's tourist industry, on the other hand, is less than desirable and leaves much room for improvement. In fact, a clear and positive tourist image of China has yet to be truly established. Unfortunately, a successful tourist image, which embodies the diversity of tourist resources and attractions, as well as the features of the political and economic systems, cannot be established or manipulated easily. The Han Chinese culture, and the many spectacular natural attractions, should always remain the core of China's tourism development. Although this approach is obvious from the standpoint of the international marketplace, it is unclear what the role of ethnic minorities, and the peripheral environment that they occupy, should be in China's tourism development. There is a real threat in China that minority traditions will be lost, or only seen and experienced in museum-like ethnic villages.

The minority ethnic groups' problem reflects the larger image problem of China in the West. The tight control that China's central government exerts over political dissent is discussed in the Western media almost as much as is the country's economic miracle. This is an important issue for some potential travelers, particularly from the

United States and Europe. No matter how many "Visit China" campaigns the CNTA plans, they may have less impact on the major international markets than images of the Chinese government presented in foreign media outlets.

Another important challenge facing businesses at the individual firm level is the need for mainland Chinese tourism enterprises to acquire market-oriented business knowledge and skills, and to adopt sound management practices that promote the profitability and sustainability of the tourism enterprises. The strong supply-side mentality that pervades China, combined with the problems and failures of many travel and tourism businesses (as described in the chapters on the theme parks industry, travel agencies, and the airline sector) point to some major problems. Tourism businesses must be based on a good understanding of market needs and the financial feasibility of business ventures must be closely examined before investment decisions are made. Accountability for business decisions is also needed and one can no longer simply pass on losses to the parent company or government agency responsible for the enterprise. This issue poses a major threat to the competitiveness of mainland Chinese tourism businesses, which is becoming even more serious now that China has joined the World Trade Organization.

Without the necessary knowledge and skills to run an enterprise on sound business and market fundamentals, China stands to lose out to more savvy and sophisticated foreign competitors. China can no longer afford to establish and support business ventures that are poorly conceived and operating unprofitably. Not only will it threaten the individual business, but it also has potential to destroy the local industry as a whole if it is not able to compete with foreign competitors. Thus, raising the level of the business acumen of the mainland Chinese is an urgent need.

Out of all of the various sectors of the tourism industry, hotel management and operations have experienced the most noticeable improvements, thanks to the transfer of management know-how through joint venture operations and foreign management companies. Travel service management and aviation operations are still lagging behind. In travel service operations, the lack of service attitude and the low productivity of tour guides are major factors hindering the improvement of visitor satisfaction (Cai and Woods 1993). The lack of a good and reliable tourism information network and a central reservation system for transportation and accommodations often causes low efficiency in operations and inconvenience to travelers. A comprehensive network of tourism information centers and systematic travel service management and operations is badly needed to improve visitor experience and satisfaction.

Regional competition exists among Asian destinations for tourism business from Europe and North America. All of the tourist destinations in the region vie with one another for the same markets with quite similar products. Although China has many advantages in its diversity of tourism resources, some emerging destinations in Indo-China and central Asia, such as Cambodia and Laos, may attract the attention of Western tourists as new and exotic adventure tourist destinations. Other well-established tourist destinations in the region such as Singapore, Thailand, and Taiwan remain strong competitors with a well-developed tourism infrastructure, quick access to information, flexible business operations, wide international connections, and effective promotion supported by substantial marketing budgets and powerful regional tourism associations.

With the opportunities and challenges of membership in the World Trade Organization, China's tourism sector will experience increasing consolidation and specialization as a result of intensified global competition in the next decade. Such consolidation has already occurred in the lodging sector as China's hotel industry provides greater potential for brand development and professional management. The consolidation trend is just beginning to affect travel agency operations as struggling travel agencies have been acquired by larger and stronger companies. This trend will only be intensified when international firms enter the China travel market.

As mentioned previously, China's transportation infrastructure has been markedly improved in the last decade, but it will continue to be a challenge for China's tourism industry. With the rapid development of domestic tourism, the current transportation facilities and services are inadequate to handle demand during the peak seasons, as evidenced during the weeklong May Day holiday in 2000. Yield management in route selection and ticket sales needs to be efficiently implemented (Bao 2000). Strategic alliances with international airlines will generate increased inbound tourism to China and could help to reduce the operating costs for the Chinese carriers in handling outbound tourists ("WTO Membership" 2000).

With increasing disposable income and free time among the Chinese people and government policies of encouraging domestic vacations, growing numbers are participating in tourism. Domestic tourism actually presents a much greater challenge than international tourism for China's transportation systems and the management of tourist attractions, especially during the long holiday periods and among the hot tourist spots. Some popular destinations are experiencing severe environmental degradation from heavy usage. Some steps in tourism planning have been taken to control the improper exploitation of tourism resources, but more needs to be done, and the sooner the better. More sustainable tourism practices need to be adopted to save and conserve China's rich tourism resources over the next twenty years.

Ecotourism development, for example, is normally low profile and low impact in its operations, and often geared toward high-end specialty tourist markets. However, the current ecotours being developed and marketed in China are aimed at the mass tourist market ("Dam Area to Establish a National Forest Park" 2000). Such promotional strategies draw concerns about simply eco-labeling tourist resources without effectively protecting them. The sheer number of mass tourism visitors could have a major negative impact on fragile ecosystems in sensitive areas. Effective education and capacity management need to be developed and implemented for ecotourism to become more than a catchword in China.

In addition to more frequent and longer domestic trips, greater openness to the outside world is encouraging, increasing relaxation of laws regulating cross-border travel for Chinese citizens. This has resulted in a steady increase in outbound international travel by Chinese citizens. In 2000 alone some 10 million departures were made by Chinese residents to international destinations (including Hong Kong and Macao). While much of this new market is in leisure travel, business travel from China continues to be strong with increasing international economic transactions and cooperation. Although a greater balance between domestic, inbound, and outbound tourism will not be realized in the short term, there will likely be a boom in outbound tourism very soon. This is a natural trend for tourism development; however, the issue must be well considered by the Chinese authorities in both economic and political terms because of its potential impact on China, Asia, and the world.

STRATEGIES

Learning from tourism development experience around the world, China needs to pay greater attention to *the management and protection of its tourism resources, both natural and cultural.* The degradation and destruction of tourism resources by careless development and uncontrolled tourist use can destroy the drawing power that pulls tourists to China in the first place. An economically sound, demand-based, environmentally sustainable, and culturally sensitive development strategy is needed to guide China's resource assessment and development. These are the issues that tourism developers are facing in many developing countries and China should actively take part in the international discussion on how to best resolve these development concerns and problems.

Given the highly centralized nature of Chinese society, even under the unprecedented reforms since the late 1970s, *appropriate government strategies and policies* will be key to the future success of the country's tourism industry. China should persist in its economic policy of developing tourism, and more supporting policies favorable to the industry should be formulated. The continued building of transportation infrastructure remains a development priority, including airport facilities, rail systems, and highway development. Only with a well-established transportation network can China efficiently move its rapidly increasing numbers of international and domestic tourists.

Instead of the current policies that focus on increasing the number of international arrivals, greater efforts should be made to *improve the productivity of the industry.* This can be achieved by enhancing human capital through training and education, and by introducing modern methods of management and supervision. In addition, laws, rules, and regulations governing tourism development should be initiated and developed. An industry code of conduct can direct business operations to be more effective and ethical, and a certified travel counselor (CTC) program, as found in many countries, can improve the management effectiveness of the travel services. Communication and education between the government and local populations should also be carried out in order to avoid or reduce the negative impacts of tourism economically, culturally, socially, and environmentally.

Choice and adjustment to *target markets* should be made according to the changing trends in international tourism, with products being introduced and renovated according to the needs of both international and domestic travelers. China needs to expand its international marketing and promotion efforts. CNTA's contact with the international market has generally been through its nonprofit overseas offices. These offices are primarily liaison offices and their marketing efforts have been limited. More aggressive marketing, including regional and international cooperative campaigns, should be undertaken. To do this, China must pay more attention to effective market studies in order to better understand international market demands and develop appropriate travel products and services accordingly. Taking advantage of entry into the World Trade Organization, China should also spare no efforts in competing with counterparts outside its boundaries.

Effective marketing needs to go hand-in-hand with effective *resource management and planning*. One example of the rapidly growing and diversifying international travel market is nature and culture-based ecotourism. However, as mentioned, ecotourism development in China has been problematic. Ecotourists are often willing to pay premium prices to experience cultures and environmental adventures in an authentic manner, yet the dominant emphasis on mass tourism that pervades most of the development in China today is anathema to the interests of ecotourists. Much of China, especially in the more peripheral regions, is still an ecotourism paradise. The Chinese government should act now to preserve the remote and fragile environments and cultures that may prove to be one of their most important tourism resources in the future. Otherwise, careless development or uncontrolled use may reduce China's attractiveness for tourists. It is essential for the development of tourism to be demand-based, environmentally sustainable, and culturally sensitive. Furthermore, input based upon international experience should also be sought.

These are issues that tourism developers are facing in many developing countries, and China should actively take part in the international discussion on how to best resolve these problems. A good initiative is to invite international professional tourism consultants to prepare tourism master plans for some promising provinces in China; however, the combination of both external and Chinese expertise may be the best solution for a good and workable plan. In addition, all the stakeholders, including the local community, should be invited to take part in the planning process, something that is often overlooked in the rush to plan.

It is strongly recommended that China take greater steps to provide better *quality guest service* to improve the visitor's experience and satisfaction. The concept of service is still not well accentuated in China's tourism industry, and visitor discontent and complaints often derive from the poor attitudes and service they encounter. Now that most service employees regularly expect and accept gratuities from international tourists, they must begin to provide the level of services acceptable by international standards. Otherwise, unhappy visitors will further tarnish the image of China and the country will lose repeat business, as well as potential new visitors. Service is really an attitude. The teaching and training of service at schools and workplaces needs to focus on developing proper attitudes in tourism workers.

To improve the efficiency and effectiveness of tourism promotion, *modern information technology* should be utilized for marketing and managing tourists and the industry. Requirements for visa and frontier controls could be made more efficient, possibly enabling their relaxation. Alliances of various tourism-related sectors should be advocated and supported. In addition to the centralized CNTA advertising approach, tourism authorities and the private and semiprivate hospitality industry need to impress upon the government the importance of political stability to their success. As tourism becomes increasingly more important, perhaps its voice on these issues will have greater influence.

With the continuing gradual transition from a centrally planned economy to a market economy, the *needs of the private sector* for effective laws and regulation and a stable and predictable economic environment needs to be given greater consideration by governments, and the public and private sectors should work together to realize the common goal of tourism development. Last, but not least, *regional cooperation* in tourism development is of great importance for the future of tourism in Asia. China should work with regional partners to develop promising tourism zones such as the Mekong River area, Tumen River Area, Silk Road, and the Pearl River Delta.

CONCLUSION

China's entry into the World Trade Organization is a double-edged sword in terms of tourism development. It will create new opportunities, and at the same time, it will introduce fierce competition. A kind of "neocolonialism" by the great powers of tourism may emerge with visitors using their own country's tour operators for package tours, flying to China on their own country's airlines, staying in hotels owned and managed by their own country's hotel groups, and shopping in the shops run by their fellow countrymen. As a result, the lion's share of the tourist expenditures may flow back to their own countries, leaving marginal taxation revenue and a great amount of problems for the host destinations. China's homegrown tourism industry will need to sharpen its business acumen very quickly to solidify its presence in this new international marketplace.

After more than two decades of international tourism development, China's tourism has reached maturity in many areas, such as lodging and perhaps for some travel agency operations. Now China's tourism industry must reflect on past development experience and look forward to the next twenty years of growth. Appropriate government strategies and policies will be key to the future success of the country's tourism industry as market demands change and global competition increases. The next five years will be crucial for China's tourism industry as a member of the World Trade Organization. Its ability to absorb and respond to global competition will determine the successful transition of China's domestic tourism into the global tourism industry. Well-managed companies will take this opportunity to strengthen their positions in the market and emerge as the leaders of the next generation of tourism enterprises in China. Poorly managed companies will be forced out of business or absorbed by other competitors. Through such intense competition and consolidation, China's tourism industry can be become a major force in global tourism.

A long-term, sustainable development approach, supported by adequate infrastructure, well-trained human resources, and an aggressive marketing plan could bring international and domestic tourism development in China to new heights in this new century. The realization of China's ambitious goal to become the world's leading international tourist destination by 2020 will require tough choices by both the Chinese government and people, as well as their collaboration and cooperation with the rest of the emerging global village.

REFERENCES

Air China and Foreign Airlines Jointly Operate China-Europe Routes (2000). *Travel China* 12(7-8): 4.

Anhui's Ecotour Products Go on the Market (2000). *Travel China* 11(8): 2.

Bao, Dao (2000). CAAC Turns Loss into Gain. *Travel China* 12(9-10): 4.

Cai, Liping and Robert Woods (1993). China's Tourism-Service Failure. *The Cornell Hotel and Restaurant Administration Quarterly* 34(4): 30-39.

China's Tourism Industry Sets Goals for the Next 20 Years (2000). *Travel China* 12(7-9): 2.

Dam Area to Establish a National Forest Park (2000). *Travel China* 11(8):2.

He, Guangwei (2000). *The Yearbook of China Tourism Statistics.* Beijing: China Tourism Press.

Lew, Alan A. (1995). Overseas Chinese and Compatriots in China's Tourism Development. In Lew, A.A. and L. Yu, eds., *Tourism in China: Geographical, Political, and Economic Perspectives* (pp. 155-175). Boulder, CO: Westview Press.

Opportunities and Challenges from WTO Membership (2000). *Travel China* 12(9-10): 8.

Sinclair, Kevin (2000). Age of Aviation Industry. *Travel Asia* October 18-21, 8.

World Tourism Organization (1997). Travel to Surge in the 21st Century. *WTO News,* November 5, pp. 1-2.

WTO Membership and China's Tourism Industry (2000). *Travel China* 12(9-10): 8.

Appendix:
Acronyms and Glossary

ACRONYMS

ADS: Approved Destination Status: foreign countries approved by the Chinese government for China's outbound tourism, also referred to as "tourism liberating countries"

ASEAN: Association of South East Asian Nations

BTT: Bureau of Travel and Tourism

CA: Air China

CAAC: Civil Aviation Administration of China

CCP: Chinese Communist Party

CIS: Commonwealth of Independent States

CITS: China International Travel Service

CJ: China Northern Airlines

CNTA: China National Tourism Administration (Same as SATT, State Administration for Travel and Tourism)

CTC: Certified Travel Counselor

CTS: China Travel Service

CYTS: China Youth Travel Service

CZ: China Southern Airlines

DPLE: Department of Personnel, Labor, and Education

FCTA: First Category Travel Service

FEC: Foreign Exchange Certificate

FIT: Foreign Independent Traveler

FYP: Five-Year Plan

GATT: General Agreement on Tariffs and Trade

GCR: Great Cultural Revolution

GDP: Gross Domestic Product

GIT: Group Inclusive Tour

GLP: Great Leap Forward

IMF: International Monetary Fund

MU: China Eastern Airlines

NTO: National Tourism Organization

OTS: Overseas Travel Services

PATA: Pacific Asia Travel Association

PLA: People's Liberation Army

PRC: People's Republic of China

PSB: Public Security Bureau

RMB: Renminbi

ROC: Republic of China

SAD/SAR: Special Administrative District/Special Administrative Region: refers to Hong Kong and Macao since they have been returned to mainland Chinese governance

SATT: State Administration for Travel and Tourism (same as CNTA, China National Tourism Administration)

SEZ: Special Economic Zone

SCTA: Second Category Travel Service

SZ: China Southwest Airlines

TCTA: Third Category Travel Service

TIR: Tourism Intensity Rate

VFR: Visiting Friends and Relatives

WH: China Northwest Airlines

WTO: World Tourism Organization

WTTC: World Travel and Tourism Council

XO: Xinjiang Airlines

GLOSSARY

autonomous region: One of China's administrative divisions, usually designating provinces in which ethnic minorities predominate. There are five autonomous regions in China: Neimenggu (Inner Mongolia) Autonomous Region, Guangxi Zhuang Autonomous Region, Xizang (Tibet) Autonomous Region, Ningxia Hui Autonomous Region, and the Xinjiang Uygur Autonomous Region.

Chan Buddhism: A form of Chinese Buddhism that emphasizes meditation and contemplation. It was influenced by Daoism and formed the basis of Japanese Zen Buddhism.

compatriots: Ethnic Chinese who are citizens of Hong Kong, Macao, and Taiwan.

Confucius (Kongfuzi, 551-479 B.C.): Classical philosopher who propagated a philosophy of life that established clearly defined rules governing social relationships and behavior.

Daoism (Taoism): A classical school of philosophy founded on the teachings on Lao Zi, which focuses on the search for harmony with the Dao (the "way"). It stresses the relativity of values and the smallness of human endeavors within the working of the universe.

filial piety: Chinese cultural value that emphasizes obedience, respect, and caring for one's parents and grandparents, or in the case of married daughters, parents-in-law.

first category travel services (FCTS): Chinese travel services that are authorized by the China National Tourism Administration to have direct business contact with overseas travel operators and receive foreign visitors, overseas Chinese, and compatriots from Hong Kong, Macao, and Taiwan.

Foreign Affairs Office: Local Chinese government department that is in charge of diplomatic relations with foreign governments and official, government-sponsored visitors.

foreign exchange certificate (FEC): China has been practicing a dual currency system since the late 1970s. The FEC yuan (¥) is issued for use by foreign visitors. The Chinese government stopped issuing new FEC¥ in early 1994, with the intention of eventually ending the dual currency system.

foreigners: Overseas visitors who hold foreign passports. This excludes citizens of Hong Kong, Macao, and Taiwan.

Four Modernizations: Modernization policies initiated in 1978 by Deng Xiaoping, which essentially overturned the approaches emphasized under Mao Zedong. The four areas of modernization were industry, agriculture, science and technology, and national defense.

Grand Canal: A man-made canal initially begun in the fifth century B.C. and completed in the Sui Dynasty (A.D. 581-618). It facilitated travel and trade between north and south China. The southern section of the canal has now become a major tourist attraction.

Great Cultural Revolution (1966-1976): A political ideological campaign launched by the Communist Chairman Mao Zedong to eradicate revisionist and bourgeois capitalist elements in the Communist Party and Chinese society.

Great Leap Forward: A nationwide campaign initiated by Mao Zedong in the late 1950s to rapidly collectivize and increase China's industrial and agricultural production in order to move China into a communist society. Failures of the policy resulted in factories and communes making false reports about production levels, and many thousands of peasants died of starvation in rural China.

ground service: Travel companies that provide the land portion of travel arrangements—air travel arrangement is not included.

group inclusive tours: Packaged tours that include all travel arrangements for a group of tourists, including transportation, accommodations, meals, and local tour services.

Huan Baohai Tourism Circle: Regional tourism development that integrates tourism projects in the three Bo Hai Bay provinces of Liaoning, Hebei, and Shandong.

inbound tourism: Foreign tourists coming to visit a host country.

Jinggangshan Revolutionary Base: The base of the Chinese Communist Party in Jiangxi Province. The communist party mobilized hundreds of peasants in this poverty-stricken province prior to the Long March, and defeated four major attacks by the Nationalist Chinese forces. It is now a major historical attraction for domestic tourists.

joint venture hotels: Hotels built jointly by Chinese and foreign developers. Both parties share the profits and losses according to their proportion of the investment. The Chinese joint venture law stipulates that the investment rate of the foreign partner should not be less than 25 percent of the hotel's total investment.

Long March (1934-1935): The Chinese Red Army led by the Communist Party escaped encirclement by Nationalist forces and took a 6,000-mile march from Jinggangshan in Jiangxi Province to Yanan in Shaanxi Province.

management contract agreement: Chinese hotels that are contracted to a foreign hotel management company for operation. It is a form of technology transfer in which the foreign hotel management company introduces new reservation and operation systems and trains the Chinese staff. The Chinese side maintains complete ownership of the hotel.

Miao Pale: Mountainous region of southwest China, extending into northern Vietnam, Laos, and Thailand in which the Miao ethnic minority group live. The Miao are also known as the Hmong.

outbound tourism: Citizens of a country going to visit one or more other countries.

overseas Chinese: This term has two meanings: (1) Official Chinese government statistics consider "overseas Chinese" to be Chinese nationals who reside in foreign countries, but maintain People's Republic of China citizenship and a PRC passport; (2) the popular use of "overseas Chinese" refers to ethnic Chinese who are citizens of countries outside of China, Hong Kong, Macao, and Taiwan. These overseas Chinese do not hold PRC passports.

Qingming Festival: A traditional festival celebrated in the spring to honor the dead.

renminbi (RMB) yuan: China's currency.

second category travel services (SCTS): Chinese travel services that are not permitted to have direct business contact with overseas travel operators. However, they can conduct sightseeing tours for overseas tourists organized by first category travel services.

special economic zone (SEZ): Cities and regions designated by the Chinese central government to experiment with free-market economic systems (similar to Hong Kong's economy). The SEZs are mostly on the coast and have experienced tremendous economic growth and international investment in the past ten years.

special municipality: Three major Chinese cities, Beijing, Shanghai, and Tianjin, have the administrative status and privileges of a province because of their political and economic importance.

star-rated hotels: The Chinese government's National Tourism Administration introduced the five-star hotel rating system in 1990 to ensure management standards and service quality. Most of the hotels used by foreign visitors participate in this star rating program.

state council: The administrative body of the People's Republic. It is headed by the premier and oversees the day-to-day administration of the country.

third category travel services (TCTS): Travel services in China that are not permitted to receive foreign tourists or provide services to them. They can only handle domestic tourists.

Third Front Policy: An economic development plan initiated by the Chinese government in 1964 that emphasized military defense through state investment in basic industry (agriculture, mining, and heavy industry) over the production of consumer goods, and on relocation of coastal industry to the interior and remote regions.

Tiao Tiao Kui Kui: Vertical and horizontal integration, or fitting closely and nicely—similar to the English phrase "to fit like a glove."

Tourism and Vacation Zones: A recent tourism plan proposed by the China National Tourism Administration to develop approximately a dozen tourist resorts throughout the country.

Zhongqiu Festival (mid-autumn moon festival): A major Chinese festival to celebrate the fall harvest. It is popularly known as the Mooncake Festival in the West.

Index

Page numbers followed by the letter "f" indicate figures; those followed by the letter "t" indicate tables.

THE HAWORTH HOSPITALITY PRESS®
Hospitality, Travel, and Tourism
K. S. Chon, PhD, Editor-in-Chief

TOURISM IN CHINA edited by Alan A. Lew, Lawrence Yu, John Ap, and Zhang Guangrui. (2003). "Aside from guidebooks, there are few widely accessible sources in English that address the broad aspects of tourism in China. So, this work constitutes an extremely useful point of departure for those interested in gaining a current and critical understanding of tourism in this important, but poorly understood, part of the world." *Geoffrey Wall, PhD, Associate Dean, Graduate Studies and Research, Faculty of Environmental Research, University of Waterloo, Ontario, Canada*

SPORT AND ADVENTURE TOURISM edited by Simon Hudson. (2003). "This book incorporates the most recent information and real-world case studies to inform the reader of the importance of sport and adventure tourism. The publication is rich in knowledge and provides the reader with innovative models, useful resources, and invaluable references for further study and research." *Wayne G. Pealo, PhD, Professor, Recreation and Tourism Management, Malaspina University College*

CONVENTION TOURISM: INTERNATIONAL RESEARCH AND INDUSTRY PERSPECTIVES edited by Karin Weber and Kye-Sung Chon. (2002). "This comprehensive book is truly global in its perspective. The text points out areas of needed research—a great starting point for graduate students, university faculty, and industry professionals alike. While the focus is mainly academic, there is a lot of meat for this burgeoning industry to chew on as well." *Patti J. Shock, CPCE, Professor and Department Chair, Tourism and Convention Administration, Harrah College of Hotel Administration, University of Nevada–Las Vegas*

CULTURAL TOURISM: THE PARTNERSHIP BETWEEN TOURISM AND CULTURAL HERITAGE MANAGEMENT by Bob McKercher and Hilary du Cros. (2002). "The book brings together concepts, perspectives, and practicalities that must be understood by both cultural heritage and tourism managers, and as such is a must-read for both." *Hisashi B. Sugaya, AICP, Former Chair, International Council of Monuments and Sites, International Scientific Committee on Cultural Tourism; Former Executive Director, Pacific Asia Travel Association Foundation, San Francisco, CA*

TOURISM IN THE ANTARCTIC: OPPORTUNITIES, CONSTRAINTS, AND FUTURE PROSPECTS by Thomas G. Bauer. (2001). "Thomas Bauer presents a wealth of detailed information on the challenges and opportunities facing tourism operators in this last great tourism frontier." *David Mercer, PhD, Associate Professor, School of Geography & Environmental Science, Monash University, Melbourne, Australia*

SERVICE QUALITY MANAGEMENT IN HOSPITALITY, TOURISM, AND LEISURE edited by Jay Kandampully, Connie Mok, and Beverley Sparks. (2001). "A must-read. . . . a treasure. . . . pulls together the work of scholars across the globe, giving you access to new ideas, international research, and industry examples from around the world." *John Bowen, Professor and Director of Graduate Studies, William F. Harrah College of Hotel Administration, University of Nevada, Las Vegas*

TOURISM IN SOUTHEAST ASIA: A NEW DIRECTION edited by K. S. (Kaye) Chon. (2000). "Presents a wide array of very topical discussions on the specific challenges facing the tourism industry in Southeast Asia. A great resource for both scholars and practitioners." *Dr. Hubert B. Van Hoof, Assistant Dean/Associate Professor, School of Hotel and Restaurant Management, Northern Arizona University*

THE PRACTICE OF GRADUATE RESEARCH IN HOSPITALITY AND TOURISM edited by K. S. Chon. (1999). "An excellent reference source for students pursuing graduate degrees in hospitality and tourism." *Connie Mok, PhD, CHE, Associate Professor, Conrad N. Hilton College of Hotel and Restaurant Management, University of Houston, Texas*

THE INTERNATIONAL HOSPITALITY MANAGEMENT BUSINESS: MANAGEMENT AND OPERATIONS by Larry Yu. (1999). "The abundant real-world examples and cases provided in the text enable readers to understand the most up-to-date developments in international hospitality business." *Zheng Gu, PhD, Associate Professor, College of Hotel Administration, University of Nevada, Las Vegas*

CONSUMER BEHAVIOR IN TRAVEL AND TOURISM by Abraham Pizam and Yoel Mansfeld. (1999). "A must for anyone who wants to take advantage of new global opportunities in this growing industry." *Bonnie J. Knutson, PhD, School of Hospitality Business, Michigan State University*

LEGALIZED CASINO GAMING IN THE UNITED STATES: THE ECONOMIC AND SOCIAL IMPACT edited by Cathy H. C. Hsu. (1999). "Brings a fresh new look at one of the areas in tourism that has not yet received careful and serious consideration in the past." *Muzaffer Uysal, PhD, Professor of Tourism Research, Virginia Polytechnic Institute and State University, Blacksburg*

HOSPITALITY MANAGEMENT EDUCATION edited by Clayton W. Barrows and Robert H. Bosselman. (1999). "Takes the mystery out of how hospitality management education programs function and serves as an excellent resource for individuals interested in pursuing the field." *Joe Perdue, CCM, CHE, Director, Executive Masters Program, College of Hotel Administration, University of Nevada, Las Vegas*

MARKETING YOUR CITY, U.S.A.: A GUIDE TO DEVELOPING A STRATEGIC TOURISM MARKETING PLAN by Ronald A. Nykiel and Elizabeth Jäscolt. (1998). "An excellent guide for anyone involved in the planning and marketing of cities and regions. . . . A terrific job of synthesizing an otherwise complex procedure." *James C. Maken, PhD, Associate Professor, Babcock Graduate School of Management, Wake Forest University, Winston-Salem, North Carolina*